THE UNITED STATES AND
IMPERIALISM

Problems in American History

Series editor: Jack P. Greene

Each volume focuses on a central theme in American history and provides greater analytical depth and historiographic coverage than standard textbook discussions normally allow. The intent of the series is to present in highly interpretive texts the unresolved questions of American history that are central to current debates and concerns. The texts will be concise enough to be supplemented with primary readings or core text-books and are intended to provide brief syntheses of large subjects.

Already published

Jacqueline Jones	*A Social History of the Laboring Classes*
Robert Buzzanco	*Vietnam and the Transformation of American Life*
Ronald Edsforth	*The New Deal*
Frank Ninkovich	*The United States and Imperialism*

In preparation

Tom Purvis	*Causes of the American Revolution*
Norrece T. Jones	*Slavery and Antislavery*
Jack Rakove	*The American Constitution*
Robert Westbrook	*America and World War II*
Amy Turner Bushnell	*The Indian Wars*
Fraser Harbutt	*The Cold War Era*
Peter Onuf	*Jeffersonian America*
J. William Harris	*The American South*
Anne Butler	*The American West*
Richard Ellis	*The Jacksonian Era*
David Hamilton	*The American State*
Lacy K. Ford, Jr	*Journey to Civil War*
Donna Gabaccia	*Migration and the Making of America*

THE UNITED STATES AND IMPERIALISM

Frank Ninkovich

St John's University

First published 2001

2 4 6 8 10 9 7 5 3 1

Blackwell Publishers Inc.
350 Main Street
Malden, Massachusetts 02148
USA

Blackwell Publishers Ltd
108 Cowley Road
Oxford OX4 1JF
UK

Library of Congress Cataloging-in-Publication Data

Ninkovich, Frank A., 1944-
  The United States and imperialism / Frank Ninkovich.
      p. cm. — (Problems in American history)
    Includes bibliographical references and index.
    ISBN 1-57718-055-0 (acid-free paper) — ISBN 1-57718-056-9
(pbk.: acid-free paper)
      1. United States—Foreign relations—20th century. 2. United
States—Territorial expansion. 3. Imperialism—History—20th
century. 4. Anti-imperialist movements—United States—History
—20th century. 5. World politics—20th century. I. Title. II. Series.
    E744 . N544 2001
    325′.32′0973—dc21
                                                                00-010179

British Library Cataloguing in Publication Data

A CIP catalogue record for this book is available from the British Library.

Typeset in 11 on 13 pt Sabon
by Ace Filmsetting Ltd, Frome, Somerset
Printed in Great Britain by T.J. International, Padstow, Cornwall

This book is printed on acid-free paper.

To Amanda, Richard, and Marina

Contents

Acknowledgments   viii

Introduction   1

1   Imperialism and National Identity in the 1890s   9

2   Failed Expectations: The Civilizing Mission in
    the Philippines   48

3   America's Caribbean Empire   91

4   The Modernization of China and the Diplomacy
    of Imperialism   153

5   Imperialism and Anti-imperialism in America's
    World Policies   200

6   Beyond Imperialism: The Empire of Modernity   247

Notes   255

Index   290

Acknowledgments

I would like to express my thanks to some of the many people who have contributed to the making of this book. Although I had long been thinking of writing about the US and imperialism, without Jack P. Greene's offer to join his series I am not certain that I would have started such a project on my own. The editorial staff at Blackwell – Susan Rabinowitz, Ken Provencher, and Leanda Shrimpton – have been very helpful and patient, despite occasional grumpy outbursts and protracted silences from the author. Sue Ashton was especially good-natured and efficient in copy-editing the volume, saving me from many stupid mistakes.

My wife, Carol, who suffered in silence for the entire period in which I was actually enjoying myself in composing this work, showed great patience. I have said this many times before, but it bears repeating: the study of history is a communal enterprise. Without the work of hundreds of scholars, not all of whom have been acknowledged in these pages, this book could not have been written. I am especially grateful to Robert David Johnson, a pioneer in the study of anti-imperialism. It is fair to say that without the benefit of his scholarly contributions this book would have been far less sophisticated conceptually. In addition, his close reading of the manuscript saved me from many errors. Akira Iriye was kind enough to look at the manuscript at a late stage and to explain my arguments to me at a time when I was beginning to wonder how cogent they really were. For a variety of reasons, I did not follow all the helpful advice offered by these two scholars. Thus I bear full responsibility for all remaining sins of commission and omission.

"Another Old Woman Tries to Sweep Back the Sea' – *New York Journal*, in *Review of Reviews*, May 1898. In the aftermath of the sinking of the *USS Maine*, many Americans accused a cautious President McKinley of engaging in an unmanly attempt to hold back the irrepressible tide of a warlike public opinion.

"How Some Apprehensive People Picture Uncle Sam after the War" – *Detroit News*, 1898. Even among those who approved of the new overseas acquisitions, there was a sense that the administration of empire would not be easy.

"The White Man's Burden" – Thomas May of the *Detroit Journal*, as reprinted in the *Literary Digest* 18 (February 18, 1899): 180. This cartoon reinforces the commonplace view that modernity had to be introduced forcefully to pre-industrial societies.

"After the First Mile" – W. L. Evans (?), *Cleveland Leader*, 1903. Americans were at first well satisfied with the results of the reforms introduced during the military occupation of Cuba.

"Held Up the Wrong Man" – William Allan Rogers, *Harper's Weekly*, November 21, 1903. Many Americans believed Colombia to be in the wrong in the Canal Zone episode.

"The Open Door that China Needs" – *The Brooklyn Eagle*. Reproduced from the *Literary Digest* 21 (July 14, 1900): 34. The great powers in China, here symbolized by the broom of "civilization," are shown sweeping away superstition, intolerance, bigotry, xenophobia, and traditionalism from a pre-modern Middle Kingdom.

"Breaking the Speed Laws" – Shiras in the Pittsburgh *Gazette Times*. Reproduced from the *Literary Digest* 43 (October 1911): 721. Here a youthful, modernizing China overturns an old China still saddled to a dragon.

"In the Wilds of Nicaragua" – Fitzpatrick in the St Louis *Post Dispatch*, January 14, 1927. By the 1920s, the red menace was already something to be guarded against in American dealings with Central America.

The Philippine Islands. The conquest of the Philippines was made possible by America's long-established imperialist position in the region as one of the "treaty powers" in China. To protect American interests in China and East Asia, the US navy's Asiatic squadron had maintained a steady presence in the area since 1842.

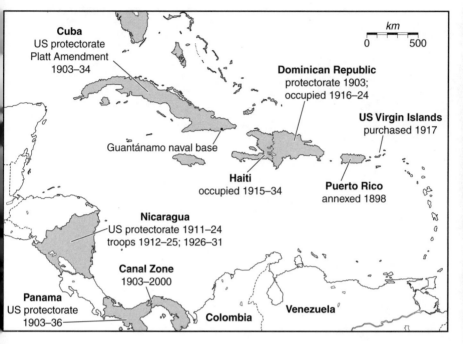

US imperialism in Central America and the Caribbean. With the exception of Puerto Rico and the Virgin Islands, the American empire in the Caribbean was administered by methods that stopped short of outright colonialism. The Panama Canal Zone was leased, countries like Cuba and Nicaragua were protectorates whose external relations were controlled by the US, while other nations were forced to submit to periods of US military occupation and governance.

Introduction

I had three goals in mind in writing this book. The first was to provide a brief survey of the ways in which the United States acquired, administered, and took leave of its various imperial possessions. As this work is intended first and foremost as an introduction to the topic, I understand only too well that I have presented some very complex events in a highly compressed manner. But even if I had wanted to unpack all the intricate details, limitations of time and space would have prevented me from going much farther than I have. The book is long enough as it is and would have grown to elephantine proportions had I chosen to explore all the scholarly labyrinths that branch off from its central theme. Besides, because facts can be collected *ad infinitum* without necessarily arriving at something called the truth, one always has to draw the line somewhere, otherwise nothing would ever get written. The trick, for any historian, lies in knowing when to stop.

A second purpose was to offer a new and more persuasive interpretation of how and why America became an imperialist power. Though it is possible to tell the story of just about any set of events in more than one way, this book was not conceived as an exercise in interpretation for interpretation's sake in which innovation comes at the expense of progress. Even though the inadequacy of our existing explanations amply justifies striking out in a new direction, venturing a new interpretation would be pointless unless somehow it served to advance our understanding. The challenge in writing history is always to tell the story in a more convincing fashion by combining novelty with knowledge.

Because the shortcomings of the traditional narratives about American imperialism will be addressed in some detail in the text and notes, only their general weaknesses need to be noted here. To begin with, at the bricks-and-mortar level, the familiar old building blocks – the rise to world power, the pursuit of economic interests, racism, and social Darwinism – fail individually to hold up under the stress of examination, thus making for an explanatory structure that is quite rickety and unstable.[1] But that is only the half of it. Quite apart from the poor quality of the individual construction materials, the conceptual architecture that we have relied upon to build our explanations also happens to be flawed. The chief design problem in mainstream accounts of United States imperialism appears to be the hard-edged emphasis on international struggle and self-interest, an approach to the topic that is out of tune with the liberal, generally optimistic tone of American foreign relations.

In my account, therefore, the usual suspects that one tends to find in historical line-ups called for the purpose of identifying the causes of imperialism have deliberately not been rounded up. Instead, they have been replaced by concepts with less familiar faces: civilization, identity, the civilizing mission, and great power cooperation.[2] Casting the story in this way allows the plot to unfold in a manner that is more consistent with America's liberal sensibility, even as it leaves plenty of room to take into account the decidedly unsavory aspects of the imperialist experience. The end result is, I hope, more convincing than the current tale in which America's explosive rise to world power is followed by a squib of a sequel in which this alleged new status as a power failed to make itself felt. Even if readers disagree with my slant on things, I would be pleased if this book stimulates some fresh critical thought on the question of imperialism. It would be more pleasing still if someone came up with a better explanation.

This interpretive departure, in which imperialism takes on a liberal face, pointed naturally to a third goal. I have tried to outline (realistically, no more than this was possible) the place of imperialism within the broader sweep of modern US foreign policy, to suggest some of the ways in which imperialism has been woven into the conceptual tapestry of America's international relations. For a number of reasons that should be made clear in the text, pursuing this question requires taking into account the role played by anti-imperialism. For this reason, the title of the book suggests a somewhat broader approach to the topic than one customarily finds in the many works that focus exclusively on "American imperialism."

To my knowledge, no one thus far has attempted to do this, even though there are some excellent books that deal with anti-imperialism. It is only a guess, but my sense is that this state of affairs is the result of the tendency among diplomatic historians either to dismiss imperialism entirely as an aberration or to make it the nucleus of US foreign relations around which all else revolves. In the former case, geopolitics tends to hog the limelight and issues related to imperialism are elbowed aside; in the latter, putting imperialism center stage eliminates anti-imperialism entirely from the cast of characters. Either way, there is no problem of "fit" that needs explaining.

Because this book's argument falls somewhere between these two extremes, some readers may conclude that I overemphasize the importance of imperialism, while others may feel that I fail to give imperialism its rightful due. Although formal imperialism has occupied a relatively small place in the big picture of US foreign relations, to leave it at that would be to miss the significance of the underlying belief in civilization that made American imperialism possible, and it would also make it difficult to understand the close link between anti-imperialism – which was a basic feature of America's experience with imperialism – and America's world policies. As I hope to show, imperialism, anti-imperialism, and geopolitics, which at first sight would appear to be very different phenomena, were in fact closely related elements within a common matrix of global civilization. As with the famous Picasso sculpture that looks like a strange bird from a frontal view but, from another angle, reveals the unmistakable profile of a woman's head, the meaning of the sculpture can be found in the artistic vision that provides it with an overall unity. In like fashion, there is a coherence to these apparently dissimilar elements of foreign policy. If this larger civilizational perspective did in fact allow for a number of incongruous possibilities, imperialism was far from being an "aberration" (an explanation favored by desperate historians who don't know how else to explain it), but neither was it an inevitable result of built-in cultural or economic programming.

For those who believe that all US foreign policy, despite its relatively modest colonial career, is imperialist to the core, a demonstration of that proposition would require a history of US foreign relations in their entirety. Even if I agreed with that thesis, which I do not, it would have been impossible for me (or anyone else) to prove it in a single book. Nevertheless, I have tried to grapple with the larger meaning of imperialism in a way that looks beyond the openly imperialist phase of American foreign policy. The last two chapters of this book should make clear that American imperialism, by virtue of its connections to anti-imperialism, world politics, and globalization, forces one to confront the meaning of American foreign relations as a whole, and in ways that historians have generally neglected to consider in their conceptual and practical interrelations.

While it is generally understood that American foreign policy in the twentieth century was global, all too often one gets the sense from far too many historical accounts that it was an undiscriminating, one-size-fits-all globalism. Fitting imperialism and the diplomacy of imperialism into the picture should help to show that this globalism was in fact quite nuanced and complicated. By looking at the connections between the diplomacy of imperialism and the balance of power, as well as the links between civilization and the civilizing mission, the end result, I hope, will be some degree of clarification of the complex interrelations between American policy toward Europe, Asia, and the Caribbean region.

In general, this book follows the interpretive scheme that I have laid out in two earlier works, *Modernity and Power* and *The Wilsonian Century*.[3] In keeping with the conceptual framework used in those books, I have treated imperialism as an element of the geopolitics of modernity. It was an important element, to be sure, but in the end it was still only part of the larger picture. In other words, I assume that a framework with imperialism at its center is akin to a conceptual peep-hole that offers too narrow a view of the playing field to be of much help in understanding either the game of imperialism or the foreign policy that produced it. Instead, I have argued that changes in the perception of imperialism's role as a force for stability and progress in modern civilization provide a superior perspective – box seats, as it were – for observing imperialism's ups and downs in the history of US foreign relations. Also consistent with my earlier writings is my treatment of American imperialism as an outcome of ideologically conditioned choice as opposed to brute necessity.

A few words about my rather broad definition of imperialism are also in order. Imperialism is one of those topics whose meaning has been endlessly argued about, in part because, like other political key words, it carries different meanings for different people.[4] Though there is, by definition, no single correct meaning, for my purposes imperialism exists when an important aspect of a nation's life is under the effective control of an outside power. It can range from the exercise of complete sovereignty via colonialism to control over only some of the functions of government normally associated with sovereignty, as was true of many protectorates. Control can be informal as well as formal, i.e. it may be exercised through the workings of private social forces without overt political control from the outside.

By this broad definition, American imperialism includes not only the formal annexation of colonies in 1899, but also the exercise of effective control of certain governmental functions in Caribbean and Central American nations, participation in the treaty system that denied sovereignty to China, and, in some cases, economic control. It also includes control of cultural institutions, though I doubt that the idea of cultural imperialism can be stretched to include control of another culture. Imperialism is a form of power, but if there is any one area of our life-world that is able to resist physical power and often defeat it, it is culture. Admittedly, cultures do change as a result of contact, including imperialistic contact, but superior power alone is a poor tool for effecting cultural transfers. It is, moreover, a crude and impoverished view of the human condition that imagines externally stimulated cultural change as the social equivalent of forced brain transplants performed upon helpless patients. If the emphasis is simply upon power, however defined, "cultural imperialism" is a questionable concept of doubtful utility.

Another point of definition is especially important to this study. For the most part, imperialism and colonialism tend to be used interchangeably as synonyms. Usually there is no harm in using the words in this way, but in certain cases it is vital to distinguish between the diplomacy of imperialism, i.e. the great power competition that often came along with territorial expansion, and the relationship between colonizer and colonized. We will see time and again in this book how it was possible to oppose one while supporting the other. Keeping this distinction in mind is crucial to understanding US policies in the Caribbean and in China and to grasping how and why the enthusiasm for imperialism eventually gave way to anti-imperialist outlooks.

Finally, I feel an obligation to make clear at the outset my views on some moral issues connected with this topic. In the course of my reading, I have come across many self-consciously critical accounts of United States imperialism. The nub of this point of view, in one author's words, is the claim that "the essence of imperialism, regardless of the economic system from which it proceeds, is the unjust bargain."[5] I agree with the position that imperialism was immoral because it forcefully, and oftentimes cruelly, imposed alien rule upon peoples without their consent. But I am not convinced that a tone of moral reprobation is appropriate as the dominant theme in one's historical view of imperialism. My ethical obligations as an historian are to be as impartial as possible by adhering to the rules of evidence and by being fair to my historical subjects. I am aware of nothing in my professional training that certifies me to pronounce with any authority on the issue of whether imperialism was, in the long run, good or evil – indeed, I am uncertain whether it even makes sense to put the issue in this way. The point is that imperialism is a many-sided phenomenon, one that is as much a function of the inequalities of size, power, wealth, and national resources that are built into the international system as it is a cause of those inequalities.

Unfortunately, playing the role of hanging judge also makes for some methodological problems. A critical scholarly anti-imperialism may get in the way of a better understanding of history, if only because what was immoral and evil from the standpoint of the relationship between ruler and ruled may not hold true for its consequences. In some cases, imperialism can clearly be a good thing, at least on the face of it. Notwithstanding their brutalities, one thinks of the Roman empire, the Austro-Hungarian empire, and the British empire as imperial units that also brought many advantages to their subjects.[6] One can even argue, as some historians have, that Hitler's domination of Europe (a bad thing) laid the foundations for post-World War II European integration (a good thing).[7] Of course, the converse is also true: moral relationships may have nasty consequences. But there is no doubt that imperialism has been a major contributor to modern globalism. Indeed, it is hard to imagine a *world* history having emerged in the absence of imperialism.

In the case of American imperialism, my sense is that a verdict on its consequences cannot help but be less than clear cut. This judgment will not sit well with scholars who advertise their critical stance toward imperialism, but I doubt that they can produce solid credentials as historical ethicists or demonstrate that non-imperial alternatives would have been better in the long run. As the saying goes, it is much easier to be critical than to be correct.

This work consists of six chapters. The first describes how imperialism emerged out of the identity concerns of the 1890s.

The next three chapters show how imperialism had quite different meanings in each area where the American flag was planted. In the Philippines (chapter 2), the US was committed to "pure imperialism." In the Caribbean (chapter 3), American policy emerged out of a more complex mixture of motivations: a fear of European expansion, the desire for economic gain, and an eagerness to promote political and cultural reform. The American involvement in China (chapter 4), which was rooted in a limited form of imperialism that dated to the middle of the nineteenth century, displayed even greater cultural ambition and put the United States in direct and continuing contact with other imperial powers. Chapter 5 deals with the emergence of anti-imperialism as a major element of America's global foreign policy following World War I. The final chapter argues that this journey away from imperialism attached the United States more firmly than ever to the idea of civilization that had originally prompted its experiment with empire.

This book is dedicated to my nextdoor neighbors: my daughter, son-in-law, and newborn granddaughter. Scholarship has its pleasures, but they pale before the other rewards that life has to offer.

1

Imperialism and National Identity in the 1890s

American imperialism was part of a surge of colonialism that washed over the world in the late nineteenth century, a wave of territorial expansion that differed quantitatively and qualitatively from countless earlier instances of empire-building. Traditional empires, however vast, had always run into limits of one sort or another, but this imperial flood tide was global in amplitude. By 1878, paced by the fantastic expansion of the British empire, Europe and its former settler colonies controlled 67 percent of the earth's surface; by 1914, 84 percent – some 57 million squares miles in all. The most dramatic example of this outburst was the partitioning, by the 1890s, of nine-tenths of Africa, which only a few years earlier had been a mysterious and largely unexplored "dark continent," but significant chunks of Asia were absorbed as well. Only in 1920 did the tide peak as the remnants of the Ottoman empire were parceled out among the victors in the wake of the First World War. With the exception of the western hemisphere, most of the world was under European control.[1] As a result of this explosion of western power, according to one historian, "the world was united into a single interacting whole as never before."[2]

Qualitatively, too, this outbreak of imperialism was unlike its historical predecessors. The European states were able to project their power by converting industrial technology and science into a new kind of war-making capacity that non-industrial societies could not hope to match. It was more than a matter of military power, however. The British political writer Walter Bagehot explained that "[western] power is not external only; it is also internal."[3] Because power inhered in the institutions and ideologies of the westerners, they brought with them not only their military might, but a radically new way of life associated with the industrial revolution. The result, as Theodore Roosevelt noted, was "not merely a political, but an ethnic conquest."[4] The expansion of what westerners called "civilization" conquered hearts and minds as well as territory, thereby producing ruptures in traditional societies between those who clung to tradition and those who succumbed to the many temptations and pressures to adopt modern ways. Imperialism as a global phenomenon thus exhibited an unprecedented diffusion of both power and culture.

Looked at from afar, the ingredients of American imperialism appeared to resemble those that made up the European experience. The United States possessed the same technological and scientific superiority that made the European conquests relatively painless. Pretty much the same kinds of special interest groups were at work behind the scenes. And, as in Europe, where the introduction of mass suffrage gave public opinion greater weight in foreign affairs, empire had some popular appeal. Nevertheless, American imperialism was not simply a copy of the European original. America's imperial surge came late, at the high-water mark of the global tide, was more limited in its territorial sweep, and broke up more quickly on the rocks of history than its European counterpart. On the ideological side, significant differences of outlook between the United States and Europe made American imperialism a much more unsettling and problematical undertaking than it had been for the Old World powers.

Imperialism, like crime (or any human endeavor, for that matter), requires means, motive, and opportunity. In the 1880s, the United States acquired some significant new military capabilities when Congress, which was looking for ways to use up some large budget surpluses, splurged on a modern steel navy. The Civil War navy, which at its zenith had been one of the world's most imposing fleets, went to rot following Lee's surrender at Appomattox. Had it been preserved, it would have been quickly outmoded in any case by a revolution in naval architecture that replaced wooden-hulled sailing vessels with a new breed of steel warships – heavily armored, powered by coal-burning boilers, and equipped with powerful new rifled cannons set in deck turrets. By starting afresh and relying upon the latest technology, the United States navy leapfrogged many other fleets to become number three in the world by 1900. But this up-to-date navy was intended primarily for defensive use in North American waters. There was no indication at the time of its construction that it was intended for use in support of anything as far-reaching as a program of imperialism.[5]

It was not long before opportunities for overseas expansion presented themselves. The first opening came courtesy of the McKinley tariff of 1890, which raised American duties on imports to their highest rates ever. Imported sugar was an exception, but its inclusion on the free list was accompanied by an arrangement to compensate domestic beet sugar producers by paying them a bounty of 2 cents per pound. The passage of this tariff bill had important consequences in Hawaii, an independent chain of tropical islands some 3,000 miles west of California. By putting Hawaiian sugar at a competitive disadvantage in the all-important American market, the McKinley tariff caused a depression in the islands and set off a chain of events that raised the question of annexation.

In January 1893 the white planter elite, much of it descended from New England missionary stock, organized a *coup d'état* against the native queen Liliuokalani in the hope that quick annexation to the United States would follow. Hawaii had lived in the economic sunlight of the US for some time thanks to commercial treaties that tied it to the American economy. Formal annexation, the planters reasoned, would restore the privileged access to US markets that the McKinley tariff had taken away. A sympathetic and enterprising American minister in Honolulu, John L. Stevens, expecting quick annexation,

conspired with the revolutionaries by landing American marines, hoisting the American flag, and declaring Hawaii a protectorate of the United States. Two weeks later, a treaty of
annexation was signed with the new Hawaiian republic.

News of the "revolution" roused considerable sentiment for
annexation within the country, but the annexationists failed
to reckon with the incoming Democratic president, Grover
Cleveland, in whose lap the problem was dumped. Cleveland,
who was by conviction an adherent of the Cobden–Bright liberal school of free trade which viewed empire more as an economic burden than an addition to national wealth, refused to
be swept away by pro-annexationist excitement. Instead, he
withdrew the treaty and authorized an investigation which
concluded that the revolution had been a shameful affair orchestrated by a small, special interest group. Going along with
the conspiracy, said *The New York Times*, would "sully the
honor and blacken the name of the United States." In any
case, the United States had no need to annex Hawaii. With
the rights to build a naval base at Pearl Harbor buttressing its
commercial presence, it was well understood, as one official
had put it, that "commercially speaking," the Hawaiian
islands were "almost an American possession." Thus, for the
time being, the Hawaiian republic was on its own.

If Hawaii demonstrated the absence of a consensus on overseas expansion, another foreign-policy crisis that exploded
shortly thereafter revealed the existence of a deep hostility to
the idea of European imperialism in the western hemisphere.
The Venezuela crisis of 1895 erupted, quite unexpectedly, from
a long-simmering boundary dispute between Venezuela and
British Guyana, the British colony directly to the east. Thanks
to the recent discovery of gold in the region, the source of the
Orinoco river, which was the key to determining the boundary, had become a lively subject of contention between the
British and the Venezuelans. Quite unexpectedly, the United
States intervened in the crisis, telling both parties that if the
boundary were not settled through arbitration, the US would
run the line itself. America's right to impose this solution was
justified, according to Cleveland's secretary of state, Richard

Olney, by the fact that "today the United States is practically sovereign on this continent and its fiat is law" – language that Olney later admitted was "undoubtedly of the bumptious order." [6]

Quickly dubbed the "Olney Corollary" to the Monroe Doctrine, the Cleveland administration's action was prompted by an opposition to the diplomacy of imperialism. The only region of the world thus far untouched by the wave of European empire-building was the western hemisphere. Olney proposed to keep it that way by making clear that the Monroe Doctrine of 1823, which had unilaterally declared colonization in the hemisphere to be at an end, would now be vigorously enforced, unilaterally if need be. As Senator Henry Cabot Lodge (soon to become a leading expansionist) explained, "if Britain can extend her territory in South America without remonstrance from us, every other European power can do the same, and in a short time you will see South America parceled out as Africa has been." [7] In his annual message to Congress in December 1895, Cleveland warned: "This is the precise action which President Monroe declared to be 'dangerous to our peace and safety'." Thus, in the Olney Corollary the United States was announcing its commitment to an assertive hemispheric anti-imperialism on the very eve of its own imperial debut.

By throwing cold water in the face of Great Britain, Olney's action had excited much favorable public approval. It did not strain the imagination to foresee that the "free security" long enjoyed by the United States in the Caribbean region might, if precautions failed to be taken, end up in a dangerous European-style balance of power. In appealing to this sense of hemispheric privilege, a lobbyist hired by the Venezuelan government to influence American opinion shrewdly titled a pamphlet "British Aggressions in Venezuela, or the Monroe Doctrine on Trial." Though much irritated by what seemed an unprovoked display of American assertiveness, the British Foreign Office under Lord Salisbury chose wisely to play down the affair. More pressing problems in Europe with an ambitious Germany and in South Africa with the rebellious Boers convinced the British to submit the dispute to arbitration, as the Americans wished.

The Hawaiian episode and the Venezuela crisis demonstrated that overseas expansion and the diplomacy of imperialism were by no means universally attractive. But they did point up the emergence of an important new phenomenon that would have to be reckoned with in the years to come: an active and excitable public opinion. With the occasional exception of special interest groups, such as the American Irish and their hatred of all things British, public opinion normally did not play a large role in foreign policy – indeed, US foreign relations had for some time been so placid that there was little to be excited about. During the 1890s, however, a charged public opinion became an important source of the political energy that propelled the nation to empire.

Arousal of the people was made easier by the newly aggressive communications media. Access to overseas news had been improved by the laying of underseas telegraph cables and by the creation of global news-gathering organizations like the Associated Press and the United Press. A sensationalist "yellow press," seeking to increase daily circulation, found foreign affairs to be an ideal source of provocative headlines. Trying to account for the public uproar in the wake of the Venezuela crisis, Harvard President Charles W. Eliot remarked that:

> there has been brought forcibly to our notice a phenomenon new in our country, and perhaps in the world – namely, the formidable inflammability of our multitudinous population, in consequence of the recent development of telegraph, telephone, and bi-daily press . . . our population is more inflammable than it used to be, because of the increased use in comparatively recent years of these great inventions.[8]

This was neither the first nor the last oracular comment about the unsettling impact of modern mass media and communications technology on public opinion in foreign policy. But newspaper technology and breathless coverage of events alone, while significant, fail to account for the "inflammability" of this new mass opinion. In the same way that matches need combustible material, a sensationalist press needs a susceptible public. As it happened, the public's sensitivity to foreign-policy developments was heightened by a number of identity issues that emerged in the 1890s. In conjunction with new opportunities that emerged out of the Spanish-American War, these identity concerns would provide the hitherto missing motive for empire.

Cuba and the Domestic Identity Crisis of the 1890s

Although American imperialism was the principal outcome of the Spanish-American War of 1898, it is important to keep in mind that it was not an anticipated result of that conflict. Because few people, if any, foresaw a colonial future in Asia emerging out of the conflict with Spain, the causes of the Spanish-American War need to be disentangled from the rationales for empire that appeared only subsequently. Initially, Americans could not see beyond the conflict with Spain; only after they had scaled that peak did the summit of imperialism come unexpectedly into their range of vision. But American military successes did not force the United States to press forward and clamber up the pinnacle of empire as well. That would be a separate decision, made for a different set of reasons.

Any explanation of why the United States acquired an empire from Spain needs to deal with one overwhelming truth: America's security and its vital interests were not at risk.[9] Neither economic needs nor external dangers compelled the nation to go to war with Spain or to go imperial in the 1890s.[10] To be sure, historians have turned over some rocks and found scurrying beneath various special interests that supported colonial expansion – especially that familiar but incongruous threesome of businessmen, missionaries, and military lobbyists – but they did not play a decisive role.[11] And even if, for the sake of argument, one were to concede that they had been responsible, that would only underline the point that imperialism was not determined by inescapable compulsions of *national* interest.[12] Either way, whether one views it from the standpoint of the national interest or of narrow interest groups, imperialism was not a make-or-break question of national existence.

The absence of concrete interests or structural determinants did not mean that there was no compelling basis for an imperialist foreign policy. On the contrary, subjective worries about self-definition and identity provided more than enough energy and motivation for the imperialist outburst. Social scientists agree that "people will fight to assert or protect who they are as readily as they will to save their standard of living or their property rights."[13] Identity issues, in contrast to concerns for national security, focus on less tangible, but nevertheless vital, internal questions of self-definition and external problems of "fit" in the world of nation-states. Identity matters because it orients a nation to the international environment and predisposes it to behave in certain ways.

An identity crisis is a period of disorientation in which values and relationships once taken for granted are thrown into question. Questions of self-adjustment that bedevil individuals caught up in an identity crisis like "Who am I?" and "Where do I belong?" also beset societies that begin to doubt the principles that shape the national character and guide relations with the outside world. In reflecting upon the nation's social psychology at the turn of the century, William James sensed the pervasive presence of such self-doubt when he wrote about "fear regarding ourselves now taking the place of the ancient fear of the enemy."[14] If the nation's existence was not in question in the 1890s, its essence was, to the extent that the concern for identity far outweighed the pursuit of hard interests.

A number of congenital weaknesses made the nation particularly susceptible to identity crises. The USA was, first of all, an ideologically created state that depended on ideas to justify its existence. Legitimacy had always been defined ideologically and through public opinion rather than through custom or reliance on absolutist symbols of sovereignty. As the Civil War had shown, these core ideas could become the object of fratricidal contention. Even though the need to grapple with the problems of industrialization had stimulated the growth of the national government after the Civil War, the

US remained a weak state that had difficulty in maintaining order in times of crisis.[15] While this soft political and administrative chassis made the United States less rigid and brittle than other societies, it also made for some unstable handling in periods of ideological transition.

Circumstances exacerbated this built-in frailty. The United States in the 1890s was thrown off balance by a combination of events that brought into question the coherence of American society and its ability to function effectively. The most obvious and serious problem was the depression of 1893. The plight of farmers in particular, aggravated by a continuing decline in prices for agricultural goods for the better part of two decades, led to a burgeoning third-party movement. Seeking relief through price inflation, the recently formed People's Party or Populists called for an expansion of the money supply by making silver legal tender and allowing for its unlimited coinage. Besides challenging the sacred cow of the gold standard, the agrarian radicals advocated other startling measures, including federal ownership of all transportation and communication lines, a graduated federal income tax, and direct election of all US senators.

This rural political ferment posed some unsettling ideological problems. In the popular mythology of democracy, yeomen farmers were supposed to be the nation's cultural backbone, the basic source of its civic and moral values. But here they were, acting in some contradictory and quite unsettling ways. On the one hand, they were fire-breathing radicals apparently hell-bent on disrupting the established order. On the other, they seemed quixotically bent on preventing the country from becoming a modern urban, industrial society. By 1896, when much of the Populist political agenda was adopted by the Democratic Party under the leadership of William Jennings Bryan, the divisive chasm of party politics had opened wider than at any time since the Civil War.

The situation in the industrial cities was no less turbulent as labor strife often verged on outright class warfare. In 1892, a strike at the Carnegie steel plant outside Pittsburgh resulted in seven killed when strikers engaged in battle with Pinkerton detectives hired by the company. Federal troops had to be dispatched to the silver mines in Coeur d'Alene, Idaho, following an outbreak of violence between miners and strike-breakers. Most spectacular of all was the nationwide boycott of Pullman railway cars by the American Railway Union in 1894, which threatened to paralyze the nation's transportation system. This action was broken up by federal troops, which were ordered by President Cleveland to safeguard the mails and interstate commerce, and by the federal courts, which issued an injunction against the union prohibiting behavior that was said to violate the Sherman Antitrust Act.

Immigration created yet another set of worries about the national character. Congress had enacted oriental exclusion legislation in 1882 in response to protests from the west over the influx of Chinese, who only a few years earlier had been encouraged to immigrate to provide cheap labor for the construction of the transcontinental railway system. By the 1890s, the focus of concern shifted eastward in response to immigration from southern and eastern Europe. It was not so much the volume of immigration, which actually declined from the numbers posted in the 1880s, as the character of the new entrants that concerned old-line Americans. Often illiterate and ethnically and religiously different from the country's dominant Anglo-Saxon Protestant stock, these new immigrants generated worries about the country's core values in the future. A vigorous anti-immigration movement sprang up in an attempt to raise the drawbridge against further newcomers.

The tide of eastern European immigration merely added to the racial and cultural insecurities that were already besetting the country. In the South, the Populists were making common cause politically with black farmers. Despite the military victory of the unionist principle in the Civil War and the end of congressional reconstruction in 1877, North and South were still very different regions that lacked a common sense of nationalism. It was clear that the nearly mortal wound of the Civil War, the most grave identity crisis of all, had not yet healed. Indeed, the scab was picked off each election by the Republican Party, whose orators resorted to "waving the bloody shirt" as a reminder to the many Union veterans and families of fallen soldiers of the treachery of southern Democrats.

Somehow, this unstable social atmosphere produced a storm of hyper-aggressive nationalist public opinion known as jingoism. Jingoism was no stranger to American politics in the past, but rarely if ever does it appear to have blown through Washington with the kind of hurricane force that it mustered in the 1890s. To ask what motivated this excitable hyper-patriotism is to inquire into the murky depths of mass psychology, which in the absence of modern public opinion surveys and experimental methods of social science is not easy to plumb in retrospect. Even today, with state-of-the-art methods of public opinion polling at our disposal, connecting psychological dispositions with distant political events is a problematical task.

Nevertheless, analysis of the political rhetoric used in connection with the Cuban crisis suggests strongly that gender concerns, specifically a concern with masculinity, provided a powerful motivation. According to one historian, many American males felt threatened by the inroads of feminism. Many men who had suffered a body blow to their self-esteem in the depression of 1893, when their identity as family providers had been called into question, were now also being challenged on the political front by the growing strength of the suffrage movement. As some anti-suffragists put it, "the transfer of power from the military to the unmilitary sex involves a change in the character of the nation. It involves in short, national emasculation." Concerns of this sort may have contributed to the rise of the jingoes, people who "regarded war as an opportunity to develop such 'soldierly' attributes as strength, honor, and a fraternal spirit among men."[16]

Less speculative is the role played by language, which is, after all, a form of behavior. Without a doubt, the language of American politics was preoccupied with manhood. "Honor," in particular, was a powerful concern of the jingoes. When newly elected President William McKinley failed to act assertively enough to suit them, his manhood was thrown into question. Theodore Roosevelt's classic insult, his reference to McKinley having "no more backbone than a chocolate éclair," epitomized a good deal of newspaper criticism of the president's cautious handling of foreign policy. Whether or not anxieties associated with the changes in male and female roles produced by industrialization were specifically responsible in this case, its seems likely that the need to assert vicariously one's manhood was a powerful motivational factor in the crisis. We know that machismo can be a source of violence among individual males in a broad range of group contexts. There is no reason to think that the masculine rhetoric of international relations, whatever its source, is any less potent in stirring aggressive feelings.[17]

In the case of the nation's elites, the connections between identity concerns and foreign policy are more readily established. Assaulted by radicals from below, they were also afflicted by deep misgivings about the changes taking place in the nation's values. One of the most outspoken members of the patrician set was Theodore Roosevelt, a rising political star, who lamented the disappearance of the classical republican virtues of civic mindedness and heroic self-sacrifice and their replacement by a new business morality that appeared to put individual selfishness and pecuniary gain above all else. The spectacularly sumptuous life-styles of this wealthy new business class, which exceeded in many cases those of the decadent European nobility, were a reproach to the ideals of unpretentious wealth and commitment to the common good by which people like Roosevelt lived. Though they still profited from the social cachet of a long pedigree, people of his kind were being replaced on the social ladder by the rapacious and self-indulgent new breed of businessman.

Many liberals called this progress, but Roosevelt saw it as degeneration or decadence. The values that had made the country great and would continue to be necessary for the future maintenance of greatness were now being forsaken in favor of lives of indolence and self-indulgence. "The really high civilizations," thundered Roosevelt, "must themselves supply the antidote to the self-indulgence and love of ease which they tend to produce."[18] For Roosevelt, it was clear that war, the exercise of the martial virtues, was an essential ingredient of national self-renewal. In a speech at the Naval War College in 1897, he told the audience that the "fight well fought, the life honorably lived, the death bravely met . . . count for more in building a high and fine temper in a nation than any possible success in the stock market."[19]

At a time when nationalism was on the rise throughout the world, this tangle of problems made it increasingly difficult for the United States to define itself as a nation, or what one historian has called an "imagined community."[20] The nation appeared to be coming apart at the seams as a result of all these tensions, with no common agreement on how to stitch it back together. In response, some sought to preserve the nation's essence, some hoped to redefine it, while others looked beyond the nation's borders for solutions. It would be going too far to assert that these assorted identity concerns led inevitably to war with Spain. But they did contribute to a build-up of anxieties and jingoist emotion that could easily be ignited by events and further inflamed by opportunistic political decisions.

As is so often the case with individuals and societies that face formidable internal problems, a sense of purposeful cohesion, however fleeting and insubstantial, was purchased at the expense of outsiders. Unfortunately, identity formation through negation, self-validation through denial of the worth of the other, is a pathological form of behavior for which foreign policy often provides an attractive outlet. This appears to be the kind of sensibility that R. A. Alger described to Henry Cabot Lodge in 1895, when he noted that "[foreign policy] more than anything else, touches the public pulse of today."[21]

It took a rebellion against Spanish rule in Cuba that broke out in February 1895 to put the match to this combustible mixture of public resentments. As in Hawaii, American tariff policy played a part in stimulating revolutionary unrest. The Wilson–Gorman tariff of 1894, by restoring the duty on sugar, cut into Cuba's sugar exports to the US and depressed the island's agricultural economy. But this insurrection was only the last in a series of revolts, the most serious of which was a 10-year insurrection that had finally been squelched in 1877. Under the field leadership of General Máximo Gómez, the rebels resorted to guerrilla warfare, avoiding direct confrontations with Spanish troops while destroying sugar plantations and wreaking as much economic havoc as possible. Although this revolt was not unlike earlier outbreaks of unrest in Cuba, it is indicative of the change in American thinking that the United States chose not to exercise the self-restraint that the Grant administration had managed to muster two decades earlier. As the violence intensified, the feeling grew that the United States had to do something.

But why? What exactly was at stake for the United States in Cuba? US investments on the island totaled about 50 million dollars. Admittedly, American investors in Cuban sugar and Spanish securities were suffering losses from the rebellion. But the protection of these endangered economic interests did not point clearly toward intervention, and even if one assumes that they did, special interests have yet to be discovered pulling strings behind the scenes. Though some American businesses were suffering from the unsettled conditions in Cuba, others stood to be hurt even more by a war. Probably the best solution from a business standpoint would have been for Spain to quash this rebellion as firmly as it had suppressed previous uprisings.[22] From a broader perspective, few people of any ideological stripe looked to war as a means of stimulating economic expansion abroad as a remedy for the economic depression. The American economy could best be revived by domestic measures like changes in tariff policy and monetary legislation.

Following this reasoning, and fearful that a war would jeopardize a budding revival of industry, the American financial and business community favored a Spanish restoration of order. Political spokesmen for big business, such as Senators Mark Hanna, Nelson W. Aldrich, and Orville H. Platt, counseled caution. In keeping with this circumspect pro-business reasoning, the Cleveland administration, which frankly admitted the nation's "large pecuniary stake in the fortunes of Cuba," pursued a policy favorable to Madrid by refusing to recognize the belligerency of the Cuban rebels. Recognition would have made the United States technically neutral in the struggle, but politically it would have placed the insurgents and the Spanish on the same footing.

In the absence of powerful pecuniary compulsions, it was not surprising, as one historian has noted, that "hot-blooded interventionists like Theodore Roosevelt and Henry Cabot Lodge decried 'the money power' and the cautious McKinley as the major obstacles to war."[23] "We will have this war for Cuba despite the timidity of the commercial interests," promised TR in a speech.[24] At the height of the excitement, following the sinking of the battleship *USS Maine*, the New York press lambasted "the eminently porcine citizens who – for dollars in the money-grubbing sty . . . consider the starvation of . . . innocent men, women and children and the murder of 250 American sailors . . . of less importance than a fall of two points in a price of stocks." Peace, said one historian, "had become a symbol of obedience to avarice."[25]

Rather incongruously, sordid jingoism was allied to saintlier humanitarian calls for intervention. The pro-interventionist uproar began in 1896, following the arrival in Cuba of General Valeriano Weyler as governor and captain-general. Weyler quickly adopted a *reconcentrado* policy that was designed to deny the *insurrectos* their base of popular support in the countryside. Cubans were ordered to assemble in towns occupied by Spanish troops or else be treated as rebels. By concentrating mostly women and children in towns and villages with inadequate food supplies and terrible sanitary conditions, Weyler created human cesspools of disease that caused large numbers of Cuban civilians to perish. Havana province alone counted more than 50,000 dead. A report by a presidential investigator in June 1897 found Cuba "wrapped in the stillness of death and the silence of desolation."

As reports of the island's misery began to come in, Cuba became a party issue, with Bryan Democrats in particular clamoring for action. Feeling the heat from radicals on his left, in April 1896 Cleveland offered to mediate an end to the struggle by suggesting autonomy for Cuba, an offer that Spain declined. By December, in response to congressional rumblings about using force if need be to settle the matter, he warned Madrid that Spanish sovereignty might be superseded by "higher obligations, which we can hardly hesitate to discharge." Given the intensity of public sentiment, the Republicans could not afford to be left behind. Unfortunately for them, the newly elected president was the cautious William McKinley. Once in office, the joke making the rounds was: "Why is McKinley's mind like a bed? Because it has to be made up for him every time he wants to use it."

Although McKinley opposed any "jingo nonsense," there is no doubt that he began to feel the heat, as influentials in his own party began to exert pressure on him to take action. Lodge warned him of a political calamity if nothing were done:

> If the war in Cuba drags on through the summer with nothing done we shall go down to the greatest defeat ever known . . . I know that it is easily and properly said that to bring on or even to threaten war for political reasons is a crime & I quite agree. But to sacrifice a great party & bring free silver upon the country for a wrong policy is hardly less odious.[26]

Prominent New York attorney Elihu Root argued similarly that a failure to act in Cuba would have disastrous domestic consequences: "Fruitless attempts to hold back or retard the momentum of the people bent upon war would result in the destruction of the President's power and influence, in depriving the country of its natural leader, in the destruction of the president's party, in the elevation of the Silver Democracy to power."[27] Politically, then, confronting Spain over Cuba was a way for the Republican Party to blunt an alarming challenge from radical forces on the political left.

At first, McKinley urged Spain to grant Cuba autonomy or independence, with the understanding that if the Spanish did not soon solve the problem one way or another, the United States would. A new liberal ministry in Madrid did grant autonomy to the island in December 1897, but by this time it was too little too late, as the rebels were determined to settle for nothing less than independence. In the United States, too, time worked against a peaceful resolution. McKinley's domestic space for maneuver disappeared altogether as contingencies – chance, luck, unanticipated ironies – intervened unexpectedly and whipped public opinion into a lather.

The slide down the slippery slope to war was greased by a number of dramatic surprises. On February 9, a cable critical of President McKinley, written by Spain's ambassador in Washington, Enrique Dupuy de Lôme, was intercepted by Cuban revolutionaries and released to the press. In the course of candidly sizing up the president, the embarrassed emissary referred to McKinley as "a would-be politician who tries to leave a door open for himself while keeping on good terms with the jingoes of his party." However accurate this and other indiscreet remarks may have been in describing the president's political style, they did not sit well with American hotheads who perceived an insult to national honor. The publication of the letter ignited a political firestorm.

On February 15, only a week later, the battleship *Maine*, which had been sent to Havana harbor to demonstrate American concern with events on the island by "showing the flag," exploded and went to the bottom with 260 seamen aboard. An American court of naval inquiry determined that the explosion had been caused by a submarine mine, while the Spanish attributed the sinking to an explosion in the forward magazine. Although a number of subsequent inquiries have failed to establish the definitive cause of the explosion, the most likely explanation is that the blast was set off by a fire in the coal bunkers that ignited powder magazines in nearby compartments, a distressingly common problem in American warships of the day.[28] But, for the jingoes, the Spanish were automatically assumed to be guilty of treachery and "Remember the *Maine*!" became a powerful rallying cry. For most members of Congress, the Spanish were culpable, if not necessarily for causing the explosion, then certainly for failing to assure the safety of an American vessel in their waters.

War might well have come even without these inflammatory events. Public opinion had already been aroused by a press that was frantically doing its best to act as a provocateur. A circulation war between the Hearst and Pulitzer tabloids in New York City led both sides to concoct ever more sensational headlines about the most recent Spanish outrages in Cuba. They dwelled, according to one survey, upon "the execution of prisoners of war, starvation, the plunder and murder of defenseless *pacificos*, the inhuman treatment of women, attacks upon hospitals, the poisoning of wells, and the killing of children."[29] On occasion the dueling papers were not above creating their own incidents when the real-life situation failed to provide drama enough. "You furnish the pictures and I'll furnish the war," William Randolph Hearst instructed the artist Frederick Remington when sending him off to Cuba to render drawings of the situation.

With opinion in the Democratic Party, and increasingly among Republicans as well, for war against Spain, on April 11, 1898, McKinley finally submitted a message to Congress in which he recommended forcible intervention as the only solution to the Cuban problem, despite the fact that Spain's resistance to his demands had softened considerably.[30] Two weeks later, Congress declared war on Spain.[31] The war over Cuba provided a welcome distraction from all the problems affecting the country, especially as the Spaniards seemed unlikely to offer any serious military resistance. For those to whom such things mattered, honor would be redeemed. For those concerned with the decline in military valor, Cuba would offer the chance to hone the dull edge of martial virtue. If an excessive regard for pecuniary gain was a problem, Cuba offered an opportunity to act on behalf of a noble humanitarian cause. For those preoccupied with issues of class, intervening in Cuba would aid the underdogs. Not least, a war would promote some badly needed national unity.

The war-fighting strategy adopted by the US had far-ranging unforeseen consequences.[32] In June 1896, naval planners formulated a contingency plan for attacking the Spanish fleet in the Philippines and Spanish possessions in the Caribbean in the event of war, a strategy that was confirmed the following year by a navy board. As the crisis with Spain intensified, Roosevelt, then assistant secretary of the navy, ordered Commodore George Dewey to prepare his Asiatic squadron, whose chief mission was to patrol the China coast, to confront the small Spanish naval force in Manila in the event of war. Originally drawn up without imperialist intent as a way of placing additional pressure on the Spaniards to concede defeat in Cuba, this contingency plan itself created an historical contingency. Its success forced the US to answer a question previously unasked: what to do with the Philippines?

The progress of the naval war promptly demonstrated the existence of a huge technological gap between Spain and the United States. With American ships faster, better armored, and enjoying superior long-range firepower which guaranteed virtual invulnerability to the Spanish guns, the Battle of Manila Bay (interrupted by a three-hour break for breakfast) lasted only seven hours. At its conclusion, the 10 Spanish vessels had been destroyed, silenced, or captured and the Spaniards had lost 381 dead. Dewey's six ships, meanwhile, suffered no damage, and casualties were a mere eight wounded. In the Caribbean, the decisive naval battle outside Santiago harbor on the south-east coast of Cuba was no less lop-sided. On July 3, in a battle lasting four hours, Admiral Cervera's fleet of four cruisers and three destroyers was wiped out while attempting an escape to open sea. The Spaniards lost 474 killed and wounded and 1,750 were taken prisoner. By contrast, US casualties, in what one seaman described as "a big turkey shoot," amounted to all of one killed and one wounded.

The war on land was a different story. Whereas Congress had force-fed the new steel navy, the US army was fiscally malnourished in the years following the Civil War, having been allowed to dwindle to a tiny body of 26,000 men whose chief challenge was chasing down the last resisting Indians in the Great Plains and the far west. To take on the numerically superior Spanish forces, McKinley called for 125,000 volunteers. The willingness to accept a relatively untrained regiment like Theodore Roosevelt's "rough riders" was symptomatic of the lack of modern professional organization. The new recruits used black powder rather than the new smokeless powder, were encumbered by winter uniforms ill-suited for campaign-

ing in a tropical environment, and had to resort to the requisi-
tioning of pleasure craft in Florida for transport to Cuba. According to a Spanish spy in Florida, the American troops were
"badly fed, badly clothed, and all are weak, poorly trained
. . . Discipline is poor and everyone drinks heavily."[33]

Once landed on the island, the progress of the campaign
was far from smooth. The Americans were fortunate that their
landing at Daiquirí, which was secured beforehand by Cuban
rebel forces, was uncontested; otherwise there might have been
significant carnage on the beachhead. Disease took an appalling toll, accounting for more than 90 percent of all casualties.
Eventually, though, in the Battle of San Juan Hill on July 1,
American troops secured the commanding heights overlook-
ing Santiago which enabled their artillery to place the city and
the Spanish fleet under bombardment.

US forces also invaded Puerto Rico. The desire to deprive
Spain of a major base in the Caribbean provided the strategic
rationale for conquering the island. The high priest of navalism,
Captain Alfred Thayer Mahan, had noted that leaving Puerto
Rico to Spain "would enable her practically to enjoy the same
advantage of nearness to the great scene of operations that
the United States [has] in virtue of our geographical situation."[34] However, inasmuch as the end of the war was already
in sight when troops were dispatched from Florida, the conquest was probably not without political motivation. "Puerto
Rico is not forgotten and we mean to have it," Lodge promised his imperialist soul-mate, Theodore Roosevelt. Advocates
of a "large policy" counted on controlling Puerto Rico, which
lay astride the central naval routes into the Caribbean, as a
strategic possession after the war, when it was widely assumed
that an isthmian canal under American control would at long
last be constructed. The island was taken without incident, at
a cost of only three killed and 40 wounded, and with a minimum of public discussion.

Before it was over, the war settled the status of Hawaii,
where the US no longer enjoyed the advantages of control
without any of the administrative headaches. In 1897, a crisis
with Japan flared up when the government in Honolulu re-

fused to permit a shipload of Japanese laborers to disembark. Over the years, the racial composition of the islands had become predominantly Asiatic. As native Hawaiians died off in large numbers from exposure to western diseases against which they had no immunities, the plantation owners compensated by importing contract laborers from Japan and China to work the burgeoning plantation economy. Now, however, the planter oligarchy feared that continued immigration would lead eventually to Japan asserting a controlling influence in the islands. The American government backed the Hawaiians, and McKinley in 1897 let it be known that annexation by the US was only a matter of time. Though the *Shinshu Maru* incident led to some testy messages between Washington and Tokyo, the threat of a foreign takeover finally pushed the US to re-evaluate its position in the islands. In July 1898, a joint resolution of Congress annexed the Hawaiian island chain to the United States. In this case, McKinley accurately described the annexation as "not a change" but "a consummation."

John Hay, then ambassador in London, described the conflict with Spain as a "splendid little war." Hostilities lasted from April 25 to August 12, 1898. Its cost in lives and money was relatively modest and its four-month duration was admirably brief.[35] It appeared to do wonders for national unity, finally creating a solid national identity out of the fragile constitutional entity that the Civil War had kept intact by military means. As Lodge stated hopefully: "the war of 1861 was over at last and the great country for which so many died was one again."[36] The lyrics to a song composed for the occasion, "He laid away a suit of gray to wear the Union blue," well conveyed that idea. More helpful was the end of the depression, thanks in part to rising prices caused by the infusion of more gold into the world economy as a result of some major discoveries.

But this harmony was short lived as the imperial aftermath of the war raised troubling new issues of identity. According to one historian, the Spanish-American War "divided America more than any other between Appomattox and Vietnam."[37] These divisions were the result of McKinley's decision to demand the cession of some major Spanish colonies with a view to creating a new American empire.

The Philippines and America's New International Identity

The sweet taste of victory following the Spanish-American War failed to quench the thirst for national self-definition. Far from resolving all questions of national character, the success of the war focused the nation's attention on yet another set of identity issues that came to the forefront in a debate about imperialism. The Spanish-American War originated in an internal crisis of national character; imperialism, by contrast, was externally oriented, the product of uncertainties about the nation's status as a member of the family of nations. Whereas the nation's inner make-up was the central concern in the period leading up to the war, outer identity issues played a much more prominent role in debates about how the peace should be shaped. Thus a series of events that originated in a domestic identity crisis wound up raising outward-facing questions of international identity.[38]

In the war with Spain, Americans had tried to resolve their identity problems in negative terms, by imagining themselves to be everything that the Spaniards were not. But identity, personal or cultural, is never a matter solely of negation. It is also shaped positively, through identification with others who serve as a reference group or as role models.[39] Unlike the urge to go to war with Spain over Cuba, the desire for empire was not the result of a domestic crisis or, for that matter, any crisis at all. It was the product of what seemed a heaven-sent opportunity, what McKinley called "a gift from the gods." In the debate over empire, the chance to pursue seductive and self-flattering visions of the nation's new standing in the world became the chief force behind the adoption of an imperial identity.

These very different kinds of identity issues were brought into play by the nation's military triumph in the Philippines.

"If old Dewey had just sailed away when he smashed that Spanish fleet," mused McKinley, "what a lot of trouble he would have saved us."[40] But it was less Dewey's continuing naval presence in Manila Bay than McKinley's decision to dispatch an expeditionary force of 11,000 troops to the Philippines that brought the question of empire to the forefront and, to a significant extent, predetermined the outcome. Based on the same strategic logic that had dictated Dewey's naval encounter, the decision to take Manila was conceived as a way of forcing Spain to sue more quickly for peace. As Secretary of the Navy John D. Long put it, an American-held Manila was intended to be "one of the most strenuous elements which brought Spain to terms." In a comic opera staging in which the Spanish garrison satisfied its honor with only a symbolic show of resistance, Manila was taken on August 13, the day after the armistice was signed. But the city's seizure had enormous political consequences that had not been thought through in advance. Writing to McKinley, the New York businessman Oscar S. Straus predicted correctly that "entanglement and embarrassment" would be the result.[41]

Setting sail on a voyage to empire had not been on the foreign-policy horizon prior to a war in which the island of Cuba had been the sole object of attention. Although there was little enthusiasm in some quarters at the prospect of a Cuban republic dominated by the *insurrectos*, annexation was never on the table. McKinley told Congress in his war message that "forcible annexation . . . cannot be thought of. That, by our code of morals, would be criminal aggression." To demonstrate the purity of America's intentions, Congress agreed and attached the Teller amendment to the war resolution, which repudiated any annexationist aims. It was all the more astonishing, then, that the United States should decide to keep Puerto Rico and the Philippines.

McKinley may have been exaggerating when he later admitted that "I could not have told where those darned islands were within 2,000 miles",[42] but it is not likely that acquisition of the Philippines was an unstated initial war aim. Even enthusiastic expansionists like Roosevelt and Lodge jumped aboard the Philippine bandwagon relatively late, only after the possibility of annexation came somewhat slowly into focus; shortly after Dewey's victory, talk had centered mainly on demanding a coaling station. Consistent with these more modest ambitions, McKinley at first toyed with the possibility of retaining only Manila; by September, he was thinking of keeping the island of Luzon.

Nevertheless, although some other terms were clearly stated in the armistice agreement, McKinley's decision to defer judgment on the fate of the Philippines until the opening of the peace conference suggests that he was already considering keeping much more than Manila. Annexation was already weighing heavily on his mind when he appointed the peace commissioners in August, most of whom were expansionist. How and when he decided to demand all the islands is not known, but the constraints under which he operated are fairly clear. Once American soldiers were in control of Spanish territory, it became extremely difficult to dislodge the US presence for any but the most compelling reasons. And those reasons could not be produced in the debate over empire.

McKinley's famous explanation of his reasoning to a group of Methodist clergymen visiting the White House deserves repeating:

> I thought first we would take only Manila; then Luzon; then other islands, perhaps, also. I walked the floor of the White House night after night until midnight; and I am not ashamed to tell you, gentlemen, that I went down on my knees and prayed Almighty God for light and guidance more than one night. And one night late it came to me this way – I don't know how it was, but it came: 1) that we could not give them back to Spain – that would be cowardly and dishonorable; 2) that we could not turn them over to France or Germany – our commercial rivals in the Orient – that would be bad business and discreditable; 3) that we could not leave them to themselves – they were unfit for self-government – and they would soon have anarchy and misrule over there worse than Spain's was; and 4) that there was nothing left for us to do but to take them all, and to educate the Filipinos, and uplift and Christianize them, and by God's grace do the very best we could by them, as our fellow-men for whom Christ also died. And then I went to bed, and went to sleep and slept soundly.

Whatever the spontaneity of this account, it does give an accurate indication of the kinds of thoughts that were bouncing around in the president's mind.

Though McKinley would have been satisfied at first with only a naval base, pursuing that option depended on the ability of the Filipinos to maintain their independence; otherwise the islands might be swallowed up by one of the imperialist sharks that cruised the region. The possibility of another nation acquiring the Philippines was real enough. The British were interested in the event that the United States decided against annexation. A prominent German official believed that German warships were lingering around Manila Bay – all too provocatively, in Dewey's opinion – "to seduce the Filipinos into believing that other Gods besides the Americans could be had."[43] After the fall of Manila, the German Foreign Ministry launched a diplomatic campaign intended to secure the islands. The Japanese, too, discreetly expressed an interest in the archipelago. But selling the islands to another nation would have meant that America had fought a war to aggrandize the position of one of the imperial powers in the region.

Allowing Spain to maintain sovereign control might lead to the same result, given Madrid's shaky hold on the islands. Summing up these possibilities, Albert Beveridge said: "Shall we turn these peoples back to the reeking hands from which we have taken them? Shall we abandon them, with Germany, England, Japan, hungering for them? Shall we save them from those nations, to give them a self-rule of tragedy?" To ask the question was to answer it. "Then," Beveridge concluded, "like men and not like children, let us on to our tasks, our mission, and our destiny." A protectorate – granting domestic freedom while maintaining control of external relations – was considered, but McKinley saw this as the worst of all worlds. By October, conversations with individuals personally familiar with the islands led McKinley to doubt the democratic bona fides of the revolutionaries, their capacity for self-rule, and the degree of popular support that they commanded.

In the end, for all the possibilities, the issue came down to an all-or-nothing choice – independence for the Filipinos or annexation of the islands as an outright colonial possession. Early discussions in McKinley's cabinet indicated that most officers favored keeping some part of the islands, but this minimalist approach was ruled out because of uncertainty about the fate of the remaining portion. Thus, the decision to keep the entire archipelago had less to do with expansionist greed than with the absence of better options. As McKinley said afterwards, despite his many doubts and lack of enthusiasm, "in the end there was no alternative" to keeping the islands."[44] By the end of October, he instructed his peace commissioners to demand them all. In his final instructions, he explained that "the war has brought us new duties and responsibilities which we must meet and discharge as becomes a great nation on whose growth and career from the beginning the ruler of nations has plainly written the high command and pledge of civilization . . ." With reluctance, the Spanish complied in the Treaty of Paris in December 1898 and agreed to accept 20 million dollars in compensation. In addition, the Spanish ceded Guam and Puerto Rico to the US.

A large measure of the president's indecision had been due to uncertainty about how imperialism would be greeted by the public. Having recently been singed by the hot blast of opinion over Cuba, it was only natural that he should be sensitive about an adverse popular reaction. But the public opinion that became a crucial factor in the decision to annex the Philippines was very different in its make-up from the kind of pressure he had encountered in the Cuban crisis. The volcanic, fire-breathing jingoism that had overpowered McKinley earlier in the year had settled down. With confusion having taken the place of compulsion, the president's instinct was to put his ear to the ground, not to reach for earplugs.

Not until an electoral speaking tour in October did he realize that annexation would not be a political albatross. As early as May, Senator Lodge, in a letter to his fellow expansionist, Theodore Roosevelt, reported that "the feeling of the country is overwhelming against giving the Philippines back to Spain . . . We shall sweep the country on that issue in my judgment. Republican conventions are all declaring that where the flag once goes up it must never come down."[45] Lodge's prediction was on the mark, for the people did indeed appear to be smitten by the allure of empire. Anti-imperialist Democrats like former president Grover Cleveland were amazed by the change in the public temper, complaining that "the ears of our people are closed to reason."[46] The most striking indication of this new enthusiasm for imperialism was the election to the US Senate of a strident pro-imperialist from Indiana, Albert Beveridge. Indiana! Beveridge was a Johnny One Note, singing a monotonously simple tune of imperialism that was, somehow, catchy enough to get him elected.[47]

Imperialism was possible because it was in the air. Prior to the 1890s, Americans held mixed views on imperialism that prevented its adoption in the few cases when the issue had come up for policy discussion. While they tended to approve of colonialism on the whole as a way of spreading civilization, just as often they condemned European methods of colonial administration. For example, the travel writer Bayard Taylor, commenting on British rule in India, was quite critical of the racism and exploitation that he encountered there. Nevertheless, "in spite of [a] spirit of selfish aggrandizement," he concluded that "the country has prospered under English government."[48] In South Africa, a US mining engineer called the British presence "a blessing, not only for the whites, but for the natives as well."[49] The distinctions ran finer still. Though Americans were often critical of their methods of administration, the British tended to be perceived as "good" colonizers when measured against the efforts of other imperial powers.[50]

Despite its positive aspects, for the United States imperialism would have violated the tradition of republican expansion whereby new territories in North America had been added with the expectation of eventual admission to the union as states. There were a host of reasons why Americans felt no need to follow in the footsteps of the Europeans, but identity concerns were at the top of the list. The refusal of the Senate to agree to the annexation of the Dominican Republic during the Grant administration was the chief post-Civil War example. While its large negro population made statehood unthinkable, the alternative of annexing the Dominican Republic as a colonial dependency seemed too radical a departure from the tradition of republican expansionism.[51] "We cannot have colonies, dependencies, subjects, without renouncing the essential conception of democratic institutions," said the New York *Tribune*, when the Johnson administration, pushed by the expansionist Secretary of State William Seward, had first sought to purchase the nation.[52]

But as times changed, so too did opinions. Thanks to industrialization and democratization, the United States and Europe were becoming more alike. As one historian has noted of the end of the nineteenth century, "underneath the political and the aesthetic contrasts, there was neither Old nor New World, but a common, economy-driven new-world-in-the-making."[53] Herbert Croly, the oracle of progressivism, believed that "the distance between Europe and America is being diminished." The democratization of Europe and the lessening of ideological distance with America were creating "a condition which invites closer and more fruitful association with the United States."[54] Another historian, writing in 1902, expressed this theme of democratic universality a bit differently: "The story of America and the story of modern world history are the same story."[55] This sense of historical convergence gave rise to all kinds of common interests between Europe and the United States, not least of which seemed to be a common way of handling their foreign relations.

With imperialism all the rage in Europe, an increasing number of cosmopolitan Americans who kept abreast of developments on the continent saw imperialism as the initiation rite that would admit the nation into the great power fraternity. Identity is defined to some extent by identification with role models or reference groups. As Ernest May has argued, "International fashions in thought and events on the world scene could have had a decisive influence on men of the establishment." These establishment men "belonged both to their own country and to a larger Atlantic community."[56] For people of this kind, America's international identity was a matter of growing concern, and with good reason. As an economic giant in the world revolution of industrialization, the US led the pack in just about every quantitative measure of industrial prowess, but it exercised little international influence in shaping the military, political, or ideological direction being taken by that revolution.

For people who were concerned about securing America's place in the modern world, imperialism was a form of internationalism. Whether it was undertaken for reasons of national pride or international duty, imperialism would clarify America's international identity, by confirming the nation's new standing and place at the forefront of civilization. According to Richard Olney, momentarily seduced by the vision of imperialist internationalism, "both duty and interest required us to take our true position in the European family."[57] Formerly an unorthodox notion, the idea of imperialism began to appeal to a growing number of people who thought seriously about foreign relations. The prophet of navalism, Alfred Thayer Mahan, put the connection between imperialism and internationalism in its simplest terms: "I am an imperialist simply because I am not an isolationist."[58]

The breakdown of the long-standing consensus on the undesirability of imperialism and the emergence of a rift within the foreign-policy elite provided imperialist ideas with an appeal that they had not formerly enjoyed. But the inroads made by these ideas were only partial. Because the question of empire was so hotly contested among the elites, public opinion became a decisive consideration. In the absence of united counsel from those who traditionally set the agenda of foreign policy, politicians were forced to take their bearings from the *vox populi*. And the public, influenced by events abroad and by opinion-makers at home who were enamored of imperialism, seemed to want an empire. The more the issue was discussed, the more people clambered aboard the bandwagon.

So too did special interest groups. American business leaders, who had generally opposed the war with Spain and the acquisition of colonies, changed their minds in the aftermath of victory and came down in favor of retaining the Philippines. Business organs like the New York *Journal of Com-*

merce argued that giving up the islands "would be an act of inconceivable folly in the face of our imperative future necessities for a basis of naval and military force on the Western shores of the Pacific."[59] Typically, the Philippines were not seen as valuable in themselves, but as a "way-station" to the China trade – "insular stepping stones to the Chinese pot of gold"[60] – an American Hong Kong.

Where there is political enthusiasm, there is money, but in this case one should be careful about attributing imperialism to economic interests. This rainbow, like all rainbows, was an optical illusion and the China arguments were most illusory of all from the standpoint of national interest. There was but a small though vocal group interested in the China market, and its economic arguments were rather doubtful. For one thing, at the time there was little money to be made in China. If anything, China's attractiveness and profitability as a site of investment had declined in the second half of the nineteenth century. By the late 1890s, China absorbed only about 2 percent of American exports. Its huge population did give rise to some grand dreams of cashing in on a limitless China market, but there was no indication that China would soon begin to industrialize and develop a standard of living capable of absorbing vast amounts of foreign goods. If anything, the prevailing image of China was that of a culturally comatose country. Given these practical limitations, one can only conclude that the special interests in this case were dreamers with ideas far removed from interests as they are commonly understood.

Another source of concern for some expansionists was the possibility that the Chinese empire would soon be carved up by the European powers, in which case the United States might have been excluded from a potentially lucrative trade. But in that case, how exactly would Manila serve as an entrepôt? And if that misfortune did not come to pass, why was Manila necessary in the first place?[61] Some wanted the Philippines as an outpost of American power in the region, on the assumption that trade would not flourish "without influence and power in back of it."[62] But this presumed the willingness of the United States to use force and power to elbow its way into the commercial action in China, something that even the pro-imperialists refrained from advocating. As events in China would soon confirm, the US was simply not prepared to leap into a dangerous diplomacy of imperialism from which it had shied away in the past.

The discussion was blanketed by a dense fog of ignorance about an island group located more than 6,000 miles away from the west coast. So meager was their knowledge about the Philippine islands that Americans relied on a few alleged British experts to provide them with much-needed information. To illustrate the geographical absurdity of annexing this new object of fascination, the anti-imperialist Republican speaker of the House, Thomas "Czar" Reed, stretched a string across a globe to get some sense of where the Philippines were located. Unlike Hawaii, where a large, influential, and vocal community of Americans had been pressing for US annexation for years prior to 1898, there were few Americans in the Philippines. Although a few merchants had taken up residence in the nineteenth century, in 1889 the US consul in Manila counted only 23 American citizens residing there, six of whom were members of his immediate family.[63]

The scarcity of concrete interests suggests that more rarefied ideological considerations were uppermost in the minds of McKinley and his advisers. In his speeches on the topic, the president stressed the country's need to abide by its obligations to civilization. It was "a holy cause" to advance "the banner of liberty" across the Pacific. "We must be guided only by the demands of right and conscience and duty," he told an Iowa crowd in October. In Atlanta, he claimed that "by meeting present opportunities and obligations we shall show ourselves worthy of the great trust that civilization has imposed upon us." Of course, the president was not above trying to place a divine sanction upon the enterprise. "The Philippines, like Cuba and Puerto Rico, were entrusted to our hands by the providence of God," he told a Boston audience in February 1899. McKinley was not alone in thanking Providence. Religious groups, Protestant and Catholic alike, warming to the idea of accepting the "responsibilities which God lays on," expressed a sudden interest in plowing the new evangelical fields opening up before them.[64]

Far from being interested in the Philippines, as such, Americans had fallen in love with the *idea* of empire as part of a broader historical outlook that caused people to thrill to McKinley's summons to "duty." More than any other argument, it was the call of duty and civilization, the internationalist rhetoric of empire, that appears to have had the greatest impact. Their imperial moment was understood by Americans in a global context, without which America's imperial expansion would probably not have taken place. The British arch-imperialist Cecil Rhodes once said that "I would annex the planets if I could." Though the Philippines were only a small asteroid in the imperialist solar system, for the moment their annexation was sufficient to give many Americans a sense of cosmic purpose.

Some historians have argued that the decision was influenced by a competitive ideology of international relations, a social Darwinist creed of the "survival of the fittest" that prompted the nation to seize its share of colonial booty or be left behind in the international struggle for existence. But social Darwinism, in the American context, was almost exclusively a domestic doctrine that extolled the virtues of a *laissez-faire* economy and society. Strictly speaking, it was not Darwinist at all, but Spencerian, after Herbert Spencer, the British sociologist who developed a complex philosophy that justified a dog-eat-dog competitive capitalism as the best prescription for progress. The international counterpart of this classical liberal domestic outlook was not great power competition for colonies, but the anti-colonial "little England" views of Cobden-Bright free-trade liberalism. Not surprisingly, then, a sizable number of prominent so-called "social Darwinists" were actually opposed to militarism and imperialism, including the granddaddy of them all, Herbert Spencer.[65]

But even the pro-imperialists failed to talk about joining the international competition for the simple reason that there was no cause for them to do so. After all, the United States was not threatened. Acquiring the Philippine islands was not a response to international competition. The Venezuela crisis and the Olney Corollary, which demanded the retraction of European power from the western hemisphere, had been the nation's answer to *that* kind of challenge – and it was not an imperialist answer, at least not yet.

Far from suggesting international strife, imperialism conjured up images of a communal enterprise. As one historian has noted, "the powers of the late nineteenth century – including, briefly, the United States – all claimed essentially the *same* ideological justification."[66] Because the spread of civilization was a process that could not be described solely in nationalist terms, its rhetoric implied that imperialism was a common undertaking of the developed nations, a form of internationalism that was helping to build a common, better world. Annexationists hoped that the adoption of an imperialist style would be connected to substantive changes in the conduct of international relations. Imperialism was emblematic of an optimism about the nation and the modern, progressive world of which it was now clearly a member. Somehow, the burst of enthusiasm for the idea of promoting civilization through imperialism tapped a hidden reservoir of popular sentiment.

Anti-imperialism and America's National Identity

As always in US foreign relations, an American president had to deal with two adversaries in negotiating a peace treaty: the defeated foe and the United States Senate, which was often the more powerful opponent. By virtue of its constitutional obligation to advise and consent to treaties by a two-thirds' majority, the Senate, normally a more independent-minded body than the House, would have to be convinced of the desirability of empire. All indications were that it was going to be a hard sell, especially as the Democratic Party under Bryan's leadership, which had been outspoken in its advocacy of war over Cuba, had taken a position against imperialism.

The ratification of the treaty showed once again the extent to which the process of acquiring an empire was affected by haphazard developments. This time, party politics and political miscalculation had an enormous impact. When it came time to consider the treaty in the Senate, the commanding role played by an unpredictable party politics in shaping the outcome demonstrated that there was no overwhelming wave of sentiment for empire. On paper, at least, the coalition of anti-imperialist Republicans and Democrats seemed to add up to a solid majority against imperialism. But once again military events influenced the final outcome. Two days before the Senate voted on the treaty, the US forces in Manila found themselves at war with the forces of Emilio Aguinaldo's independence movement.

Remarkably, it was Bryan himself who was largely responsible for the Senate's approval of the Treaty of Paris (by a 57–26 vote, one more than the two-thirds' majority necessary for ratification).[67] Bryan, in his capacity as party leader, instructed his troops to vote *for* the treaty. Despite having taken a firm stance against imperialism as a matter of principle, it appears that he did not want to make a political football of the treaty process. He reasoned that once the Democrats were returned to power – it was hoped in the election of 1900 – the islands could quickly be given their independence. As 11 Democrats followed Bryan's lead and voted for the treaty, the imperialists marveled "at seeing an opponent fall on his sword."[68] In the end, the Republicans did a better job of maintaining party cohesion by using promises of patronage and even offers of money to reel in the waverers from the other side of the aisle, which might well have done the trick even without Bryan's accommodating tactics.

But the close call in the Senate did not mean that imperialism had a clear field before it. After the treaty was passed, a resolution calling for early Philippine independence produced a tie vote in the Senate, which was broken only by the vice-president's deciding ballot. With the favorable Senate vote, the anti-imperialists shifted their attention to the election of 1900. Bryan and the Democrats opposed imperialism in the campaign, as the Democratic platform called the Philippines a "burning" and "paramount" issue of the day. Meanwhile, an anti-imperialist league, which had been formed in Boston in November by liberal Republican types, or "Mugwumps," had organized a nation-wide opposition to the acquisition of the islands.

Debates about fundamental issues are rarely conclusive, but they do tend to be quite informative in revealing the basic assumptions of the two sides. And so with this debate. The anti-imperialists had a battery of arguments to hurl against the imperialists. They believed that imperialism would involve the country in power politics and allow militarists too much influence in the US government. Commerce? Trade was developed "not by the best guns, but by the best merchants," they insisted. The China trade? It seemed clear to them that "one European customer is worth more than twenty or thirty Asiatics." World power? "We *are* a world power now, and have been for many years," they claimed. With respect to the civilizing mission, was it absolutely certain that the Filipinos were unfit for independence? "This is their affair and . . . they are at least entitled to a trial," said one. As for coaling stations, they could be had aplenty without resorting to empire.

There was also an important racial critique of imperialism which, in the past, had been played as a trump card in opposition to annexationist projects."[69] In some respects, the anti-imperialists took a generous view of Filipino capabilities, most notably so when they questioned the presumption that the Filipinos were unfit for self-government. "There is an overwhelming abundance of testimony," said Carl Schurz, "that the Filipinos are fully the equals, and even the superiors, of the Cubans and the Mexicans." But that was to damn them with faint praise, for few believed that they were the equals of the white man. "That the islanders are not qualified for American citizenship is everywhere acknowledged," said one anti-imperialist.[70]

For the more liberal anti-imperialists and for African-Americans, the sorry record of the United States in dealing with its negro population was hardly an endorsement of the country's ability to treat the Filipinos in an enlightened manner. "It is a sorry, though true, fact that wherever this government controls, injustice to the dark race prevails," said one observer.[71] And even if the proponents of the "white man's burden" were taken at their word, the connection between climate and racial degeneracy seemed an insurmountable barrier to racial uplift. One anti-imperialist senator maintained that "you can no more produce a white man, a man of our blood, in the Tropics than you can a polar bear." It seemed silly to talk about uplift for the Filipinos when many anti-imperialists worried that life in the tropics would lead to degeneracy among the white colonists. Given this pronounced aversion to the idea of annexing non-white peoples, it may well be, as one historian has suggested, that racism was "a deterrent to imperialism rather than a stimulant to it."[72]

Many imperialists also appealed to racial inferiority, but it was an appeal that painted a more optimistic picture of racial possibilities. As an example, take the famous suggestion by Albert Beveridge that giving independence to the Filipinos would be "like giving a razor to a babe and asking it to shave itself." This quotation is usually found in contexts that stress the patronizing adult–child contrast but ignore the fact that babies do eventually grow up to wield razors successfully. Thus Beveridge's caustic remark, which suggested the capacity of non-white peoples eventually to become civilized through tutelage, actually exhibited a softer form of racism than the hard-edged arguments of many anti-imperialists.[73] On balance, however, race – persuasively deployed against annexation for much of the century – had become simply an inconclusive argument used by both sides. By itself, racism did not point clearly in the direction of imperialism."

To the extent that race did influence the debate, it is more likely that the *intra-racial* doctrine of Anglo-Saxonism – which was, to be more precise, an expression of inter-cultural solidarity based on affinities of language and institutions – had a greater impact on the outcome. Anglo-Saxonism was an approving expression of the trend toward reconciliation between England and America, but its new-found attraction derived largely from the seductive internationalist packaging that appealed to some key features of America's new global self-image. "The two countries which stand best for a free civilization have all their interests in common," said one journal. "Together they can do much for the world." Thoughts about marching arm in arm with the formerly despised mother country, England – according to John Hay the two nations were "joint ministers in the same sacred mission of freedom and progress" – also implied a readiness to transcend purely national concerns. For example, Richard Olney pointed to "a patriotism of race as well as of country – and the Anglo-American is as little likely to be indifferent to the one as to the other."[74] At the margins, this patriotism of race shaded into a sense of affinity for other civilized powers like France and Germany.[75]

While the anti-imperialists had responses to all of the imperialist contentions, their strongest and most passionate arguments emphasized the poisonous effect of colonialism upon the national character. If, as one author has suggested, "imperialism is government of other people by other people for other people," there was indeed an ideological discordance between empire and democracy.[76] Pointing up this incompatibility, Schurz argued that "a democracy cannot so deny its faith as to the vital conditions of its being." Senator George Hoar of Massachusetts, one of the more eloquent anti-imperialist Republicans, put the concern squarely when he described imperialism as "a greater danger than we have encountered since the Pilgrims landed at Plymouth – the danger that we are to be transformed from a republic, founded on the Declaration of Independence, guided by the counsels of Washington, into a vulgar, commonplace empire, founded upon physical force." As historian Robert Beisner has suggested, the "Mugwump" anti-imperialists worried that "the more America departed from her original character, the more it seemed . . . that she began to resemble the old nations of Europe."[77]

Resorting to rhetoric that was reminiscent of the anti-slavery crusade, Hoar argued that "No man was ever created good enough to own another. No nation was ever created good enough to own another."[78] Though such identity-based arguments tend to be associated with Republican anti-imperialists, they were also prominently on display in the rhetoric of that ostensible insurgent, William Jennings Bryan, when he insisted that "the highest obligation of this nation is to be true to itself." Anti-imperialism appealed, in William James's phrase, to "every American who still wishes his country to maintain its ancient soul – soul a thousand times more dear than ever, now that it seems in danger of perdition."[79] Adopting the new other-directed international identity would irreparably warp the nation's innate inner-directed character.

Perhaps the most telling indicator of the mentality of the avid anti-imperialists was their advanced age – the average age of leading anti-imperialists in one study was 69. These men had cut their political teeth in an earlier era as abolitionists, radical republicans, and civil service reformers. The generational difference was underscored by Roosevelt in a letter to Mahan. "We have in America among our educated men a kind of belated survivor of the little English movement among the Englishmen of thirty years back," he said. "They are provincials, and like all provincials, keep step with the previous generation of the metropolis."[80] By contrast, imperialism seemed more appealing to what the US consul in London described as "the younger and more active elements of the country." Thus the debate over empire to some degree reflected a generation gap between those who wanted to adhere to tradition and a younger group who believed that modern times demanded that the United States abandon its aloofness and become an active partner of the Europeans in the project of creating a global civilization.[81]

It was this international standard of civilization that made imperialism seem a good and noble policy. As McKinley told one audience in Ohio, "we must take up and perform and as free, strong brave people, accept the trust which civilization puts upon us."[82] The belief in civilization implied an unselfish willingness to undertake what Rudyard Kipling called, in a poem drafted in celebration of the Senate's ratification of the Paris treaty, the "White Man's Burden." The white man's burden was a supranational racial principle, not a nationalist conviction. As one earnest soul put it, "What America wants is not territorial expansion, but expansion of civilization. We want, not to acquire the Philippines for ourselves, but to give the Philippines free schools, a free church, open courts, no caste, equal rights to all. This is for our interest."[83] This was a position that appealed even to some prominent anti-imperialists who opposed empire for geopolitical reasons. According to John W. Burgess, "There is no human right to the status of barbarism. The civilized states shall have a claim upon them, and that claim is that they shall become civilized."[84]

In the end, the debate over empire revolved around contrasting visions of the nation's place in the world. Those who sought to fashion a new international identity for the United States saw imperialism as the price of admission into a fast-developing global society in which the United States was destined to be a leading member. Those who opposed empire did so largely because it would have been a denial of what they conceived to be the nation's unique ideological essence. The difference was between those who believed that America's place outside history was the source of its greatness and those who believed that continued exclusion from the global flow of time would marginalize the nation.

2

Failed Expectations: The Civilizing Mission in the Philippines

Like a dumb-bell, the weight of the public debate over the annexation of the Philippine islands was concentrated overwhelmingly at the extremes. At one end, annexationists foresaw an idealized outcome in which acquisition of the islands would do wonders for the national character, for the Philippines, and for America's place in the world. At the other, the antis believed that acquisition would corrupt national identity and lead to horrible entanglements in power politics. But America's actual experience as a colonial power in the Philippines bore little resemblance to the forecasts made so earnestly and confidently in 1899. In the course of a one-hundred-year process of acquisition, divestiture, and intimate postcolonial involvement, nearly every prediction about the consequences of empire, whether positive or negative, was proved wrong.

The Philippine archipelago is a group of more than 7,000 islands scattered over 115,000 square miles of the western Pacific, some 6,000 miles west-southwest of San Francisco, 4,500 miles from Honolulu, and 500 miles south of the Asian mainland. Of the fewer than 1,000 inhabited islands, 11 account for most of the total land area as well as the bulk of the population, which numbered approximately eight million at the end of the nineteenth century. The inhabitants were largely Malay in ethnic origin, with a sprinkling of Chinese and a small number of aboriginal Negritos. Linguistically, the islands were more diverse, with more than 70 tongues in all, though Tagalog in the north was the primary dialect. Ninety percent of the people were Roman Catholic Christians, but there was a sizable Muslim population (called Moros after the Spanish Moors) in the southern islands of Mindanao, Palawan, and the Sulus. In some of the remoter areas, animist beliefs predominated among the so-called "wild tribes."

The Philippines had been ruled by Spain since the 1570s with what one historian has called "that curious mixture of brutality, mild beneficence, and ineptitude ever typical of Spain's colonial venture."[1] Little development took place under Spanish rule as, typically, the holding of public office in the islands was considered a personal prerogative that entailed no obligation to promote the public good. Because the corruption of the Spanish government was offset by its feebleness, the most powerful force on the islands was actually the church, its on-the-ground embodiment being the Spanish friars who owned much of the land, monopolized education, and performed many governmental functions. In seeking to preserve the status quo in the countryside, the friars tried to isolate the natives from contact with the outside world on the supposition that their weak culture could not survive the shock of impact. This enforced cultural isolation, fortified by a mercantilist trading system that confined commercial access to the non-Spanish world in a regulatory straitjacket, effectively kept the Philippines outside the main currents of modern world history. The sight of a people so "idle and dissipated" was, for one travel writer, "a remarkable and instructive example of 'age-reared priestcraft and its shapes of woe.'"[2]

But the Spaniards could not stifle all change. A native intelligentsia, the *ilustrados*, or enlightened ones, emerged in the nineteenth century. By the end of the century, this Spanish-educated native elite was smitten by the allure of nationalism. With writers like José Rizal fanning the desire for independence, the Philippines, like Cuba, were in a state of rebellious ferment when the Spanish-American War broke out. An independence movement called the Katipunan, or Patriots League, led by some of the local elite in Manila, had been created in 1896. After a promising beginning, the revolution faltered militarily and an uneasy armistice was signed with Spain early in 1898. According to its terms, the rebel leaders agreed to relinquish their arms and leave the country in return for some money, an amnesty for their followers, and vague promises of reforms. Following the conclusion of this deal, the leaders of the insurgency took refuge in Hong Kong.

Commodore Dewey, who was aware of the independence movement's existence, arranged to transport its leader, Emilio Aguinaldo, to Manila on the chance that he might prove politically useful against the Spaniards. Impressed by the rebel leadership, Dewey noted that "these people are far superior in their intelligence and more capable of self-government than the natives of Cuba." For his part, Aguinaldo accepted oral but wholly unofficial assurances from the American consul in Hong Kong, subsequently denied by the official, that the US intended to hand the islands over to the Filipinos after delivering the death blow to Spanish rule. Operating on the assumption that the Americans would leave following the conclusion of a peace treaty, Aguinaldo organized an army upon returning to the islands and, on June 12, 1898, declared a provisional government that was independent – of Spain and, presumably, of everyone else.

"All empires have been cemented in blood," said Edmund Burke. As it became clear that Washington was leaning toward proclaiming an American-controlled future for the islands, relations between Aguinaldo's forces and the Americans began to deteriorate and were further strained when Aguinaldo's forces, having surrounded Manila, were not allowed to participate in its capture. Over the course of the following months, Aguinaldo sought fruitlessly to negotiate with American military commanders who had been given strict instructions against engaging in parleys. When Aguinaldo learned in January 1899 that the Treaty of Paris had ceded the islands to the Americans, he called upon his people to declare their independence. On February 4, following increasing tension, open conflict broke out between Filipino forces and their new colonial overlords. Ironically, the insurgents were newly armed with weapons from the Cavite arsenal that had been made available to them by Dewey before the falling-out.

Of all the forecasts made about America's future in the Philippines, William Graham Sumner's proved to be the most clear-sighted. "The most important thing which we shall inherit from the Spaniards will be the task of suppressing rebellions," predicted the social Darwinist foe of imperialism. Referring to Filipino resistance to annexation, former president Cleveland said that "our imperialistic enthusiasm should not be checked by the prospective necessity of destroying a few thousand or a few hundred thousand Filipinos. This should only be regarded as one stage in a transcendentally great movement, a mere incident in its progress."[3] Cleveland was being sarcastic, but his comments cut close to the bone.

Crushing the Filipino rebellion proved to be far more difficult and costly than defeating Spain. "They wanted to drive the Americans into the sea and kill every white man in Manila," claimed General Elwell S. Otis.[4] By mid-November 1999, after his army had suffered repeated defeats at the hands of American forces in conventional battles, Aguinaldo switched to guerrilla tactics. This second and more brutal phase of the war lasted another three years. Neither the failure of the Democrats to win the election of 1900 nor Aguinaldo's capture in March 1901 persuaded the rebels to end their insurgency.

Ultimately, the US poured 70,000 soldiers into the war. At least 16,000 Filipino insurgents died, and probably far more than that, since that was only the number counted by the Americans. At least 200,000 civilians perished, perhaps as many as 700,000 according to one estimate, though this catastrophe was the result of malnutrition and epidemic disease that could be traced back to "preexisting epidemiological and ecological conditions."[5] The Americans, meanwhile, suffered a total of 4,200 dead in the islands and 2,800 wounded. The monetary price paid to suppress the rebellion was about 600 million dollars, far more than the cost of the entire Spanish-American War.

For imperialists like Theodore Roosevelt, who traded on

the glory gained in Cuba to gain first the vice-presidency and then the presidency following McKinley's assassination in 1901, resistance deserved to be met only with brute force. "With such peoples – half-caste Christians, warlike Muslims, and wild pagans – weakness is the greatest of crimes," he declared. "The resistance to American authority is nothing but a conspiracy of murder and assassination," said William Howard Taft in refusing to dignify the nationalist political goals of the rebels.

It was a squalid little war. Whenever the mutilated bodies of dead American soldiers were discovered, American forces engaged in fierce reprisals against villagers who were assumed to be accomplices of the guerrillas. American troops killed domestic animals, burned crops, and summarily shot natives believed to be aiding the guerrilla chieftains. One general, whose excesses led to a court martial and forced retirement, ordered that the island of Samar be turned into "a howling wilderness." To deprive the guerrillas of local support, the Americans resorted to a version of the *reconcentrado* policy which only a few years earlier had been condemned as bestial when applied by the Spanish in Cuba. Rural populations were herded into designated security zones, where they fell victim to food shortages and outbreaks of disease.

The fighting, which at times degenerated into sheer savagery, was often compared to America's Indian wars. One soldier who wrote home predicted that the islands "won't be pacified until the niggers are killed off like Indians."[6] But this conflict was different from the police action of the wild west. It was impossible to distinguish civilian from insurgent, as Aguinaldo's forces had stopped wearing their uniforms. Sometimes the rebels lured the Americans into traps by using white flags. The American troops, in contrast to the professional soldiers used in Indian warfare, were for the most part volunteers not noted for their discipline. The "take no prisoners" approach of many American units meant that the numbers of dead rebels exceeded the number of wounded, in marked contrast to the usual casualty ratios. Prisoners were routinely starved and mistreated. One particularly gruesome form of torture designed to elicit information from captives, known as the "water cure," caused a scandal when its techniques were revealed back in the United States. It consisted of holding open the victim's mouth, pouring gallons of water down his throat, then kneeling on the stomach to force it back out. The process was repeated until the victim either talked or died.

Many imperialists had maintained that acquiring the Philippines would be an uplifting and ennobling experience for the Americans engaged in bringing civilization to the islands. But the unrestrained ferocity of the fighting made a mockery of arguments that imperialism would be a school for building character and manufacturing manhood. Wherever one looked, nearly everything about the Philippine war pointed to the conclusion that the end result, for the young American males engaged in combat, was degeneracy rather than revitalization.

To start with, the climate was inhospitable. It was a staple of late nineteenth-century geographical lore that white men were not well suited to life in the tropics. Prior to the rediscovery of quinine in the mid-nineteenth century, the life expectancy of Caucasians in equatorial regions was astonishingly short. And sure enough, a wide variety of tropical diseases soon began to take their toll.[7] The heat, humidity, and rain, far from being invigorating, produced a state of torpor among the troops. The rigors of battle, on the other hand, appeared to stimulate cruelty among the soldiers. "This is not civilization. This is barbarism," complained one Congressman. "We are taking the boys who left Christian homes, full of love of country, of patriotism, and of humanity, and brutalizing them."[8] Unfortunately for the jingoes, mounting revulsion against the methods used to suppress the rebels saw their emphasis on manliness turned against them.

To the dismay of moralists back home, the climate also seemed to stimulate sensuality among the soldiers as the restraints of civilization were sloughed off and the lust for empire gave way to a coarser lust. Doing what military men away from home have done ever since the dawn of warfare, American troops sought sexual consolation among local women and prostitutes. "The life of soldiers is in every sense animal," said one commentator, "and venereal pleasures are foremost among its relaxations."[9] On the assumption that prohibition of sexual contacts was unrealistic and unenforceable, the army had licensed brothels with a view to reducing the incidence of venereal diseases, only to succumb to shrieks of outrage when reports made their way back home of standing room only in the houses of prostitution in Manila. Reports of "bodies damaged for life" led the War Department to forbid further inspection of prostitutes by army surgeons, thus aggravating the public health problem.

Worse yet, at a time when most scientists were convinced that miscegenation produced racial degeneration, reports of mixed-race sexual contact fed fears of racial decline at home. The perils of drink ran a close second to the evils of sex. Campaigning against the "shameful spread of the saloon," temperance reformers forced the army to suspend operation of the army canteen in the Philippines.[10] After a few years, one historian has concluded, "the Philippines no longer seemed, to most Americans, a glorious opportunity to build manhood."[11]

Still, the Republican Party had too much political prestige invested in the islands to think about cutting them loose. The war was an unpleasant shock to Americans, to be sure, but its sordid features never generated criticism potent enough to reverse the decision for empire. McKinley's imposition of censorship helped somewhat, but it was only a holding action. To draw some of the sting from the reproaches of anti-imperialists at home, General Arthur MacArthur announced a general amnesty in 1900. Once Aguinaldo was captured in 1901, the rebellion began to sputter and ended the following year with the surrender of the rebel forces. Though it would take a number of years of continued fighting in the outer islands before the Moros and "wild tribes" were subdued, the US was able to shift its attention to the less controversial task of shouldering the white man's burden.

Occupation and Accommodation

Once pacified, the islands had to be governed. True to the rhetorical declarations of the debate on empire, the chief objectives of the occupation were to prepare the Filipinos for independence, develop the economy, and educate the masses for life in a modernizing society.[12] William Howard Taft, the first governor of the islands, was more serious about this civilizing mission than most. "We hold the Philippines for the benefit of the Filipinos," he said, "and we are not entitled to pass a single act or to approve a single measure that has not that as its chief purpose."

Some early talk of preparing the Filipinos for statehood was quickly squelched. The new secretary of war, Elihu Root, a prominent New York attorney who had been appointed to oversee the creation of a system of colonial administration, told a visiting delegation from the islands that "statehood for Filipinos would add another serious race problem to the one we have already. The Negroes are a cancer in our politics, a source of constant difficulty, and we wish to avoid developing another such problem."[13] Given the conspicuous lack of interest in racial uplift at home, politicians were not prepared to commit themselves to granting equality of statehood to a distant non-white possession. The Philippines would be an outright colony, managed by a Bureau of Insular Affairs whose bureaucratic home was in the War Department.

Policies were being discussed and decided even as all-important legal questions remained in suspense. Indeed, it was not even certain that the Constitution allowed the US to become a colonial power. Anti-imperialists had argued strenuously that it could not. The text of the Constitution was mute on this question, but the Supreme Court read between its lines in a series of decisions known collectively as the Insular Cases. In *Downes* v. *Bidwell* (1901), the justices ruled, by a one-vote majority, that Congress had the right to impose a tariff on Puerto Rico, which implied that the island was not a part of the United States. The criterion for determining whether the

Constitution was fully applicable (and whether statehood was ultimately in the cards) depended on whether the territory was unincorporated or incorporated. Puerto Rico was not a foreign country, but neither was it wholly domestic, either. In the labored language of the court, it was "foreign to the United States in a domestic sense, because the island had not been incorporated into the United States, but was merely appurtenant thereto as a possession."

This line of reasoning was subsequently extended to the Philippines, which were also denied incorporated status by Congress. Among other things, this meant that while certain fundamental provisions of the Constitution – freedom of speech, religion, the press, etc. – applied to all territories, operational provisions did not. The court, as one historian described it, had "hit upon a clever plan for enabling the United States to acquire and govern colonial possessions without the necessity of at once extending citizenship, jury trial, and free trade with the United States to populations unprepared for those privileges."[14] Thus it gave to Congress considerable latitude to legislate for the colonies, which included also the important power eventually to get rid of them. What survives today of these slippery legalisms is Elihu Root's clever summary of the court's rulings. "The constitution follows the flag," said Root, "but it does not catch up with it."

Irreverent though he was, Root fully agreed with the court that the Bill of Rights was applicable to the Philippines, but not the right to democratic self-rule. "Government does not depend upon consent," he insisted in 1900. The great majority of Filipinos, he believed, were "but little advanced from pure savagery." They were like children in their "lack of reflection, disregard of consequences, fearlessness of death, thoughtless cruelty, and unquestioning dependence upon a superior."[15] Most interested observers agreed. "It would be wrong to try to give the same government now to the Philippine islands as we enjoy who have been schooled for centuries to the use of our liberties," said Woodrow Wilson, then a professor at Princeton.[16] The Filipinos had "yet to learn the lessons of political honesty, thrift, and of self-reliance," said one economic adviser.[17] These kinds of values would have to be instilled in them by an apprenticeship in democracy, but at the same time, Root believed that inherent cultural and racial differences made it necessary for American measures "to conform to their customs, their habits, and even their prejudices." This meant that the Filipinos would be introduced to democracy, but on training wheels.

To chart the course of imperial administration, in 1899 McKinley appointed a Philippine commission headed by Jacob Gould Schurman, the president of Cornell University and a former opponent of empire. The commission concluded that the Filipinos could not be granted independence any time soon. "Their lack of education and political experience, combined with their racial and linguistic diversities, disqualify them, in spite of their mental gifts and domestic virtues, to undertake the task of governing the archipelago at the present time," said its report. Because the war was still raging, the commission heard primarily from conservative Filipinos, who feared that a successful rebellion might explode into a full-blown revolutionary threat to their own interests. They obligingly suggested that a period of American tutelage would be necessary to lay the foundation for eventual democratic self-rule. "The very thing they yearn for is what of all others our Government will naturally desire to give them – religious liberty, fundamental personal rights, and the largest practicable measure of home rule," the commissioners reported approvingly.

Thus was born the policy of "attraction" that sought to make collaborators of the ruling classes of the Philippines. The policy is usually credited to Taft, who headed a second Philippine commission in 1900 and later in the year was appointed the first civil governor general of the islands. This second commission was empowered to take over all civil authority from the military and to create a new government for the islands. Like Schurman, Taft had originally opposed imperialism, only to be swayed by the practical realization that the US had to make the best of a policy that was not likely to be reversed.

Taft outlined his strategy in testimony to a congressional

hearing. "The reliance of the Commission is on the small educated portion of the community," he said. "With this as a
nucleus and with the aid of American control we think a stable government can be erected."[18] For Taft, there was no alternative to this partnership with a collaborationist elite. Like
most Americans, he believed that the common people were
ignorant and, as one report put it, that it was "more or less a
matter of indifference to them what their government is so
long as it is not repressive."[19] The rebellion was explained by
attributing it to a miscreant minority – "unscrupulous plot-
ters and desperate men," in Taft's words – who had temporarily attracted the people to their cause by unjustly confusing
the Americans with the Spaniards.

As the war continued and the violence spread throughout
the countryside, more and more Filipinos of all persuasions
began to conclude that collaboration rather than resistance
was the preferred way of dealing with the Americans and protecting their interests. Even before the Americans took over,
conservatives in the independence movement like Aguinaldo
had sought to prevent their colonial rebellion from becoming
a social revolution of the kind that more radical leaders like
Andres Bonifacio had sought to promote. Convinced that they
were the rightful inheritors of the prerogatives once enjoyed
by the Spanish, they had taken measures, even prior to the
rebellion against the United States, to safeguard their interests. Thus a constitution drafted in Malalos in 1898 was heavily
biased in favor of the wealthy landholders and the middle
classes.

For the elites, accommodation proved to be the ideal form
of resistance. As a result of the policy of attraction, the political future of the islands was mortgaged to a class who had
little interest in changing the social and economic status quo,
the "sixty families" who would continue to dominate the country in neo-feudal fashion. From the very beginning, then, the
United States was not in a position to impose a far-reaching
program of social transformation of the kind envisaged by
enthusiastic promoters of the gospel of civilization. By giving
the US army all it could handle, the Filipino rebels, though

failing to achieve independence, had at least induced their conquerors into ruling with a light hand. Although the American enthusiasm for the civilizing mission in the Philippines was not extinguished, as it receded from public consciousness it became the ongoing concern of a small number of bureaucrats and special interests with limited resources and narrower agendas.

Because only societies with a fairly equitable distribution of income can be both stable and democratic, it is evident that the Americans from an early date had seriously compromised their ability to restructure the economy and society of the Philippines. However, it is probably a mistake to think that they had a choice between a conservative policy of co-optation and a progressive policy of reform. In their minds, law and order was the *sine qua non* of development. And, in fairness, it is not clear what a radically progressive program might have looked like, nor is it certain that it would have had a better outcome had it been applied. The Americans cannot fairly be criticized for failing to modernize the Philippines because they did not know how to achieve that goal – no one did. And to accuse them of failing to push forward a social revolution that violated their precepts of law, order, and propriety is to suggest that they could have jumped out of their Republican skins. But in the short term, the policy of attraction, when combined with the forceful suppression of the rebellion, formed a brilliant carrot-and-stick strategy that succeeded in stabilizing the islands.

The Americans moved most decisively and sure-footedly in their introduction of democratic representative institutions. The Organic Act of 1902 provided for general elections for the lower house of the Philippine legislature, with the commission serving as the upper chamber. Elections were scheduled to take place every two years. The first assembly was elected in 1907 by a vote of 3 percent of the population, since the franchise was based on literacy or tax payments, which meant that politics was dominated by the upper classes. The assembly's speaker, Sergio Osmeña, quickly became the most influential native politician. As one commissioner put it, "the

Filipinos regarded him as the real head of the government."[20]

In September 1901, three Filipino members were appointed to the commission with a fourth being added in 1908, making the balance four Filipinos and five Americans. Beginning in 1913, Woodrow Wilson's appointee as governor, Francis Burton Harrison, accelerated the process of Filipinization by giving Filipinos a majority on the commission and by replacing Americans with natives in the bureaucracy – much to the displeasure of the American colonial community in Manila. In 1916, the commission was replaced by an elected senate and all literate adult males became eligible to vote. However, legislation could still be vetoed by the president, and the US Congress continued to have the last word in Philippine policy.

A nominal two-party system emerged early on, though politics was soon dominated by the Nacionalistas, who exercised domestic hegemony until independence was achieved. The Nacionalistas, occasionally challenged by minority parties the way mosquitoes challenge a rhinoceros, originally differed from their opponents by urging "immediate" as opposed to "ultimate" independence. But there was less here than met the eye, since immediate independence was being advocated only as a matter of political expediency. Although the Filipino politicians made a great show of exaggerating differences between parties, it is hard to see them as anything but the political equivalent of Tweedledum and Tweedledee. Loyalty was determined largely by personal allegiances among the great families and by considerations of patronage. Because the Nacionalista Party was a neo-feudal patronage machine, fealty resided ultimately in personal loyalty to a single leader.[21]

American influence was greatest in the first decade, after which Washington's power began to decline. The door to rapid independence even swung open briefly with the election of a Democratic president, Woodrow Wilson, in 1912, but the Filipino elites backed away from the prospect. They could not come out and say so publicly, for it would have been political suicide to advocate a continuing American overlordship, but privately they feared that sudden independence might unleash radical populist forces that they would not be able to control.

By guaranteeing their local dominance, the Americans had made it difficult for the elites to demand independence with a straight face. Alluding to this problem, the Nacionalista leader Manuel Quezon once said: "Damn the Americans, why don't they tyrannize us more?"

Although a sizable number of American carpetbaggers came from the States to administer the islands, the actual experience of governance deflated the expectations of those who believed that colonialism would be a training ground for America's elites. From the start there was a reliance on Filipinos to staff the majority of government posts, though for the first decade the top administrative positions were dominated by Americans. And those Americans who did come were hardly the best and the brightest. As early as 1903, Taft was complaining about graft that was "due to the temptations to dishonesty that beset young Americans removed from the restraints of home life, without their families and with a disposition to gamble or drink or lead a lewd life."[22] This shortage of qualified Americans meant that from the beginning the Americans were willing to give control of municipal government to the Filipinos. By 1921, only 614 of more than 13,000 civil servants were American.

The Americans installed an honest judicial system in which, according to one historian, "for the first time a Filipino without money or influence could hope for justice in the courts."[23] They also sought to transfer their conception of impersonal and honest bureaucratic administration, a principle only recently adopted by the US federal government and which the progressive movement was trying to install at the state and local levels. This was a huge change from the pattern under Spain, in which public office was considered a personal franchise with no thought whatever to efficiency, honesty, and expertise. However, giving offices to the Filipinos as a way of gaining their tacit acquiescence in American rule had a downside, for it allowed the Filipinos to develop a patronage system in which progressive conceptions of good government were irrelevant. As one historian concluded, "while the Americans came to the Philippines espousing the principles of the

Civil Service League, they left the place looking worse than Tammany Hall."[24]

The bureaucracy did what modern bureaucracies do. Transportation was improved by the building of roads and railroads. Harbors were dredged. A Bureau of Agriculture sought to promote scientific methods of farming. Modern sanitation and public health programs based on modern scientific medicine were introduced. In short, a modern governmental apparatus was installed. With the exception of free defense supplied by the US army and navy, the Philippine government was self-supporting. No doubt this set an example to the locals and neutralized any criticism of imperial extravagance in Washington, but administering the islands on a pay-as-you-go basis also ruled out massive fiscal inputs, whether to relieve distress or to jump-start the island's economic development.

Religion and Land Reform

It quickly became evident that the limitless new fields for evangelization and Christianization were neither as extensive nor as fertile as Protestant mission enthusiasts had hoped. The islands had already been made an object of successful mission activity, albeit by the Roman Catholic Church. As one historian described the islands under Spanish rule, they were "really an enormous mission, rather than a colony operated for commercial ends."[25] Although main-line Protestant denominations as well as smaller sects set up outposts in the islands, their success was limited. By the 1980s, only about 3 percent of the Filipino population was Protestant in confession. Although some historians have suggested that these small numbers conceal a greater overall impact,[26] it would seem that the Protestant churches were more successful in promoting the American colonial mission than in achieving their goals of spiritual and political transformation.

Once the policy of political accommodation was in place, politicians in Washington sought to make their peace with the spiritual status quo. "The Commission did not come here to change the religion of anybody," insisted Taft.[27] President McKinley made overtures to the papacy and ultimately won its endorsement for his Philippine policy by promising to settle the vexed friar question. The friars, who owned more than 400,000 acres of the richest agricultural land in the country, had for centuries been the most powerful force in the countryside, enjoying *de facto* independence from both Rome and Madrid. Consequently, much of the resentment within the Philippines against Spanish rule was in fact directed at the power of the Spanish religious orders. There was a good deal of anti-Catholic sentiment in the country that denounced the "priest-ridden, defrauded, revolting adherents of a formal religion."[28]

Despite occasional attempts to install native priests, of which there were increasing numbers, the power of the friars increased in the nineteenth century. They minimized the introduction of new, secular ideas and blunted all hopes for modernization and change. Censorship was designed, according to a member of the first commission, "to keep the few Filipino readers of inquiring minds, so far as possible, from excursions into the bibliography of modern thought."[29] Not coincidentally, the provinces in which the friar lands were located had been hotbeds of the revolution prior to the arrival of the Americans.

The Organic Act of 1902 empowered the government to dispose of their lands. At the end of 1903, a deal was cut with Pope Leo XIII in which the US paid the Vatican a little more than seven million dollars for approximately 400,000 acres of land. The friar lands were supposed to go over to the 60,000 tenants for annual payments little more than those currently being paid in rents. Their disposition was intended to be part of a larger program of land reform in which more than 16 million acres of public land acquired from the Spanish were to be sold off in 40-acre parcels, in the spirit of the Homestead Act. Even squatters who had farmed lands not their own for a minimum of five years were to be made eligible for ownership with payment of a small registration fee. But these efforts were frustrated by the Filipino legislature, which saw to it that large blocks of land would be sold instead to the planter elite. Despite stated intentions of making land available to peasant smallholders, fundamental land reform never took place. Indeed, the percentage of tenant farmers doubled during the period of American rule.

Trade and Economic Policy

Commercially, the Philippines disappointed the expectations of the pro-imperialists. Despite the fact that interest in China continued to evolve following the acquisition of the islands, Manila never became the entrepôt for the China trade that enthusiasts had expected. The promise of neo-mercantilists that colonies would provide markets for export industries and sources of raw materials not available elsewhere also fell far short of expectations. If one defines imperialism in narrowly economic terms as the use of coercion "to extort profits above what simple commercial exchange can procure,"[30] there is room to argue, oddly, that the American presence in the Philippines was not imperialistic.

Notwithstanding all the enthusiastic talk of the riches of the islands, Washington's first concern was that the islands might become an economic liability. There was a determination to make the Philippines pay their own way and, initially at least, special interests feared that American markets would be swamped by cheap Filipino exports. Thus Congress was originally reluctant to grant unfettered access to the American market for Filipino goods, despite Taft's desire to use tariff preferences as a way of jump-starting economic development in the islands. Free trade, Taft argued, would "have a tendency to develop that whole country, of inviting the capital of the United States into the islands, and of creating a trade between the islands and this country which can not but be beneficial to both."[31] He even intimated that the benefits of free trade would kill off any desire for independence among the Filipinos.

But Congress gave way only grudgingly, preferring to protect domestic interests that feared injury from cheaply priced Filipino competition. Reciprocal free trade was established only by the Payne–Aldrich tariff of 1909, with the exception of quotas on certain sensitive commodities such as sugar, cigars, and tobacco. Had anyone other than Taft been president, these concessions to the Philippines in what was otherwise a high-tariff measure would probably not have been granted by Congress. The quotas on tobacco and sugar were dropped altogether in 1913, when the Underwood tariff eliminated most restrictions on trade between the mainland and the islands.

The Filipinos, led by Manuel Quezon, at first objected to the policy of free trade. Quezon believed that as American commercial interests moved into the islands they would insist on American protection, thus making independence less likely. And that was without taking into consideration the economic domination of American capital. "That the coming of large American companies would bring as a result the monopoly of wealth of the country by them is a fact that is beyond doubt; they would first take possession of our market, through lack of competition, and then of our agriculture," he argued.[32] But the objection of the Filipino assembly was overridden by the veto of governor W. Cameron Forbes and sustained by the American Congress. Believing that only American capital was capable of providing the necessary investments for development, Forbes predicted that free trade would "bring the Filipinos from poverty to prosperity, to make of these struggling, half-starved, half-clothed millions a great, strong, robust, well-nurtured, and well-developed people."

The result was a division of labor in which the Philippine economy was encouraged to produce primary commodities like sugar, hemp, and coconut oil that enjoyed secure access to the large American market in exchange for imports of US consumer goods. Thus the output of sugar, which would account for 60 percent of all Philippine exports, increased from 194,000 short tons for the period 1890–4 to 345,000 for the years 1910–14, to 820,000 tons for 1925–9. The total percentage of Philippine exports to the US and imports from the US increased dramatically, in effect integrating the Filipino economy with that of the mother country. By 1930, the Philippines depended on the US mainland for 79 percent of its exports and 63 percent of its imports.

Contrary to the fears of Quezon and members of his class, most of the profits from these primary product exports remained in the hands of Filipinos rather than flowing to absentee owners abroad. In this way, the policy of free trade, by allowing the crops of the planter class free access to the American market, reinforced the policy of attraction by promoting the continued dominance of the Filipino agrarian elites. Philippine labor remained concentrated in agricultural production, as fully 10 million of 16 million Filipinos in 1940 depended for their incomes on the export to the US of sugar or coconut products.

As a result, says one historian, "the Philippines entered into a vulnerable, subordinate relationship that it has yet to escape."[33] But what were the alternatives? There is no assurance that another tariff policy would have produced better results; massive fiscal inputs were out of the question; and a policy of benign neglect might well have made a bad situation worse. But even if one assumes that this policy worked to the economic advantage of the Philippines, the close adaptation to the American economy practically assured that independence, when it did come, would have painful economic consequences for the islands unless continued access to the American market was assured.

As for massive US investment, that would not be forthcoming, either. Afraid of looking like an exploiter, Congress refused to approve concessions to US mining and agricultural interests. The Organic Act limited corporate tracts to 2,500 acres each instead of the 25,000 desired by business interests.[34] Harvey Firestone's attempt to secure one of the islands for a massive rubber plantation was rebuffed. Taft, fearing that development was being hampered, criticized these limitations as "obnoxious." Despite this slow start, the special interests, who were not much in evidence during the initial policy debates over acquiring the islands, soon enough saw their opportunities for profit, primarily in public utilities, sugar milling, and mining. Nevertheless, the amount of American investment came nowhere near the amount required for economic take-off.[35] By the mid-1930s, it totaled no more than 160 million dollars, which came to only 22 percent of total US investments in Asia and approximately 1 percent of all investments abroad.[36] If there was surplus capital "congested" in the United States, it did not find its way to the Philippines.

If capital exports were disappointing, so too was the discovery that the Philippines were a puny market for American goods. "With our protective tariff wall around the Philippines islands, its 10 million inhabitants, as they advance in civilization, would have to buy our goods," Lodge had predicted to McKinley.[37] But by 1917, US exports were only 28 million dollars and did not reach 100 million until 1940. In fact, in the pre-World War II years, the balance of trade ran heavily against the United States to a total of 400 million dollars.

Having failed to find El Dorado in the islands, domestic opposition to the policy of free trade and economic integration never went away. The stretch run toward Philippine independence in the 1930s was to a great extent explainable by the desire of Americans, ravaged by the great depression, to close the American market to Philippine sugar, cordage, and immigrant labor. Freeing the Philippines would free Americans from their economic competition. President Franklin D. Roosevelt made no bones about it. "Let's get rid of the Philippines," he told some Congressmen, "that's the most important thing. Let's be frank about it."[38] Economic frustration also sheds light on why the divorce settlement was less than generous. Even though the economy of the islands also suffered during the 1930s, leading to a good deal of internal unrest, the Tydings–McDuffie Act (1934), which began a 10-year countdown to independence, provided for free trade only until 1940, with quotas on exports to the US, but with no limits on US exports to the islands.

It is true that the islands were locked into an agrarian pattern that reinforced the rule of the elites and foreclosed alternative paths to development. But it is also true that the islands prospered economically during the period of American rule.

In some ways, the economic regime installed by the United States was clearly beneficial. The period of American rule resulted in a significant increase in rice consumption and access to consumer goods – which could not be said of Japanese rule in Korea.[39] According to one estimate made in 1943, the standard of living in the Philippine islands was three times higher than that of neighboring countries of the Far East. Americans felt that they had done such a good job that, in the midst of World War II, they felt free to brag about their experience as a model for other Asian colonial powers to emulate.

Education

In their thinking about education, Americans would certainly have agreed with Napoleon, who in 1807 said: "Of all our institutions public education is the most important. Everything depends on it, the present and the future." Although the Spanish had begun the process of installing a system of primary education in the late nineteenth century, it had been administered by the friars only in some of the wealthier areas so that in 1898 there were fewer than 7,000 students enrolled in elementary, secondary, and collegiate schools. The great mass of the Filipinos, according to Taft, were "still in a hopeless condition of ignorance, and utterly unable intelligently to wield political control."[40] A US senator described the Philippines as "tenanted by a very peculiar mass, a heterogeneous compound of inefficient humanity."[41] The census of 1903 revealed that 55 percent of the population over the age of 10 was illiterate in any language.[42] Education, Americans believed, would promote Filipino cultural cohesion, encourage democracy and civic-mindedness, liberate individual talents, and help to create a sense of national and global identity.[43]

The Taft commission was instructed to give priority to "the extension of a system of primary education which shall be free to all" in order "to fit the people for the duties of citizenship and for the ordinary avocations of a civilized community." Of course, the new system would have to be secular. At the same time, bowing to the fact that the overwhelming majority of Filipinos were Catholics, the US allowed for religious instruction three times weekly for those students whose parents desired it. Not surprisingly, much of the Catholic hierarchy in the islands hated the new system, arguing that "the native teachers were exercising a perverting influence religiously."[44] Despite some half-hearted resistance, the Filipino elites fell behind the idea of secularization.

Given a massive shortage of teachers, Americans were often called upon to fill the gap. Hundreds crossed the Pacific on the *Thomas* and became known as Thomasites. It took a full decade before most of the instruction was done by native Filipino teachers, with Americans generally serving in a supervisory capacity. Although instruction was originally supposed to be in the vernacular, for a number of reasons English was made the language of instruction: English was the language of administration, it would be easier for the American teachers with no knowledge of Spanish or native tongues, and many Filipinos, when asked, seemed to be in favor of learning English as the key to advancement. As Finley Peter Dunne's Mr Dooley put it: "we'll larn ye our language, because 'tis easier to larn ye ours thin to larn oursilves ye'ers." The assembly passed a bill in 1908 which would have made the vernacular the language of instruction, but it was rejected by the commission. However, Spanish remained the official language in the Philippine courts and in the assembly until 1920 because the Filipino elite had been educated in the old imperial tongue.

The first superintendent of education, Fred W. Atkinson, was concerned about "overdoing the matter of higher education and unfitting the Filipinos for practical work." His curricular model was based on the system of industrial education installed at Tuskegee Institute, which was then in vogue as the best approach to educating African-Americans recently liberated from the bonds of slavery. Its most famous exponent, Booker T. Washington, believed that African-Americans needed first to acquire elementary skills before aspiring to advanced education. Although this emphasis on manual and vocational training was opposed by W. E. B. DuBois, who argued that the creation of an educated African-American elite was indispensable to racial progress, the Tuskegee approach became the *fin-de-siècle* standard for educating people of color.

"Education in the Philippines must be along industrial lines," Atkinson told Booker T. Washington.[45] This approach was congenial to Americans because of its modest, non-radical character and because it coincided nicely with the reigning scientific view of race known as Lamarckism. Named after the French zoologist Jean-Baptiste Lamarck (1744–1829), this view held that races differed markedly in their innate abilities, but it also conceded the possibility of racial improvement through education, as learned characteristics were biologically transmitted to the next generation. While this outlook meant that backward races need not be consigned forever to the lower depths of inferiority, it did not envision any dramatic improvement either, which, no doubt, helps explain its popularity among turn-of-the-century Americans.

But industrial education did not work out well – there was, after all, not much industry in the Philippines – and the Americans shifted focus to primary education, with its traditional emphasis on literacy and numeracy. Under the superintendentship of David R. Barrows, the goal became universal primary education, with an emphasis on inculcating the basic skills needed for citizenship. "Two years of instruction in arithmetic to every child will in a generation destroy that repellent peonage or bonded indebtedness that prevails throughout this country," said Barrows with characteristic optimism.[46] In addition, the students would be provided with "character training" and instruction in civic values. Americans also assumed that the lower classes, armed with the English language and a basic understanding of their fundamental rights, would be able to emancipate themselves from their landlord *caciques*.

After 1907, the pendulum swung once again in the direction of manual training. Barrows's successor believed that the program he had inherited was impractical. "We want men taught to work with their hands; and while we do not object to their learning to read and write, we want to see agricultural schools and arts and trades schools in greater abundance," he said. This new course was thought to be more in keeping with the goal of economic development, which would in turn provide the needed revenues for mass education. Henceforth less time was devoted to English and arithmetic in favor of hand weaving, gardening, and housekeeping, and elementary forms of civilized behavior like cleanliness, table manners, and acceptable public conduct. (Henry Cabot Lodge had once remarked, in the most condescending way possible, that "a native family feeds; it does not breakfast or dine, it feeds.")[47]

Given this confusion among American policy-makers about the basic mission of education, it is not surprising that serious problems emerged. As the result of this *de facto* abandonment of universal primary education, enrollments in primary schools actually decreased after a decade. Insufficiency of revenues also limited expenditure on schools. And to the extent that education had expanded horizontally, it was only by sinking shallow roots as many students received, on average, instruction for only one and a half years from poorly trained teachers, many of whom were themselves barely literate in English. The well-heeled elites, meanwhile, continued to send their children to private schools. However, the administration expanded the number of intermediate schools, where enrollments continued to climb.

Higher education had also been badly neglected by the Spanish, on the (correct) assumption that a European-style university education was likely to produce a revolutionary class among the natives. A high school was established in each province. The one university on the archipelago, San Tomas, had a curriculum and mode of instruction that harked back to the scholasticism of the Middle Ages. A new University of the Philippines, free from church control and using English as the language of instruction, was established in Manila in 1908 as the capstone of the educational system. The high schools and the university were particularly popular with the elites, who envisioned these institutions of learning as stepping-stones to advancement in the new English-language system of government. The elites also used the new graduates to demand a greater share of governmental posts from the Americans.

Although US educational policies had their shortcomings, any judgment of their efficacy needs to take into account the comparative efforts of other colonial powers. By that standard, the US did quite well. "No other colonial power made a greater priority of national education than the United States," says one historian.[48] Indeed, educational spending accounted for one-half of the governmental budget. The number of English speakers by the end of the 1930s had climbed to one-quarter of the population, while literacy had increased to over 50 percent.

The Mirage of Great Power

To hear the imperialists tell it in 1899, annexing the Philippines would bolster America's status as a great power. Speaking of the archipelago, General Arthur MacArthur waxed ecstatic, claiming that "its strategic position is unexcelled by that of any other position on the globe. The China Sea, which separates it by something like 750 miles from the continent, is nothing more or less than a safety moat."[49] Albert Beveridge touted the islands as "a fortress thrown up in the Pacific, defending our Western coast, commanding the waters of the Orient."[50] But within a few years the moat was transformed into an open invasion route as the realization dawned upon military strategists that the Philippines, far from adding to American power, were a serious liability. Indeed, it was the great power advocates who, more than any other group, recoiled from the geopolitical implications of possessing the islands.

By 1907, in the midst of an immigration dispute with Japan, tension with Tokyo over the interpretation of the "open door" in Manchuria, and some war talk among the military, Roosevelt was acknowledging privately that the islands were "a heel of Achilles" for the United States. "In the excitement of the Spanish War people wanted to take the islands," he wrote to Taft. "They had an idea they would be a valuable possession. Now they think they are of no value." TR now agreed with them: "I am bound to say that in the physical sense I don't see where they are of any value to us or where they are likely to be of any value." The Philippines, for TR were "all that makes the situation with Japan dangerous."[51]

Roosevelt may have been unduly pessimistic, but he was certainly closer to the truth than the optimists of 1898. Though the United States had built up one of the world's most powerful navies by this time, its mission was still primarily hemispheric defense and Roosevelt recognized that the Japanese navy was supreme in its home waters. A new hypothetical war plan, code named Orange, conceded this point when it concluded that the islands could not be defended against the powerful Japanese navy. Even though a decision was made early to build a naval base at Subic Bay on Luzon, the precariousness of the American military position led the Roosevelt administration to decide to locate the chief American base for the Pacific Fleet at Pearl Harbor in Hawaii, though only after the usual inter-service squabbling. In the years to come, occasional bursts of optimism among naval planners did little to change the underlying strategic facts.[52]

For a brief moment, at least, the vision of the Philippines as a base for an enlarged American role in East Asia seemed likely to be fulfilled. With the outbreak of the Boxer Rebellion in China in 1900, McKinley sent 2,500 soldiers, most of them from the Philippines – and there were precious few to spare, since the army had its hands full dealing with Aguinaldo's forces – to participate in a multinational expedition to rescue the foreign legations besieged by 140,000 rebels in Beijing. But this was a false dawn. It soon became clear that the diplomacy of imperialism, far from being a purely progressive phenomenon, was a source of tension and conflict among the powers in East Asia.

Although American diplomacy secured the fruits of ownership for the United States in the short run, it could do little to turn around a problem that, in the long term, would only grow worse. Roosevelt did cut a few deals with Japan in an attempt to shore up the US position in the Philippines, but their underlying vulnerability was heightened when Japan's acquisition of Germany's former Pacific islands in the post-World War I peace settlement effectively blocked the navy's already tenuous lines of communication. The continuing military insecurity of the islands was highlighted in 1922 by a decision made at the Washington Conference in which, in return for a naval arms control agreement, the US agreed not to strengthen its Philippine defenses for 15 years. Given the lack of confidence about defending the islands, the US gave up little in making this concession.

The widely entertained notion that American military power in the Philippines could be translated into an economic bonanza also proved to be empty. If the costs of maintaining their security are weighed against the profits derived from trade, the military investment in the islands contributed to a net loss overall. By the mid-1930s, according to one estimate, the "military cost of conquest, suppression, fortification and garrison maintenance totaled at least 500 million dollars." The enormous cost of reconquering the Philippines during World War II also needs to be factored in. By contrast, American exports to the islands over the same period amounted to roughly 400 million dollars. If one factors in profits, the duties lost from allowing Philippine exports free access, the loss of American earnings from Philippine exports, and other incidental costs, it is hardly surprising that even a radical historian was forced to conclude that "in the large view the Philippine colony was not a paying venture."[53] The "commercial opportunity" sought by President McKinley, such as it was, was enjoyed by Philippine landowners and by a small group of American special interests.

Ironically, the Philippines became economically profitable for the first time in the post-independence decade when the US ran a favorable trade balance of 1.7 billion dollars with the islands. American investment tripled in the first two independence decades. Even then, however, the amount of aid granted by the US to the Philippines, largely for strategic reasons, dwarfed the investment in the islands or the profits reaped therefrom.

The Road to Independence

In keeping with the idea that this colony was being held in trust for civilization, the ultimate goal for the Philippines was, from the beginning, independence – which was a quite advanced doctrine, for its time. TR told Congress in 1901: "We hope to do for them what has never been done for any people of the tropics – to make them fit for self government after the fashion of the really free nations."[54] The only question was when, not whether. Given the strategically disadvantageous position of the islands and the tendency of the American public to view the islands "simply as an unremunerative and indeed expensive duty," by 1907 TR had concluded that "we shall have to be prepared for giving the islands independence of a more or less complete type much sooner than I think advisable."[55]

Nevertheless, disengaging from the islands proved to be more difficult than getting in. With the victory of Woodrow Wilson and the Democratic Party in 1912, it seemed as if the timetable for independence would be advanced. Wilson had been a fully fledged imperialist in 1898, but his outlook, like that of progressives generally, gradually turned in an anti-imperialist direction. During the election campaign, he declared that "the Philippines are at present our frontier but I hope we presently are to deprive ourselves of that frontier." By 1913, Roosevelt publicly agreed, saying "I do not believe that America has any special beneficial interest in retaining the Philippines."[56]

The Jones Act of 1916 promised independence as soon as a "stable government" had been achieved. Independence might have been granted at once had it not been for the opposition of the Taft segment of the Republican Party, the Catholic church, and Manuel Quezon, the Filipino representative to the US House of Representatives. In public, Quezon advocated immediate independence. "I would prefer a government run like hell by Filipinos to one run like heaven by Americans," he said. That was for public consumption, however.

Privately, he feared being cut adrift from the American market, being exposed to Japanese power, and facing the lower classes in the absence of American support for elite rule. Although Quezon lobbied successfully against immediate liberation, in 1920 Harrison stated that the job of tutelage was complete and recommended that independence be granted forthwith.

By then, however, the pendulum of American politics had swung in the other direction. The newly elected Republican president, Warren G. Harding, declared that it would be a "national disgrace" if the Filipinos were forced "to walk alone when they had not been taught fully to creep." An investigating commission, which included former governor W. Cameron Forbes, concluded that the time was not yet ripe. Independence, it said, "would be a betrayal of the Philippine people, a misfortune to the American people, a distinct step backward in the path of progress and a discreditable neglect of our national duty were we to withdraw from the islands." More frank was Governor Henry Stimson, who opposed independence on account of the "Malay tendency to backslide" and because of his belief that independence would permanently fasten an "undemocratic oligarchy" upon the peasant masses.[57] The US needed to stay on until popular, as opposed to merely stable, government had been achieved. The institutions had been created, but the Filipinos needed time to grow into them.

With the collapse of the stock market in 1929 and the onset of the great depression of the 1930s, the tide turned once again in the direction of granting independence – for the last time. This time, powerful economic forces, particularly sugar and dairy lobbyists and agricultural interests who were opposed to Filipino imports, reinforced the Democratic animus against imperialism. Typical was the attitude of one senator, who argued that the Philippines "are hanging like a millstone about the necks of our [agricultural] producers." [58] Trade unions were outraged by the influx of Filipinos into the country, most of the 60,000 immigrants having arrived in the 1920s. And as the political skies in Asia began to darken with the Japanese invasion and conquest of Manchuria in 1931, many foresaw serious trouble ahead if the US insisted on hanging on to the islands.

For Franklin D. Roosevelt's New Deal administration in Washington, the time for Philippine independence had clearly come. After some delays caused by political maneuvering that was designed to give Quezon the credit at the expense of his political rivals, Congress passed the Tydings–McDuffie Act in 1934. This bill inaugurated the "commonwealth period," a 10-year warm-up period prior to independence in which the islands would be self-governing. The government was placed in the hands of Quezon, who won elections to the commonwealth presidency in 1935. The islands were governed by a new constitution, ostensibly based on the US model, but which placed far more power in the hands of the president. A US high commissioner exercised vestigial American sovereignty.

The decision to let the islands go was made with the knowledge that they would be easy prey for an expansionist power like Japan. As Theodore Roosevelt Jr, then governor general, predicted in 1932, "The Philippines can be independent of the United States, but there can be no such thing as an independent Philippines."[59] Recognizing that the defense of the newly independent islands would be even more problematic without an American military presence, FDR appointed General Douglas MacArthur to the thankless job of military adviser to the new regime.

The Philippines also faced severe economic difficulties in the 1930s. The world depression had sent agricultural exports into a tailspin while booming population growth (the islands, once considered underpopulated, now numbered 16 million souls) aggravated rural poverty. The islands had long been plagued with rural unrest, but in 1935 a spontaneous uprising of farm tenants and landless laborers left many dead and wounded. Though some progressive Americans insisted that "no nation can be founded on a downtrodden peasantry," the Filipino elite, concerned with maintaining its wealth and power, continued to tighten the screws. The terms of the Tydings–McDuffie Act did not help, as it provided for growing barriers to the importation of island products that formerly had

enjoyed free entry. Immigration of Filipinos was likewise severely restricted.

Independence was postponed by the outbreak of World War
II, which confirmed the long-standing assumption that the
Philippines were a strategic liability for the United States.[60]
Simultaneous with the Japanese attack on Pearl Harbor in
Hawaii, the Japanese launched an air assault against American bases in the Philippines and then followed up with an
invasion. American forces held out at Corregidor on the Bataan
peninsula outside Manila before being forced to surrender in
May 1942, but not before General MacArthur made his famous promise: "I shall return." The conduct of the war followed in general outline the premises of War Plan Orange,
which assumed that the islands would fall quickly to the Japanese and would be recovered only as American forces fought
their way across the Pacific.

Roosevelt's refusal to make a priority of supplying reinforce-
ments for the Philippines generated considerable bitterness
among the Filipino elite, who desired immediate assistance.
The choices facing them must have seemed like a replay of
1898 and 1899 as the Japanese, like the American conquerors
before them, resorted to a mixture of coercion and attraction.
In addition, however, the Japanese played the race card quite
effectively, at least at first. One Japanese officer reminded the
Filipinos: "Like it or not, you are Filipinos and belong to the
Oriental race. No matter how hard you try, you cannot become white people." During World War II, much of the oligarchy cooperated with the Japanese. In 1943, a constitution
for a puppet state was drafted and, in September 1944, the
Filipino republic was forced to declare war on the United States.
Jose Laurel explained this decision as "nothing more than a
surrender to the inevitable."

Nevertheless, as happened in the 1890s, many radical nationalists decided from the beginning to resist by joining the
Hukbalahop or People's Anti-Japanese Army. As they had
before, the guerrillas resorted to terrorism to make their point
against the Japanese – and against their fellow countrymen, if
necessary. This time, however, the moral balance swung in

favor of the resistance, thanks largely to the ferocious and exploitative nature of the Japanese occupation that caused about one million Filipino deaths over the course of the war. By the end of 1944, the guerrilla forces numbered some 180,000. Apart from the havoc they caused behind Japanese lines, they provided priceless intelligence to the returning Americans, who invaded Leyte in October 1944. By February 1945 American troops were in Manila, though they nearly destroyed the city in the process of taking it. By April, the American reconquest of the Philippines was all but over, despite lingering resistance from the die-hard Japanese.

The return of MacArthur in October 1944 provided probably the last opportunity for the Americans to impose land reform, this under the guise of punishing the planter oligarchy for its collaboration with the enemy. But the opportunity was not taken. President Osmeña was inclined to go easy on the collaborators who were, after all, members of his small and exclusive social class whose support he would continue to need in future. With independence imminent, President Harry S. Truman was not willing to take on such an explosive issue. Yet another reason for failing to act was a peasant rebellion, which included communists known as Huks, that had been gaining ground since the 1930s. MacArthur feared that destroying the conservative planter elite would only clear the way for an even more undesirable radical leadership.

The Post-independence Relationship

Decolonization, like divorce, rarely brings a clean break between the two parties. In the case of the United States and the Philippines, the terms of separation had to be worked out and new arrangements put in place to address interests, created over the course of years in a morganatic marriage, that would continue to be of mutual concern. Adding to the reasons for the continuation of a close relationship was the outbreak of the Cold War between the United States and the Soviet Union that added a new geopolitical importance to the Philippines that it had not possessed in the preceding half-century. As a result, the United States became more deeply involved than ever in Filipino internal politics and developed a stake in the modernization of the islands that took on greater importance than it had under the colonial regime. But as the foreign-policy importance of the Philippines increased, the power to achieve policy goals dwindled. Thus, despite the expenditure of much money and effort, the gap between intentions and results remained as wide as ever.

After the war, the Americans made haste to grant the independence that had been postponed by the conflict, though on less than generous terms. In the Bell Trade Act of 1946, Congress insisted on strict quotas for imports of Philippine goods, while American products enjoyed complete tariff immunity for a period of eight years. This interim period would be followed by 20 years of increasing tariffs. The US also insisted on a controversial parity amendment in which American businessmen were granted the rights of Filipino nationals while placing limits on the ability of the Philippines to control their currency's international value. Congress also appropriated funds for repairing war damage and reconstructing the Philippine economy, some 620 million dollars in all. Though some of the reconstruction aid was targeted for social measures, it amounted to only a small proportion of the total.

The Philippines became independent on July 4, 1946, but military dependency upon the United States continued. The congressional aid package provided an incentive for the Filipinos to approve not only the trade bill, but also to grant the Americans exclusive rights to create 23 military bases on the islands. The deal struck in 1947 gave Americans an extraordinary degree of control over the bases and their immediate environs, while prohibiting third powers from doing the same. As a result, the islands became, *de facto*, a military protectorate of the United States.[61]

The continuing presence of the United States was made necessary by the emergence of the Cold War in Asia. Concerned primarily with Europe in the initial stages of the conflict with the Soviet Union and its allies, the US was forced to pay more and more attention to Asia and the Pacific as the decade came to a close. With the triumph of Mao Zedong's communist forces in a long-running civil war with the Kuomintang, the entire mainland of China came under communist control by the end of 1949. The outbreak of the Korean War in June 1950 further sparked fears about the spread of communism throughout Asia.

As a result of an enormous sea-change of strategic sensibility that had taken place in Washington, the Philippines were transformed almost overnight from a military liability to a strategic asset. In the minds of American policy-makers, the loss of the islands to communism would be a major blow to American credibility that might cause an already wavering world opinion to lean in the direction of appeasing the communists throughout the world. Their former colonial status had little to do with this perception of the importance of the islands. Other obscure areas of the world in which the United States had played little or no role at all – Korea and Vietnam, for example – were even more valuable real estate according to the new definition of national security.

Even if the Cold War had not arisen, the US had determined during the war with Japan that its strategic defensive perimeter would lie in the western Pacific. Thus the US made sure to claim for itself as United Nations trust territories the Japanese-held islands of Micronesia through which American military forces had fought before launching the final offensive against the Japanese home islands. The American naval base at Subic Bay and Clark airforce base, the US's largest overseas military facility, were to provide the westernmost outposts of the new strategic position. American base rights were confirmed in 1947 and security ties between the two countries were further tightened by the conclusion of a mutual security treaty in 1951 and by making the Philippines a charter member of the South-east Asia Treaty Organization in 1954.

The economic development of the islands also continued to preoccupy American policy-makers, though now within a Cold War context in which strategic significance, and not the white man's burden, was the primary justification for modernizing policies. At base, the Cold War was seen as a contest between two competing ways of life, one based on socialist ideals and managed economies, the other on liberal-democratic values and a reliance upon the market as the regulator of economic development. In the end, the success of US strategy depended on the nation's ability to demonstrate the superior virtues of the American model of development, lest the Sino-Soviet example prove more attractive to underdeveloped countries.

A National Security Council memorandum of November 9, 1950 summarized the rationale for promoting modernization:

> The security interests of the United States require that the Philippines become and remain stable, anticommunist, pro-American, and an example for the rest of the world of the intention of the United States to encourage the establishment of progressive and responsible government. This entails the reassertion of US influence to the extent required to eliminate prevalent corruption, provide efficient administrative services, and restore public faith in the best interests of the people.[62]

Because the US could no longer exercise its sovereign will, direct tutelage was replaced by secretive attempts at manipulation by the Central Intelligence Agency (CIA), which meddled in propaganda, in elections, and in training of new reform-minded activist leaders. Not surprisingly, the failure of these covert programs was as pronounced as the shortcomings of the overt policies of the colonial period.

Reform was especially urgent because the Philippines, like many newly independent societies in the Far East, were experiencing revolutionary tremors that originated in the unstable ground on which Filipino society had been constructed. By 1950, the Hukbalahop rebellion, which had been building for some time, was cresting to the point that a US military adviser judged the situation to be "definitely out of hand." Fortunately, the pro-American Filipino minister of defense, Ramon Magsaysay, collaborated closely with the US military and the CIA. He managed to decapitate the rebellion by arresting most of its political leadership in one stroke.

Magsaysay also recognized that "it would be futile to go on killing Huks while the Administration continues to breed dissidence by neglecting the problems of our masses." Following American advice, he adopted psychological warfare techniques with some success, reined in the army (whose brutal approach to the rebellion had begun to resemble the methods of the American colonial army of occupation a half-century earlier) and resorted to harsh methods himself when necessary, such as using napalm against the rebels. Magsaysay attempted some land reform, even going so far as to promise free land to rebels who surrendered, but the reforms were frustrated by agrarian courts dominated by the powerful families. Magsaysay's election in 1953 as a reform president further de-fanged the rebellion.

Unfortunately, Magsaysay discovered once in power that running a reformist government was a more formidable task than defeating a rebellion. Despite the urging of the Eisenhower administration that he mount a "vigorous attack" on the country's social and economic problems, his freedom of maneuver was hampered by his political dependence on planters, crony capitalists, and government bureaucrats who were opposed to change. In the absence of substantially more foreign aid than the US was willing to provide, Magsaysay had little leverage to use on his colleagues. His death in a plane crash in 1957 created a legend, but it is doubtful that he could have lived up to it had he survived.

In short order, the Philippine elites re-established the old pattern of manipulating relations with Washington to their own advantage. In 1955, in the Laurel–Langley agreement, the non-tariff quotas were renewed as a reward and the limitations on Philippine sovereignty were eliminated. Between 1945 and 1958, the US made available more than one billion dollars in grants and credits, more than to any country in the region. In addition it supplied about 30 million dollars annually in military aid, some of which went into non-military purposes like road construction. Much of the aid was channeled to the uses of the ruling elite as a form of patronage that favored friends and punished enemies. Enjoying privileged access to government, the landed elite used its influence as a point of entry into light manufacturing, thereby uniting the industrial and agricultural interests of the country.

In general, the Filipino elites made the increasingly testy and truculent base negotiations a tool to strengthen their own control and to "nationalize" their economy in their own interests. In time, they managed to turn upside-down the early postwar relationship by successfully demanding protection from American exports while demanding at the same time free access for their products in the American market. Content with their own low-tech, low-growth industries, they also resisted linking their economy to Japan's, thus isolating themselves from the most dynamic force in East Asia. On more than one occasion, they shot themselves in the foot, as when they passed discriminatory legislation against the industrious Chinese and created widespread unemployment as a result. The result was growing independence, but this "industrialization without development" only further hardened the socioeconomic patterns that flourished during the colonial period.[63] As was often the case in patron–client relationships, the client managed to gain the whip hand.

The Philippines plunged into outright autocracy in 1973 when President Ferdinand Marcos, whose second and last term as president was about to expire, suspended civil liberties by declaring martial law, allegedly in order to deal with a communist threat. Marcos also justified his power grab by arguing that the Philippines were a "sick society" that could be nursed to health only through his autocratic ministrations. He was correct about the society, but totally misleading as to his reformist intentions. Instead, his personal rule broke all records for political corruption in a society where politics as a way of lining one's pockets had long been the rule. By the 1980s, helped along by a precipitous fall in commodity prices, the country was virtually bankrupt and even his former supporters were looking forward to his departure. Sixty percent of the population lived in "absolute poverty."[64] Radical insurgencies once again sprang up in the countryside.

The Marcos era ended in 1986 when the dictator made the mistake of holding an election that he believed he would win. He fled the country after having secreted abroad some six billion dollars in assets, though Americans were understandably more fascinated by the revelation that his wife, Imelda, had 3,000 pairs of shoes to choose from in her commodious closets, some of which are now on museum display in the nation's shoe-making capital. Americans took pride in the coming to power of the democratically elected and American-educated (Manhattan College) Corazon Aquino, whose husband had been murdered – the suspicion was that the deed was done at the order of Marcos or by rogue sympathizers – some years earlier. With her slogan of "people's power," she seemed bent on realizing the elusive promise of democratization. But Aquino was herself from one of the great families. Under constant pressure from the military and potent conservative forces, she neglected to press for fundamental land reforms out of the understandable fear that her rule would be undermined if she tried.

With the return of democracy, the relationship between Washington and Manila became even more rocky. Increasing Philippine nationalism, motivated in part by resentment of Washington's open support of Aquino, was matched by a growing disinclination on the part of American negotiators to make concessions to what they saw as the extortionate demands of the Filipinos. Base negotiations in 1988 resembled a game of "chicken" in which both sides backed down only at the last moment and forged a three-year interim agreement that paid the Philippines far less than they desired. In 1991, however, neither side budged and no agreement was reached. A member of the US negotiating team, fed up with what he considered to be outrageous stipulations, said that the Filipinos, "by asking for greater compensation, were acting like teenagers holding their parents' Visa card for ransom."[65]

Maybe so, but a growing number of Filipinos, feeling that the bases were symbols of a debilitating dependence upon the United States, were prepared to cut the apron strings, if necessary. "We must slay the American father image and cut him down to brotherly size," said Raul Manglapus.[66] The end of the Cold War and a volcanic eruption from Mt Pinatubo that buried Clark airforce base under a thick and nearly impenetrable blanket of ash diminished American ardor for staying on any longer, while the increasingly nationalistic Filipinos grew even more opposed to the prospect of a 10-year phased withdrawal. By the end of November 1992, Americans had evacuated the bases and the Philippines had completed their transit from strategic liability through strategic asset to strategic insignificance. With the end of the base privileges, it became abundantly clear that the US had little economic interest in the islands.

Though the Filipinos had long since regained economic sovereignty by adroitly using base negotiations to their nationalist advantage, independence provided no miracle cure for the nation's economic ills. By the end of the century, the islands had fallen far behind other East Asian societies. Ironically, former colonies of Japan like South Korea and Taiwan, which had been harshly ruled, were at the leading edge of the East Asian economic miracle. Malaysia, Thailand, and even Indonesia enjoyed higher per capita GDP than the Philippines.

Part of the problem had to do with the rapid growth of the population, which nearly quadrupled between 1900 and 1946, increasing from seven million to 27 million. By the end of the 1990s, as the number of Filipinos approached 80 million with a population density of 500 people per square mile, the Philippines ranked in the middle of the pack in the UN's human development index, seventy-seventh among 172 nations. The annual per capita GDP of 3,200 dollars was twice that of India, but less than one-fourth that of Taiwan or South Korea, and only two-thirds that of Indonesia. Compared to Central American countries, its GDP was higher than Honduras but lower than Guatemala's.

Despite attempts to break up monopolies, liberalize the economy, and establish free-trade zones, a new constitution put into effect in 1987 also incorporated some highly protectionist economic provisions that ran directly counter to the liberal global ideology of the 1990s. The nation's continuing problems became clear when some nominally impressive gains in GNP in the early and mid-1990s were negated by inflation, population growth, and a serious economic downturn that

struck Asia late in the decade. Thus Philippine growth continued to lag behind the star performers in Asia and appalling
amounts of grinding poverty remained.

It was also far from certain that the Philippines had finally
turned the corner to true democracy. Corruption and crony
capitalism were still the rule in its political and economic affairs. The election of a former movie star, Joseph Estrada, as
president in 1998 left unclear whether serious modernization
was under way or whether Philippine politics had descended
to the most trivial kind of electioneering – symptoms that were
not entirely absent from American politics, either. Despite what
one journal catalogued as "charges of incompetence, crude
nationalism, poor educational background, health problems,
gambling and adultery,"[67] Estrada continued to mesmerize the
masses. It did not take long before his political opponents,
headed by Corazon Aquino, were accusing him of harboring
Marcos-type ambitions.

In the 1990s, the relationship between the United States and
the Philippines had lost many of its points of attraction. Immigration was perhaps the most important bilateral connection.
The Philippines were the second largest source of legal immigrants to the United States, with a population of three million
already in the States and 70,000 more coming every year. But
while the Philippines celebrated the bittersweet anniversary of
1898 in which independence from Spain had been gained at
the cost of bondage to the United States, Americans barely
noticed. For the policy elite the Philippines were not nearly as
obscure as they had been in 1897, but in the minds of most
Americans it would have been hard to tell the difference.

It is clear from this account that there existed a vast gap between imperialist promise and performance. Although states are
not noted for their benevolence, it is still fair to ask: why didn't
the United States do a better job of Americanizing the Philippines? Why didn't political democracy and economic development emerge? Three basic reasons for the failure to develop the
Philippines leap quickly to mind. First, Americans had no serious desire to try very hard. Second, even if they had, they didn't

know how. And, third, in the absence of the will and the way, other priorities – first order, then security – ranked higher.

To begin with, the United States had no deep-seated need to modernize the Philippines. The relationship was the product of a temporary obsession with the notion of empire in general, not of an attraction to the Philippines in particular or an interest in the Filipinos as Filipinos. As with any infatuation, the attraction was short-lived. Because a commitment to modernization would have required much more time, money, and policy energy than Americans were willing to invest – and this kind of imperialism would have been quite thoroughgoing in its insistence on cultural transformation or deracination – it is not surprising, after the initial frisson of colonialist emotion had subsided, that American attention waned and the administration of the islands was shunted on to a rather obscure bureaucratic siding.

From the beginning, and especially once the military rebellion was subdued, the primary goal was stability. The solution adopted – the policy of attraction – was a form of backsliding in the direction of indirect rule, a way of ruling colonies with a light hand through native intermediaries.[68] Though Taft would have denied it vehemently at the time, this amounted to an abdication of the idea of an active civilizing mission. Why? Because the grudging respect earned by the Filipinos in their war for independence produced an understandable element of caution in American policy. In combination with the rapid decline in public enthusiasm for empire back home, the growing strength of anti-imperialist ideas, and the continuing potency of racial views, the requirements of pacification worked against an all-out effort at social transformation and resulted in the United States adapting to the local situation rather than vice versa.

But even if Americans had profoundly wished to modernize the islands, the absence of knowledge would have ruled out success. To change something for the better requires that you know how it works. Even today there is no instruction manual or paint-by-numbers technique that spells out, step by step, how to transmit modernity from one people to another. The critique of American tutelage assumes that where there is a will, there is a way. But all the determination in the world, combined with a willingness to throw unlimited amounts of money at the problem, would have accomplished little in the absence of knowledge.

Americans have tended to be over-optimistic about the potential of educational institutions to bring about basic cultural change in other societies. The source of this misplaced optimism was the educational analogy of "tutelage," which was of doubtful validity when applied to intercultural relations. Education is primarily enculturation, a process of intergenerational transmission of knowledge and values within a culture that begins, literally, in the home. That kind of learning, including learning about learning, is a fundamental key to formal educational achievement.[69] Intercultural education or acculturation is a different process altogether that operates on the periphery of culture, far removed from its inner bastions.

It is true, as one historian has noted, that the situation in the Far East brought about "a qualitatively new situation: imperialism as a vehicle for intercultural communication."[70] But communication across cultural boundaries is often miscommunication. And even when Americans were serious about change, their enthusiasm was tempered by a racialism that saw the Filipinos as capable of only so much modernization. Convinced that it would be, at best, a slow process, they were not inclined to push it along. For their part, the Filipinos successfully resisted the importation of value systems that Americans were reluctant to export.

Thus Americans introduced some of the superficial institutional forms associated with the American way of life without even coming close to transferring America's political culture to the Philippines. Americanization would have been impossible without destroying the native culture. But even if that kind of wholesale deracination had been contemplated, there is no assurance that it would have done the trick. As the sad example of Native Americans illustrates, the ability to destroy a culture does not mean that one can shape what remains into one's own image.

In the absence of desire and knowledge, it should come as no surprise that more traditional motives took over – stability, economy, catering to special interests, and, increasingly, security. As one historian notes about the post-World War II years, "secure bases and collective security agreements mattered more to the makers of US policy than did economic growth, land reform, or American business interests."[71]

Instead of wondering, with critical intent, why the United States didn't do a better job of preparing the Philippines for independence in a modern world,[72] it would seem more pertinent to ask why the United States took any interest at all in the development of the islands when there was virtually no pressing reason to do so. The strongest motive for development was that it seemed the right thing to do. But this altruistic rationale paled before the powerful security arguments made during the Cold War on behalf of promoting development. Even then, however, it was easier to state development as a desideratum than to impose it upon a sovereign nation skilled at playing the aid game for its own purposes.

In the end, American policies did not "fail" in any objective sense. It is only because they have been measured against the extravagant, though well-meant, rhetoric of civilization that was used to justify retention of the archipelago that they have come up short. Ironically, the notion of the "white man's burden," though thoroughly discredited for its racialist arrogance, continues to survive as the unrealistic standard against which present-day critics continue to measure America's performance in the Philippines.

3

America's Caribbean Empire

Whereas the upwelling of US colonialism in the Philippines can be traced to a relatively pure spring of imperial imagination, American behavior in the Caribbean flowed from a set of murkier sources. Curiously, one of the more powerful motives for America's acceptance of a Caribbean imperial role was anti-imperialism, in the form of an opposition to the diplomacy of imperialism. This was not as strange as it may seem at first sight because the absence of great power competitors in the Caribbean was at the same time America's greatest strategic asset and a source of considerable insecurity. Disturbed by the specter of other nations tramping through the nation's back yard, the US resorted over a span of three decades to a pre-emptive imperialism.[1]

By itself, pre-emptive imperialism, seizing a territory lest it fall into the hands of a competitor, was not unusual; indeed, it had often been the chief motive behind periodic scrambles for empire elsewhere. But American imperialism in the Caribbean basin differed from the norm in two respects. First, it was justified as an exercise of regional responsibility on behalf of civilization lest that very same civilization, in the form of European encroachment, spill over into the Caribbean. This argument from civilization, far from being a thinly veiled rationalization for more rapacious motives, needs to be taken seriously because it was the central ideological theme behind *all* of American foreign policy in the twentieth century.[2] Just as it provided a rationale for imperial control earlier in the century, under changed conditions it also provided some powerful motives for withdrawal. Second, despite a glut of potential colonies there for the taking, American control of the region was, for the most part, anti-annexationist. Though the US exercised virtually sovereign powers for varying periods of time in places like Cuba, Haiti, and the Dominican Republic, with the exception of Puerto Rico the US typically refused to assume formal colonial control.[3]

But there were other motives at work. American economic interests were more evidently at stake in the Caribbean basin than they were in the Philippines – to the point that some critics have seen nothing but economic motives at work. The Marine Corps General Smedley Butler furnished the groundhog's limited view of events when, in looking back on his career, he confessed that "I helped in the rape of a half dozen Central American republics for the benefit of Wall Street."[4] These economic interests were not very significant when compared to the stake held by the US in developed countries, but American direct investments in the region were nevertheless "greater than in any of the other developing regions of the world."[5] Of minor importance to the US in absolute terms, they often had an overwhelming impact upon the Lilliputian economies of the nations south of the border.

Though these economic inducements were by themselves not of sufficient weight to bring about intervention, when combined with other justifications they contributed heavily to a policy of pre-emptive imperialism that lasted for three decades. As one historian has put it, "US policy-makers supported US businesspeople and bankers in their efforts to compete with British and other European interests, because closer economic ties strengthened US political influence and reduced that of potential rivals."[6] Or, as an assistant secretary of state explained when reflecting upon America's meddling in the so-called banana republics of Central America: "we are after bigger game than bananas."[7]

American imperialism in the region also featured a strong emphasis on creating stable, prosperous societies in nations that seemed incapable of self-modernization. As one journalist put it, "the Central Americans are like a gang of semi-barbarians in a beautifully furnished house, of which they can understand neither its possibilities of comfort nor its use."[8] Because no one contemplated the permanent imposition of law and order by military means, meaningful stability required the promotion of some degree of political and economic development, since anarchy and revolution were usually associated with backwardness. "True stability," said Philander Knox, "is established not by military but by economic and social forces."[9] Stable polities, by keeping their noses clean, would reduce the temptation of outside powers to meddle in their affairs. Economic development would also contribute to this end, and it would also be good economically for the United States in the long run. But one should not ignore the continuing allure of the civilizing mission as a motivation. If the idea of civilization was powerful enough to get the United States involved in the Philippines, it stands to reason that it was also a significant factor in the Caribbean region.

Because the US possessed overwhelming power and there were few serious costs associated with throwing its weight around, intervention in its heyday seemed to operate as if by some involuntary conditioned reflex. But that is not to say that American power was exercised in an unthinking way.[10] The United States operated from an unquestioned presumption of imperial entitlement that most policy-makers were prepared to articulate if called upon to do so. Theodore Roosevelt cogently expressed the prevailing view that not all peoples deserved to be sovereign. "Freedom does not mean absence of all restraint," he insisted. "It can be used only by people capable of self-restraint and they alone can keep it or are entitled to it." It followed, in TR's view, that there were "nationalities and tribes wholly unfit for self government."[11] When Americans judged their Caribbean neighbors by that standard, as most did, few seemed to measure up, which was taken to mean that the United States had to do something about the situation.[12]

It would take three decades of increasingly unsatisfactory experience in imperial control, coupled with a re-examination of American thinking about the historical meaning of imperialism, before this sense of entitlement began to ebb.

The Cuban Protectorate

Given the countless expressions of interest prior to 1898 by Americans about the desirability of annexing Cuba, it is an ironic twist that the United States should have acquired the relatively unknown Philippines instead. Earlier in the century, John Quincy Adams predicted that laws of "political gravitation" would force the island, once free of its "unnatural connection" with Spain, to fall as a matter of course into America's receptive lap. Many southerners in particular coveted the island as a potential counterweight to the growing number of northern free states, but a number of attempts to purchase Cuba from Spain in the 1840s and 1850s came to nothing. Sentiment for annexation dwindled after the Civil War. Although the US nearly went to war with Spain during the Grant administration in the 1870s as a result of frictions arising from the Cuban 10-year war of 1868–78, annexation of land with a large population of negro slaves was pretty much unthinkable at a time when the US had enough racial problems on its plate.

When war broke out with Spain in April 1898, there was a good deal of sentiment in Congress for a free Cuba, but it was hardly unanimous. The Teller amendment to the war resolution, which at first sight suggested a hands-off approach to the island's postwar future, was actually a compromise between proponents of a *Cuba libre* and those who wanted to maintain American oversight in one form or another. While the amendment disavowed any American intention to exercise "sovereignty, jurisdiction, or control over said island except for the pacification thereof," pacification provided a convenient loophole for maintaining control without governing the island outright.[13] McKinley, who confessed privately that he was "embarrassed" by the amendment, made a point of not recognizing the rebels as the legitimate government of Cuba, lest he tie his hands in advance. Instead, he promised that US military control would continue until Cuba had "complete tranquility" and "a stable government."

Some important people made no secret of wanting to annex Cuba outright. Lodge and Beveridge hoped to hang on to the island. Richard Olney, secretary of state in the anti-imperialist Cleveland administration, went off the reservation in this particular case, contending that Cuba was a "natural appendage" of the United States. In his view, it remained only to make the island "in point of law what she already is in point of fact, namely, United States territory."[14] General Leonard Wood, who took command of the occupation in 1900, advocated a more subtle, indirect route to annexation, even as he assured the Cubans that they were "marching toward independence." An occupation of indefinite duration, he believed, would in time convince the Cubans of the advantages of being joined to the United States. The occupation was only getting under way, but he was already convinced that the Cubans were "rapidly realizing that annexation is the best thing for them."

But anti-annexationist sentiment was predominant. Despite its ambiguities, the Teller amendment was crystal clear on the question of annexation. Statehood seemed to be a way around the problem for some, but, as with the Philippines, this option was largely foreclosed by racial concerns. Of the island's population of 1,500,000 in 1899, about 15 percent were negroes. As John W. Foster explained: "with the negro problem in our southern states pressing upon us for a solution . . . Do we desire to aggravate the situation by adding a million more of the despised race to our voting population?" Senator Orville Platt argued that the Cuban people "by reason of race and characteristic, cannot easily be assimilated by us." Adding Cuba to the Union as a state, therefore, would be "most disturbing."[15]

Most of Washington searched for a happy medium in which the US could control Cuba indirectly. By the end of 1898, even Senator Henry Teller of Colorado, sponsor of the famous anti-annexation resolution, favored a long-term American guardianship. President McKinley, in his annual message to Congress of December 5, 1899, telegraphed his intentions when he asserted that the US had "assumed before the world a grave responsibility for the future good government of Cuba." He concluded, therefore, that "the new Cuba . . . must needs be bound to us by ties of singular intimacy and strength if its enduring welfare is to be assured." Senator Platt agreed, arguing that "a nation which undertakes to put an end to bad government in a neighboring country must also see that a just and good government follows."[16] Politicians soon began to talk about erecting safeguards against the possibility of foreign intervention in an independent Cuba.

The early stages of the occupation, before US military government had been firmly established, confirmed the low opinion that many Americans held of Cuban political capacities. "Wherever Cubans, under nominal American control, have been trusted to exercise the reigns of government, the result has been worse than failure," said one assessment.[17] Given the existence of serious doubts about Cuba's capacity for self-rule, Cuba was too important to be left exclusively to the disorderly Cubans. Should the US withdraw outright, Root argued that "it would be a most lame and impotent conclusion if, after all the expenditure of blood and treasure by the people of the United States for the freedom of Cuba . . . we should be placed . . . in a worse condition in regard to our own vital interests than we were while Spain was in possession."[18] As the *Literary Digest* soon realized, opinion in Washington was now full of "animated questionings as to whether it would be safe for the United States and safe for Cuba to let the latter start out alone upon the perilous seas of national sovereignty."[19] Obviously, the Cuban patriot José Martí had been prophetic to ask: "Once the United States is in Cuba, who will get her out?"[20]

Once it had been determined to stay on for a time, American authority over all of Cuba needed to be established. US commanders were alarmed at having to deal with another, potentially competing, source of authority as the rebels moved into large areas of the island vacated by the Spanish. As early as August 1898, General William R. Shafter was telling Washington that "A dual government can't exist here; we have got to have full sway of the Cubans."[21] Clearly, if the United States had not lingered on, the rebels would have filled the political vacuum. Indeed, it is quite possible that Cuba would have become a dictatorship under the leadership of revolutionary general Máximo Gómez.[22]

The key to preventing Cubans from seizing their independence was to disband the revolutionary armies, which were, fortunately for the Americans, in very run-down condition. The Cuban rebels, often depicted as heroic and chivalric prior to the war, were by this time reduced to stealing and begging for food, their hunger being partly due to an American blockade. They were now portrayed as anarchic "good for nothing allies" and as too black to be given total control of the reins of government. "The most inhuman and barbarous cutthroats in the world," ex-president Cleveland called them.[23]

In the hope that a display of sensible moderation would lead quickly to self-rule, the former insurgents chose the path of cooperation. Although there was some talk of another war for independence, this time against the United States, their forces were in no position to adopt such a suicidal policy. There was no realistic choice but to comply. The Americans bought them off by providing 3 million dollars in back pay that was owed to their impecunious soldiers. The rebels were talked into demobilizing their armies with the promise that the US would honor its commitment to Cuban independence. Further incentives were provided by awarding many of the positions in the new civil government to former rebel officers.

Politically, too, American oversight needed to be assured. A constitutional convention, stocked with former revolutionaries, finished its labors in February 1901 without bothering to define relations with the US. The United States decided to do the job for the Cubans with a document called the Platt amendment. Submitted as a rider to the annual army appropriation bill of 1901, it stipulated the conditions that would have to be met by Cuba before the American occupying forces would leave. Limits were set on Cuba's right to negotiate treaties with foreign powers and on Cuba's foreign borrowing. The

Platt amendment also granted the US the right to intervene when Cuba was threatened either externally or internally and gave the US rights to bases on the island (the US navy even today maintains a large base at Guantánamo Bay). Lastly, it demanded that Cuba ratify all the acts of the military government. The Platt amendment effectively made Cuba a protectorate of the United States, a state that was independent in name but less than sovereign in foreign policy and in domestic affairs. Less charitably, it created what one anti-imperialist called "a vassal state."

The reluctant Cuban political leaders were eventually persuaded by Root to adopt the Platt amendment as an appendix to the Cuban constitution and as part of a treaty between the US and Cuba that was signed in 1903. Root helped this bitter medicine go down more easily by arguing that intervention would not be promiscuous and by pointing out that the Monroe Doctrine would remain in force, with or without the Platt amendment. The amendment was, he insisted, simply "the Monroe Doctrine, but with international force." Fearful of an interminable occupation and aware of the folly of taking up arms against the colossus to the north, the Cubans signed. Interestingly, in the congressional debate, even Senator George Hoar, the formidable anti-imperialist, favored this arrangement. Though the island's status was impossible to reconcile with the spirit of the Teller amendment, few people seemed much concerned by the inconsistency.

The civilizing mission was quickly put to the test during the occupation. General Leonard Wood, appointed military governor in 1900, informed McKinley that "We are dealing with a race that has been going steadily down for a hundred years and into which we have got to infuse new life."[24] He believed that the US, by declaring war on Spain, had "assumed a position as protector of the interests of Cuba" and had become "responsible for the welfare of the people, politically, mentally and morally."[25] Cuba needed "decent, candid, courageous government; good courts, good schools, all the public work we can pay for, and a businesslike way of doing things."[26] Comments like Wood's suggest that some imperialists, at least, envisaged full equality for their charges, though only after a thorough cultural makeover.

Americans traveling abroad have repeatedly complained about the filth, squalor, and disease found in non-industrial countries; unsurprisingly, then, the US was determined to clean Cuba up and bring it up to the sanitary standards of the American middle classes. Cleanliness was a matter not only of aesthetics and a handmaiden of public health, it was also a reliable indicator of social discipline and civilized status. The first commander, General John R. Brooke, started the job by disinfecting public buildings, prohibiting city dwellers from tossing garbage into streets, and banning animals from foraging for food in town. Wood was even more energetic in his reformism, partly out of the desire to bring Cuba up to American standards in the expectation that it would soon be annexed. Trained as a medical doctor, he saw his mission as eradicating disease. For the Cubans, American-imposed cleanliness was almost as bad as their political godliness, especially as violations of the new civic code were punished with public whippings. There were some critics of this aspect of the occupation, but they were ridiculed by *The New York Times* for seeming to believe that the Cuban people "are and by right ought to be free to have all the yellow fever they want."[27]

The Americans also paid a good deal of attention to infrastructure, physical and organizational. Roads and bridges were built and major harbors were dredged. A paving and sewer project for Havana begun in 1902 was continued after the occupation's end. Wood employed Cubans in the bureaucracy but made sure that Americans were always in charge. However, his moderate treatment of Spaniards, which included keeping a number of bureaucrats in office, infuriated the Cubans. Foreshadowing US policy in future interventions, a rural guard was created to maintain order.

The American belief in the power of mass education to effect fundamental change was reflected in the occupation's attempt to transform Cuba's educational system. Before the war, the Cuban middle and upper classes had been educated mainly in private academies. Alexis Frye put together a public school system of 3,000 schools with approximately 140,000 pupils by 1902 and some 1,300 Cuban teachers were sent to the US, to Harvard University, to experience first-hand the educational wonders of an advanced society. As in the Philippines, emphasis was placed on vocational skills. Not surprisingly, given such an exponential increase, quantity prevailed over educational quality, but it was at least a beginning.

The most important goal was the inculcation of democracy. Municipal elections were held in 1900, while the constitutional convention seemed to promise a new era of democracy. Things proceeded smoothly enough so that at the end of the occupation in 1902 Wood could confidently assert that he had accomplished "the building up of a republic, by Anglo-Saxons, in a Latin country." But Wood's boast was not very close to the truth of the matter. While the Americans had imposed law and order from the outside, they were unable to transfer the American style of politics to Cuban *politicos* and candidates for office, many of them former leaders of the revolution, who seemed to view government office as no more than a source of personal gain.

As early critics of the Platt amendment had predicted, with such a zero-sum view of politics the "outs" were certain to use American intervention as a way of settling scores with the "ins." And it was not long after the American withdrawal before the turbulent politics of Cuba resulted in another American occupation. The election of 1904 was pockmarked with considerable vote fraud and violence. Supporters of the embittered loser of the 1904 election, José Miguel Gómez, revolted, and in 1906, the discontent was serious enough for President Tomás Estrada Palma to ask for American intervention.

Reluctantly, at Taft's recommendation, TR sent in 2,000 marines in September 1906, the first contingent of what became another army of occupation. The insurgents surrendered promptly, having been granted amnesty and the right to keep their horses, even if they had often been acquired by larcenous means. As usual, American soldiers had a low opinion of the revolutionaries: a "dirty rabble of Negroes armed with every type of antiquated weapon," by one account.[28] This time around, authority rested in the hands of a civilian, Charles Magoon, who had made a name for himself by his effective administration of the Canal Zone in Panama. Unlike Wood, who exercised direct military control, Magoon ruled through an established government, though a large number of American military officers looked over its shoulder as influential advisers.

In an attempt to placate the liberals and restore some administrative balance to the bureaucracy, Magoon initially favored the liberals in appointment to government posts, including many do-nothing patronage jobs which subsequently became entrenched in the Cuban government. The key to "keeping Cuba quiet", apparently, was to prevent the kind of all-or-nothing patronage situation that led to the previous insurgency. The rural guard, criticized for aiding the government, was reorganized and combined with other forces into the Armed Forces of Cuba, which in time would become the nation's dominant institution. After organizing a general election for the presidency and Congress in November 1908, the liberals – who promised the people "legal cockfighting, less work and a lottery"[29] – won a convincing victory. This led TR to announce in December the end of the occupation, though he warned that "the only way a people can permanently avoid being governed from without is to show that they both can and will govern themselves from within." Magoon departed a month later, leaving power in the hands of the newly elected Cuban government.[30]

Magoon's tenure as proconsul is the subject of considerable controversy. Americans believed that he brought honest and efficient administration to the island, reconciled the warring factions, and left Cuba in a prosperous condition. Critics, by contrast, accused him of cronyism in awarding contracts and of institutionalizing corruption in the Cuban political system. Although subsequently criticized for preferring American companies for road-building contracts, there seems little doubt that the roads were necessary and adequately constructed. And there is no doubt that he attacked a variety of problems. In

the process of fighting a yellow fever epidemic, sanitary services were nationalized. An advisory law commission codified
the laws and reorganized the legal system with a view to promoting impartiality. The executive branch of government was
reorganized and provision was made for civil service reform.
To boot, he presided over a fairly prosperous period in Cuba's history.

Though the occupations were fairly ambitious in their attempts to reform infrastructure and institutions, the paramount
aim from the beginning was maintaining stability, the rule of
law and order. "When people ask me what I mean by stable
government," General Wood explained to McKinley, "I tell
them 'money at six percent.'"[31] Stability in Cuba would guarantee the security of American investments, provide Cubans
with a favorable climate for development, and, most importantly, it would assure that domestic chaos would not invite
outside intervention.

Even after the withdrawal of American soldiers, the United
States continued to exercise a good deal of economic control.
Economically, Cuba was much more important to the United
States than the Philippines. More than 100 million dollars had
been invested in the islands by 1902, mostly in tobacco and
sugar holdings worth 45 million and 25 million dollars re-
spectively. There was also a large United Fruit operation of
200,000 acres. Everyone understood that America's economic
presence would continue to grow. *The New York Times* viewed
this inflow of money with optimism, arguing that "American
brains and American capital will work a marvelous transformation in the island. It is a paradise that has been treated as a
waste."[32]

A Reciprocity Treaty of 1903 tied the Cuban economy to
the US. Much desired by the Cubans, it provided some compensation for accepting the Platt amendment. Cuban sugar
received a 20 percent tariff preference whereas US exports to
Cuba received a 25–40 percent reduction. Although Congress
forbade the granting of economic concessions or franchises
during the period of occupation, American capital flooded in
after the soldiers departed. US investments rose to 1.5 billion

dollars in 1925 as soft drink and candy companies moved in to control the Cuban sugar industry. In addition, US investors dominated Cuban utilities and other industries.[33] By this time, about 75 percent of Cuba's imports came from the US. Americans in Cuba created exclusive enclaves and associations that exercised considerable economic and political influence. The commanding American economic presence, with its ruthless drive for more rationality and efficiency in production, led to a good deal of nationalist resentment among Cubans of all classes against what they perceived as economic imperialism.

Culturally, too, the United States continued to make itself felt on the island. Havana became a tourist destination where Americans were free to engage in activities – drinking, gambling, sex – that were frowned upon at home. For upwardly mobile Cubans, English became a second language. Cubans adopted American movies, drove American cars, played baseball with a passion, and absorbed American radio broadcasts. But this did not mean that Cuba was being Americanized. On the contrary, as one visitor noted: "It is America who is the enemy, in the mind of the average Cuban – between American and Cuban no love exists."[34]

Although the second military occupation ended in 1909, the habit of directing Cuba's affairs continued. The United States intervened briefly again during another revolution in 1912 and in future electoral crises, as in 1920–1 when proconsul Enoch Crowder revised the electoral code, dictated the choice of a president, and attempted to infuse morality into Cuban politics, all in return for a 50 million dollar loan from J. P. Morgan. Between 1919 and 1924 US marines were assigned to guard plantations in the eastern sugar-growing provinces against armed rebel bands. But in the end, American interference availed little, as the governments in Cuba became increasingly corrupt and insensitive to social conditions, thereby breeding precisely the kind of chaotic conditions that the US would have preferred to avoid.

The regime of President Gerardo Machado (1925–33) represented the nadir of this tendency. When a student revolt and general strike in 1933 brought to power a left-leaning government under Dr Ramón Grau San Martín, the Roosevelt administration, fearing that it might be too radical, used economic pressure to depose Grau in favor of a more pliable president. But in the depressed economic conditions of the 1930s, the economic discontent in the countryside and the cities was often directed against American-owned companies. Only after the security of American-owned properties in Cuba was restored was the Platt amendment finally abrogated and Cuba left to its own political devices.

Leaving America's considerable interests in the hands of faithful local leaders worked well in the short term, but over the long haul the result was a disaster for American policy. The key figure in Cuba from the mid-1930s through the 1950s, whether serving as president or behind-the-scenes kingmaker, was Fulgencio Batista, a former army sergeant. Although at first Batista was allied with the labor unions and his policies contributed to a broadly based economic growth, by the 1950s his rule ossified into a corrupt conservatism that was well suited to American interests, as long as there was no disorder. Even Grau, who defeated Batista for the presidency in 1944, forgot his former radicalism and gave way before the prevailing impulse to graft and political corruption. By the late 1950s, a deep current of discontent among the lower and middle classes made Cuba a land ripe for a revolution with an anti-American flavor.

The Panama Canal Zone

No other American action contributed as greatly to the image of Yanquí imperialism, or to the self-image of American greatness, as the construction of the Panama Canal, which one historian has called "one of the supreme human achievements of all time."[35] The idea of a canal had been a topic of conversation ever since Balboa's discovery of the 50-mile wide isthmus of Panama early in the sixteenth century. Americans first became interested in such an undertaking in the 1820s, following the collapse of the Spanish empire in Latin America.

However, formidable engineering obstacles combined with insuperable political difficulties – primarily the recognition that a canal could not be built without taking in Great Britain as a partner – limited Washington's interest in the project.

The expansion of the United States to the Pacific Ocean in the 1840s made clear that a canal, as a *de facto* extension of the coastline of the US, would be the most efficient way of unifying the eastern and western portions of the transcontinental nation. A significant political toehold on the isthmus was gained in 1846 with the signature of Bidlack's treaty with New Granada. Ostensibly a treaty of commerce, the pact also allowed the US to intervene for the purpose of maintaining open transit across the isthmus while upholding Bogotá's sovereignty over Panama. (Over the years, the US repeatedly landed troops to protect the security of the American-financed cross-Panama railroad whose construction began in 1850.) In 1850, after some fruitless attempts to secure treaty rights with Mexico and Nicaragua, a deal was struck with Great Britain. The Clayton–Bulwer treaty, which stipulated that a canal would be jointly built and remain unfortified, both advanced and limited the American cause.

The completion of the Transcontinental Railway in 1869 temporarily stanched the momentum of American diplomatic initiatives. Nevertheless, in 1879 Americans were stunned to hear that a French company headed by Ferdinand de Lesseps, the celebrated builder of the Suez Canal, had gained concessionary rights for the canal project. This coup stimulated renewed interest in an American-owned and operated canal. In 1880, President Hayes called for "a canal under American control," arguing that it would be "virtually a part of the coast line of the United States." However, American attempts to escape from the shackles of the Clayton–Bulwer pact were frustrated by Great Britain, which argued for the internationalization of the waterway (at the same time that it was intervening in Egypt and effectively seizing control of Suez). Though the de Lesseps organization foundered in 1889, a successor company gained renewed rights to a Panamanian right of way.

After many false starts, the canal project finally took on an air of urgency in the 1890s. The depression of 1893 stimulated hopes that a canal would promote trade. The Spanish-American War demonstrated in dramatic fashion how useful a canal would be in shifting the weight of American naval power from one ocean to the other. A canal would shorten the New York to San Francisco voyage by nearly 8,000 miles, but some enthusiasts were more thrilled by the prospect of a new route to China that would shave 3,000 miles off the existing eastward journey. For people like Lodge and Roosevelt, a canal would be the prime demonstration of the continued power and vitality of the United States. In contrast to former assumptions that a canal would be privately financed and constructed, opinion increasingly swung in the direction of a governmental project.

But, above all, a canal was justified as a great work of civilization. From this broader perspective, the canal would be an international public good, part of the global commons, a highway open to all. A canal had long been viewed in these cosmic terms as a route, in the words of Lewis Cass, whose "advantages should be common to all nations."[36] Philander Knox saw a classical precedent in the canal, recalling that "the march of the old Romans toward universal civilization was, to put it practically, over good roads."[37] In the words of Albert Bushnell Hart, it "is an international benefit which the United States has no right to take upon itself, except as the representative of civilized commerce. The oceans are the property of mankind."[38]

Because the emerging view of the Monroe Doctrine considered the US to be the trustee of civilization in the Caribbean, it stood to reason that a canal ought to be constructed, maintained, and defended exclusively by the United States of America. There were powerful strategic reasons for taking this line. The navy needed a canal and the canal needed a navy. Although a canal would be a wondrous instrument of global commerce, Theodore Roosevelt spoke for many when he argued that a canal not fortified by the US and with vulnerable approaches would be "a menace . . . in time of war." Thus, as Mahan argued in 1893, there should be "no hesitation about taking the positions – and there are many – upon the approaches to the Isthmus."[39] Building a canal thus entailed, for strategic purposes, controlling strong points in the Caribbean for use as bases and coaling stations and assuring that neighboring countries did not fall under the control of hostile powers – in short, a program of imperialism.

The Spanish-American War was the watershed event. The acquisition of Hawaii and the Philippine islands made clear the necessity for shorter lines of communication with the new Pacific empire. The comically long 14,000 mile voyage of the battleship *Oregon* from Puget Sound around Cape Horn to join the American fleet in Cuba underscored the advantages that an isthmian canal would bring in deploying naval power from ocean to ocean. Almost immediately, the US approached the British for a revision of Clayton–Bulwer, which was now considered an intolerable arrangement. It took two tries, however, before the British relented and, in a second Hay–Pauncefote treaty, signed in November 1901, gave the Americans the right to build and fortify a canal on their own. Challenged by Germany in Europe, by the Boers in South Africa, and by growing instability in China, Great Britain could no longer afford to dictate to the Americans about Caribbean matters.

Once released from Great Britain's ball and chain, Theodore Roosevelt, who assumed the presidency following McKinley's assassination in 1901, was free to move swiftly in bringing the project to political fruition. The first critical issue was choosing a canal route. The options were to dig through Nicaragua or through the narrower isthmus of Panama. Congressional sentiment leaned originally in the direction of a Nicaraguan waterway. The New Panama Canal Company, which had inherited the rights of the De Lesseps organization, was also asking too much money for its rights, some 109 million dollars, which everyone but the French considered flagrantly excessive. When an Isthmian Canal Commission, set up in 1899 by Congress to investigate alternative routes, suggested that 40 million dollars was a more reasonable amount, the New Panama Canal Company wisely dropped its asking price to the suggested sum.

The New Panama Canal Company was willing to take even more energetic measures to assure that its investment remained secure. After Congress authorized Roosevelt to negotiate for the Nicaraguan right of way, Mother Nature turned against the Nicaraguans. In May 1902, Mont Pelée on Martinique erupted in devastating fashion, giving rise to rumors of similar volcanic hazards in Nicaragua. Nicaraguans tried to deny it, but Philippe Bunau-Varilla, a lobbyist for the New Panama Canal Company, presented official Nicaraguan postage stamps to Congressmen and Senators which displayed Mt Momotombo erupting in all her vulcan majesty. After some mysterious backstage maneuvering, the Senate dropped its insistence upon a Nicaraguan route and authorized the president to secure the rights to an isthmian canal route.

The signature of the Hay–Herrán Treaty on January 22, 1903 gave the US a 100-year lease on a six-mile wide band of the isthmus for 10 million dollars plus annual rental fees of 250,000 dollars. The US Senate approved, but the Colombian Senate, despite warnings from Hay that rejection would result in action "which every friend of Columbia would regret," unanimously rejected the treaty. Though the Colombians claimed infringement of sovereignty and lack of US generosity, they were probably maneuvering to extract better terms from the US in renewed negotiations. Perhaps, too, they were stalling until the concession to the Panama Canal Company expired, at which point they rather than the French could claim the 40 million dollars allotted by Congress for securing rights to a route. While money talked, it did not say everything. Conceding virtual sovereignty to another power was a sensitive issue in a country that only recently had survived a civil war in which sovereignty had broken down.

Whatever the precise motive, the ploy backfired because the Colombians grossly misjudged the American leadership. Absolutely convinced that he had been double-crossed by Colombia President Marroquín, Roosevelt was furious with what he called "the Bogotá lot of jackrabbits" and "those Dagoes in Bogotá." Hay called the Colombians "greedy little anthropoids" for acting in bad faith. The anger in Washington was such that further negotiations with Bogotá were no longer in the picture. As Roosevelt later said, "you could no more make an agreement with them than you could nail currant jelly to the wall."

TR immediately began to consider alternatives, including perhaps outright seizure of Panama. Rejecting a straightforward land-grab, he chose to aid and abet a revolution in Panama with the help of some willing accomplices. Fearing that the action of the Colombian Senate would cost them the canal route, Bunau-Varilla and the New Panama Canal Company, as well as some dissatisfied residents of the isthmus, decided to foment a Panamanian revolution. It was not the first attempt at secession. The province of Panama, which was tenuously controlled from Bogotá, had frequently rebelled against Colombia. Since Panama City was separated by two hundred miles of dense jungle and mountains from Colombia and the only communications were by sea, American naval support would be critical to the success of their plans.

In October, Bunau-Varilla met with Hay and TR in Washington. Roosevelt made no promises, but Bunau-Varilla was a sharp man who sensed what the President was up to. He told his co-conspirators that the US would see to it that a revolution against Colombian authority would not fail. Meanwhile, Hay told TR that if a revolt did break out, the US had the right to intervene, "to keep the transit clear," under the terms of Bidlack's treaty. "Our intervention should not be haphazard, nor, this time, should it be to the profit of Bogotá," counseled Hay. This was, obviously, a lawyerly way of concocting a cover. The treaty had never been intended to be used against Colombia, but to provide security for life and property in the area when Colombia itself could not enforce it. If anything, from Colombia's perspective, such intervention blatantly contradicted the treaty's *raison d'être*.

Warships were dispatched to Central American waters under orders to prevent Colombia from landing troops on the isthmus in the event of revolutionary unrest. On November 3, 1903, at the instigation of the New Panama Canal Company, a revolution broke out, its shock troops being the fire department, the local police, and a Colombian army detachment whose commander had been bribed. Colombian intervention was thwarted when the US made it clear that it would not allow troops to land. It took TR only 76 minutes to recognize the new Republic of Panama and not much longer to negotiate a treaty with it. Losing no time, the new nation's first foreign minister, none other than the ubiquitous Bunau-Varilla, hurried to Washington and on November 18, 1903, just 18 days following the revolution, signed a pact that was extraordinarily generous to the United States.

The Hay–Bunau-Varilla treaty guaranteed Panama's independence and granted the US complete control of a 10-mile wide zone "in perpetuity . . . as if it were sovereign." Despite some second thoughts about having given away too much, the Panamanian junta ratified quickly. The newly declared Republic of Panama – "a kind of Opera Bouffe republic," in John Hay's words – was left, as one historian says, "with barely a shred of independence."[40] Shrugging off Colombia's outraged protests, Hay termed the revolution "an accomplished fact." As for the new republic's sovereignty, it was, Hay insisted, merely titular, a "barren scepter."[41]

Not surprisingly, there was some domestic criticism of this high-handed behavior, especially from the Democrats. One Senator accused TR of having performed a "caesarian operation" in which Panama had been ripped "alive from the womb" of Colombia. Another, marveling at the treaty's one-sidedness, said incredulously that "it sounds very much as though we wrote it ourselves" – which was uncomfortably close to the truth.[42] But Roosevelt, in his best high-horse manner, shrugged off criticisms of his behavior. In a letter to his son, he said: "this entire fool Mugwump crowd have fairly suffered from hysterics, and a goodly number of Senators even of my own party have shown about as much backbone as so many angleworms."[43]

Without any evident embarrassment, Roosevelt took the high ground in justifying his overbearing behavior by insisting that the action was "for the good of the entire civilized world." In his message to Congress in 1903 he argued that "the recognition of the Republic of Panama was an act justified by the interests of collective civilization. If ever a government could be said to have received a mandate from civilization . . . the United States holds that position with regard to the interoceanic canal." By this internationalist reasoning, the rights to a canal zone were analogous to an easement across Colombia's property. Roosevelt had a legal opinion from the State Department which argued that the 1846 treaty gave the US the right to compel Colombia to allow the US to dig a canal. In the absence of Bogotá's consent, confiscation of the property was justified by appeal to an international version of eminent domain.

Though all the talk of civilization was far from eyewash, the administration's rationalizations failed to hold up in international law. Panama was a rebellious province, it is true, but legally speaking it was still a province of Colombia when the US conspired to secure its independence. The US would have remained true to its treaty obligations only if it had restored Colombian authority after intervening. At a cabinet meeting where Roosevelt sought to persuade his appointees of his virtuous conduct, Elihu Root, the puckish secretary of war, told TR what he did not want to hear. "You have shown," he said, "that you were accused of seduction and conclusively proved that you were guilty of rape." In the 1920s, only after Roosevelt's death, the US paid Colombia 25 million dollars in thinly veiled reparation for its high-handedness.[44]

Could the US have obtained the canal by other means? Undoubtedly, but Roosevelt was impatient to "make the dirt fly." Influenced by his racialism, by his eagerness to build a record for the 1904 elections, by his serious belief that the US actually enjoyed "civilization's mandate in the Caribbean," and by his conviction that a canal was essential to his country's security and prosperity, he had no second thoughts about bulldozing the problem. To his dying day, he continued to defend his questionable maneuvers in starting "one of the great works of the world" as being in the best interests of mankind and progress. And his action was, without question, politically popular. High-minded faultfinding with his use of the "big stick" was never able to dent his enormous appeal among the voting public.

Acquiring the Panama route did not mean that the United States would actually be able to situate a canal there. Building the canal required not only digging the ditch, itself a Herculean engineering task that required the leveling of many mountains, but also arranging a complex system of massive locks to raise and lower ships over the continental divide. Despite its complexity, the lock canal was thought to be shorter, straighter, less prone to potentially disastrous flooding, and cheaper to build than the sea-level canal that the de Lesseps organization had been unable to complete.

Steam shovels and engineering wizardry could make the dirt fly and raise ships above sea level, but before work could be started an even more formidable difficulty stared the Americans in the face: vanquishing the tropical diseases that would otherwise decimate the labor force and American military garrisons. It appeared for a time that the disastrous French experience with disease, which had cost them thousands of lives, would be repeated when preliminary work had to be halted in 1905 because of a disastrously high mortality rate. Before it could resume, Colonel William L. Gorgas first had to impose a sanitation program that drained swamps and poisoned areas of stagnant water that were breeding grounds for the mosquitoes that transmitted yellow fever and malaria. Even with these successful measures, 5,600 men died from disease and accident.

Only then did TR sign a bill in 1906 that authorized the construction of a 40-mile long lock canal from Cristóbal on the Caribbean to Balboa on the Pacific side. The appointment in April 1907 of Major George W. Goethals as head of a three-member military Isthmian Canal Commission vested him with near-dictatorial powers to speed work on the canal. In response to criticism that the Canal Zone did not have a democratic structure, President Taft later said in justification that it was about "the management of a great public work, and not the government of a local republic."[45] Following the completion of the canal at a cost of 350 million dollars, the Panama Canal Act of 1912 provided for the appointment of a governor, but it was never the intention to transplant democracy to this militarily governed area.

The Panama Canal Zone was neither an incorporated territory, like Alaska and Hawaii, nor an unincorporated territory, like the Philippines and Puerto Rico. It was an "unorganized possession," with a government fixed by executive order and run by US naval officers who served as appointed governors. Its governance most closely resembled that of Guam and American Samoa, Pacific islands that had been picked up as coaling stations in the nineteenth century. Because goods imported into the Canal Zone paid no duties, the Panamanian government enjoyed no income from this source. To allay local unhappiness, President Taft allowed the Panamanian government to collect duties on all items except those that were "necessary and convenient." Meanwhile, goods from Panama were allowed to enter the US duty free. This was, in effect, an additional subsidy to the Panamanian government beyond the annual payments stipulated by treaty.

The Canal Zone and its Panamanian surroundings created a political laminate whose pieces never successfully bonded together. The construction of the waterway provided a good example of how poorly the pieces were joined. The Panama Canal, an old saying goes, was built with French brains, American money, and West Indian sweat. The workers who constructed the canal were organized by race into a "gold roll" dominated by skilled white workers and a "silver roll" of unskilled laborers who did the physically demanding pick-and-shovel work. Besides collecting higher salaries, the whites received free housing, health care, schooling for their children, and a whole list of other perks. But this paternalism came at a price as unions and strikes were not permitted. The workers on the silver roll, most of whom came from the West Indies and southern Europe – primarily Spain, Italy, and Greece – were paid less than half of the gold rate and commanded hardly any fringe benefits at all. As for the Panamanians, few participated in the Canal's construction, having been classed as hopelessly lazy and unreliable laborers by the US managers.

Panamanian merchants were also frozen out. To enable workers to buy goods without paying the high prices charged by Panamanian retailers, the commission authorized a commissary, which quickly became an organization so large that it rivaled the Panamanian economy. Indeed, the zone was an enclave of military socialism that gave short shrift to *laissez-faire* notions. Having expected an economic bonanza, Panamanians were dismayed to see themselves elbowed aside by the American stress on economic self-sufficiency. This was but one of many sore points between Panamanians and Americans in what turned into a continuing struggle for commercial control of the zone. Although in the long run the canal became a source of prosperity for Panama, accounting at one point for as much as a third of Panama's national income, it was at the same time a force that stifled local entrepreneurs.

The zone was not the only problem. If the Canal Zone was *de jure* American, the rest of the country's economy was *de facto* under American domination. The United Fruit Company controlled the nation's railroads and was the country's largest landowner. The US was the source of most of Panama's imports and took most of Panama's exports. Consequently, when the US economy suffered, as in the great depression of the 1930s, so too did Panama's. Panama's economic dependence upon the United States was symbolized by the fact that since 1904 its national currency – and separate currency is typically a basic indicator of sovereignty – was tied to the American dollar. Today its currency *is* the US dollar. While some of Panama's economic difficulties were attributable to an oligarchy that controlled the lion's share of the nation's wealth, the contrast with the standard of living in the Canal Zone provided a convenient focus of discontent for its citizens. Added to this mixture were some ill-concealed racial hatreds. According to one observer, these elements, in combination, made for "a deep, malevolent rancor that needs only a fit occasion to blaze forth in riot and in massacre."[46] And from time to time, it did.

The tension between the contrasting visions of the canal as an international public work and an extension of the national coastline became quite evident in a dispute over how tolls ought be levied. American nationalists argued that US vessels ought to pay a lower fare, whereas internationalists argued that the rates should be non-discriminatory. The Panama Canal Act of 1912 had exempted US coastal shipping from paying tolls, contrary to the internationalist spirit of the Hay–Pauncefote treaty, which had promised equality of commercial treatment to all nations. The issue was finally put to rest by Woodrow Wilson just prior to the canal's opening in 1914. Going before Congress, he insisted that the US was "too big, too powerful, too self-respecting a nation to interpret with too strained or refined a reading the words of our own promises just because we have power enough to give us leave to read them as we please." Congress finally passed the repeal bill, though only after a bruising behind-the-scenes battle between shipping and railway interests.

Over the years, the United States often played the deciding role in Panama's political affairs. From time to time, the army intervened to guarantee the fairness of elections and to campaign against vice, which was rampant in the two chief port cities of Colón and Panama City. During times of revolutionary unrest, the United States was often drawn in by the losing side. The United States also imposed economic discipline on occasion in the form of fiscal agents or "money doctors" who were appointed to minister to Panama's ailing finances. As for the zone, it was a world within a world, a slice of high-protein America inserted between two slices of low-calorie Third World bread. Just as the canal became the symbol of American imperialism, for the Zonians and for many Americans it was the pre-eminent symbol of the fundamental correctness of American behavior.

Though the zone seemed utterly American to some, by the 1930s US policy-makers had come to realize that the unusual situation could not endure forever. Thus the US agreed to revised treaties in 1936 and in 1955. In the Hull–Alfara treaty of 1936, the US admitted Panama's ultimate sovereignty over the zone and gave up the right to intervene with military force. By 1955, the annual payment had been increased to 2 million dollars. Riots in 1959 forced the Eisenhower administration to make further concessions, including the symbolically charged agreement to fly one Panamanian flag within the Canal Zone itself.

More serious riots broke out in 1964 when American students attempted to raise the stars and stripes over a high school in the zone. Following the deaths of 21 Panamanians and four US soldiers, Panama broke relations with the US and demanded a new, more favorable arrangement. Relations were restored later in the year when President Lyndon Johnson agreed to renegotiate the treaty. Though some draft treaties were in fact negotiated, for the time being ratification proved impossible for both sides. Discussions made little progress until 1974, when Secretary of State Henry Kissinger agreed to a statement of principles that any new treaty would restore the zone to Panamanian sovereignty.

Following this conceptual breakthrough, a new treaty superseding the Hay–Bunau-Varilla pact was signed by President Jimmy Carter and General Omar Torrijos in September 1977. Under its terms, the US remained in charge until 1999, when Panama finally assumed total control. In the meantime, Panama was given increasing amounts of responsibility and a growing proportion of revenues from the canal. The Panamanians promised to maintain the neutrality of the waterway, but American warships would be given priority consideration by being allowed to jump to the head of the line. Apart from the desire to improve America's image in Latin America, the decision to hand over control was prompted in large measure by the declining commercial and strategic significance of the canal. Too narrow to accommodate modern superfreighters and warships, the canal had become a declining asset for the United States.

The new treaty generated much emotional opposition within the United States, especially from conservatives who enjoyed a good deal of support from public opinion. As a result, selling the treaty proved to be a migraine for Carter compared to the more conventional foreign-policy headaches that came from maintaining the peace of the world. One senator said "we should keep [the canal]. After all, we stole it fair and square." Ronald Reagan, the movie star turned politician, declared (incorrectly) that the zone was "sovereign United States territory just the same as Alaska is." "We bought it. We built it. It's ours and we are going to keep it," he insisted. The 10,000 Zonians mobilized as a pressure group and were backed by much of the US military, which hoped to save some major bases located within the zone. Despite considerable opposition, a big public relations offensive by the president, with considerable support from swing conservatives like William F. Buckley, helped to convince the Senate to approve the treaty in 1978 by a razor-thin margin of one vote, though with a reservation that granted the US the right to intervene in the event that the security of the canal was threatened.

An otherwise orderly process of devolution was derailed by yet another American intervention in 1989, when US forces invaded to oust the dictator Manuel Noriega. Formerly linked to the CIA, Noriega in the 1980s allowed his nation to be used as a base for drug trafficking with the United States. In 1988, economic sanctions were imposed. Following his annulment of elections in 1989 and a series of incidents between Panamanian and US forces, the US invaded with 24,000 troops. After being serenaded by loudspeakers that blared non-stop rock music at ear-splitting volume, Noriega surrendered and was spirited to the US to stand trial on eight counts of drug trafficking, for which he was convicted in 1992 and sentenced to a long prison term. Although the Bush administration dubbed its invasion "Operation Just Cause," arguing that it was intended to protect the lives of American citizens and American interests, critics questioned whether it was justified under international law. Notwithstanding Noriega's admittedly unsavory character, another question of legality arose with respect to the forcible kidnapping of a head of state to stand trial within one's own country.

As for Panama, it remained to be seen whether control of the canal would substantially ameliorate its serious social and economic problems. Although the zone's economic significance had declined over time – in the 1990s only 7 percent of the country's economy depended on the canal – hopes were high that the takeover would help resolve Panama's high unemployment rate. For their part, many Americans worried that the various rationales that had justified an American-controlled canal – shortening intercoastal transport by sea, creating a highway for civilization, and enhancing security – would be undermined under Panama's stewardship. Critics argued that the cash-hungry and corrupt Panamanian government would treat the canal as a toll road rather than the non-profit international highway it had been under American administration. They also fretted about the rather unlikely possibility of the canal falling under the control of a power like Red China.

Customs Receiverships

As the hub of American policy in the Caribbean, the Panama Canal had long spokes. Writing to Root in 1905, TR confided that "the inevitable effect of our building the Canal must be to require us to police the surrounding premises. In the nature of things, trade and control, and the obligation to keep order which go with them, must come our way."[47] In other words, the US would have to intervene throughout the Caribbean basin in order to secure the approaches to the canal. In so doing, the United States would be re-learning the lesson already taught by the European experience with empire: that the securing of colonial possessions usually required more imperialism.

One of the most common and ingenious forms of control devised by the US in the first two decades of the twentieth century was the imposition of customs receiverships over small Caribbean republics – what one historian has called "managerial capitalism taken offshore."[48] The immediate purpose was to restore financial stability by assuring that import duties would be used to pay off loans that were in danger of being defaulted. The larger aim was to use the receivership as a device for forestalling the danger of foreign military intervention, by collecting debts on behalf of aggrieved bondholders. In time, customs receiverships became mechanisms for replacing European creditors entirely, thanks to consolidation loans granted by preferred American banks. In this way, economic interests grew like kudzu around the trunk of strategic rationales.

Customs receiverships were justified under the terms of the so-called Roosevelt Corollary to the Monroe Doctrine, which was first spelled out in TR's message to Congress of December 6, 1904. The occasion for the announcement was another debt collection crisis in the Caribbean. Like Cuba, the Dominican Republic, which occupied the eastern portion of the strategically situated island of Hispaniola, had long been an object of American interest. During the Grant administration, naval interests and commercial speculators had succeeded in getting the president to promote an annexation project, only to be thwarted by the Senate, which rebelled against incorporating a large, non-white population into the national polity.

In 1904, bankruptcy and civil war threatened outside intervention. The Republic's problems stemmed from racial divisions, political instability, widespread poverty, and fiscal mismanagement which was partly the responsibility of an American banking firm that had come to exercise extraordinary influence in the republic's fiscal affairs. Bankrupt, with menacing European warships in Dominican waters, and exhausted by a revolution and civil war, the Dominican president requested American assistance.

The fear of foreign intervention was more hypothetical than real. Though England, France, and Germany were exporting significant amounts of capital to Latin America, Great Britain had already made the fundamental policy decision to concede primacy in the Caribbean to the United States. As for Germany, despite some tensions with that country and occasional snits from the Kaiser about American pretensions to greatness, there was no real danger of coming to blows with Berlin over ambitions for hemispheric expansion.[49]

Nevertheless, fancies do matter, and in this case the US could afford to indulge them. The year before, TR had quietly threatened the use of force when it appeared that Germany and other creditor nations would use force to extract debt payments from

Venezuela. At first, TR had no qualms about European debt-collection procedures, which were perfectly legal under the international law of the day. "If any South American state misbehaves, let the European country spank it," he said. But on second thought, though he agreed that the Venezuelans ought to be compelled to fulfill their obligations, he feared that the Europeans, once they had a foot in the door, might not leave. Allowing European intervention might bring about, through inadvertence, the routine exercise of European power in the Caribbean region – something that Roosevelt was not about to tolerate. If anything, TR lagged behind American public opinion on the issue, which was surprisingly vehement in its opposition to European intervention.

Thus, he had to find a way to square the circle: extract debt payments while avoiding European intervention in the hemisphere. He explained his logic to Congress in this fashion:

> Any country whose people conduct themselves well can count upon our hearty friendship. If a nation shows that it knows how to act with reasonable efficiency and decency in social and political matters, if it keeps order and pays its obligations, it need fear no interference from the United States. Chronic wrongdoing, or an impotence which results in a general loosening of the ties of civilized society, may in America, as elsewhere, ultimately require intervention by some civilized nation, and in the Western Hemisphere, the adherence of the United States to the Monroe Doctrine may force the United States, however reluctantly, in flagrant cases of such wrongdoing or impotence, to the exercise of an international police power.[50]

Annexation was never at issue. Roosevelt claimed that he had "about the same desire to annex it as a gorged boa constrictor might have to swallow a porcupine wrong-end to." The purpose of intervening was, rather, to preserve American informal influence while denying the entrance of European state power on behalf of continental financial interests.

Following a naval demonstration, the Dominicans signed an agreement with the US in 1905 that made the United States responsible for collecting and disbursing customs receipts – the most lucrative and reliable source of revenue in the country, the control of which had been a chief source of political contention. Fifty-five percent would go toward debt repayment, 45 percent to the Dominican treasury. The arrangement itself reflected its internationalist pedigree, being modeled on the precedent of foreign receivership of tobacco taxes in the Ottoman empire. The Senate at first refused to approve this treaty, but TR went ahead anyway by signing an executive agreement. The Senate finally capitulated in 1907, when it agreed to give TR what he had already taken.

The resort to financial receiverships was given a new twist under Roosevelt's successor, Taft, who was eager to test his concept of "dollar diplomacy" in the Caribbean. In 1909, a US-backed conservative revolt in Nicaragua removed a quarrelsome dictator, Jose Santos Zelaya, whom Secretary of State Philander Knox had called "a blot upon the history of Nicaragua," from power in the Central American republic. After a president satisfactory to the United States had been installed – Adolfo Díaz, a former clerk at an American-owned mining company – the Knox–Castrillo convention of 1911 provided for the appointment of an American customs collector. But instead of paying off European creditors, payments were made to American bankers who had purchased the European debt. From that point on, New York bankers virtually ran the country by virtue of their control of the national bank and the railroad. Even though both were returned to Nicaraguan jurisdiction by 1920, a financial control commission continued to dominate Nicaraguan finances between 1917 and 1924.

The idea apparently was not only to rid the region of European influence, but also to take the customs houses out of politics. In the process, Taft hoped to attract foreign investment to the country. Knox explained that "by this policy we shall help the people of these rich countries to enjoy prosperity instead of almost incessant revolution and devastation."[51] The policy was aimed at "averting rather than quelling internal disturbances."[52] If all went well, economic prosperity alone would dramatically lessen the tendency for outside powers (including the United States) to militarily interfere in these countries. "We shall do a noble work," argued Knox.

The control of Nicaragua was exercised through more than

financial means, however. The Bryan–Chamorro treaty of 1916, which gave the United States an option on a Nicaraguan canal route, would have resulted in an American presence in Nicaragua not unlike that in Panama. But the military presence was already formidable enough. The marines intervened in a 1912 civil war that cost 37 American and more than 1,000 Nicaraguan casualties. Thereafter, a 100-man marine legation guard in Managua remained as a continuing reminder of the military muscle that lay behind dollar diplomacy in the region. The marines were withdrawn in 1925 after an electoral plan was worked out, only to be quickly reintroduced in 1926 following some revolutionary unrest prompted by a disputed presidential election.

Henry Stimson, who was sent in to mediate, proposed new elections and the creation of a new constabulary to maintain order. But one rebel commander, Augusto César Sandino, refused to surrender and recognize the American-backed president, the reliable Adolfo Díaz. "I want a free country or death," he declared defiantly. After some confrontations, the marine contingent grew to 1,500 men and then to 5,000 as it sought unsuccessfully to capture the by-now legendary insurgent leader. Realizing through bitter experience that a continued American presence was fruitless, policy-makers finally ordered the marines to leave after supervising the election of 1932. Sandino's insurrection was suppressed the following year and Sandino himself was gunned down in 1934 after a meeting called by Anastasio Somoza, the new strongman in Nicaraguan politics.

The last American marines departed the country in 1934, leaving the country in the grip of Somoza, the commander of the presumably politically neutral national guard created by Stimson. Somoza became president in 1936. By that time, the good neighbor policy had taken the United States out of the game of promoting democracy in the region, which meant that the locals would have to suffer their autocrats. Somoza and his sons would rule the country until 1978. This may have been disastrous for Nicaragua, but it was tolerable to the United States. As Franklin D. Roosevelt said of Somoza, "he may be a son-of-a-bitch, but he is our son-of-a-bitch."

Puerto Rico

The annexation of Puerto Rico was less talked about in 1898 than Cuba or the Philippines, but its consequences for the United States proved to be far more enduring. One hundred and eight miles long and 40 miles wide north to south, with a population of slightly less than one million in 1898, Puerto Rico lay athwart the Mona passage, a key shipping lane to Central America and the anticipated isthmian canal. Like Cuba, the island had recently been granted home rule by the liberal Spanish government in Madrid, which hoped to keep Puerto Rico within the imperial fold.

Only as war with Spain became likely was a plan formed for attacking the island on the theory that it would deprive the Spanish of an important base of operations. An American expeditionary force of 18,000 men under General Nelson A. Miles landed on July 25 to little opposition and, suffering few casualties, effectively had the island under American control in a short period of time. Perhaps because the Americans announced themselves as liberators rather than conquerors, the invasion encountered little or no resistance from the native population. As in Cuba, Americans reacted negatively to the locals. One described them as "ignorant, filthy, untruthful, lazy, treacherous, murderous, brutal, and black."[53]

Puerto Rico's value was defined almost exclusively in military–strategic terms. Alfred Thayer Mahan pinpointed the island's strategic value when he wrote in 1899 that "Puerto Rico, considered militarily, is to Cuba, to the future Isthmian canal, and to our Pacific coast, what Malta is, or may be, to Egypt and the beyond . . . it would be very difficult for a transatlantic state to maintain operations in the western Caribbean with a United States fleet based upon Puerto Rico and the adjacent islands."[54] There was almost no discussion of Puerto Rico prior to the war with Spain, though a few politicians who favored a "large policy" hoped that the island would fall into America's lap as a fruit of the war. Annexation was not decided upon, nor discussed, until June 1898.

In the record of policy debate, Puerto Rico stands out by its absence. Normally, historians look for written evidence to drive home their points, but sometimes a dearth of discussion on a major topic can speak volumes. The lack of debate about Puerto Rico's future provides a good example of the new consensus on America's expanded role in the Caribbean. Focusing their attention almost entirely on the Philippines, imperialists and anti-imperialists alike took it for granted that Puerto Rico would remain an American possession. Annexing the island seemed so natural and sensible a thing to do that it occurred to no one that taking it over was worth arguing about.

Puerto Rico represented yet another wrinkle in the far from smooth conceptual fabric of imperial administrative logic. General Miles announced to the islanders that the US had come "to promote your prosperity, and to bestow upon you the immunities and blessings of the liberal institutions of our government." But this was more easily said than done. Hawaii was an incorporated territory to which, by the Organic Act of 1900, the US constitution was extended, but Puerto Rico remained unincorporated, thus limiting its constitutional rights, even after blanket citizenship was granted to islanders in 1917. Most constitutional rights were made applicable to Puerto Ricans, with the notable exception of the right to trial by jury. General suffrage was granted only in 1936. The Foraker Act of 1900 provided for an appointed governor and council, and an elected legislature. The council would serve as the upper house, while the lower house would be chosen through popular vote. The upper house was made elective in 1917, but the first governor was elected only in 1948. The system resembled, in many respects, British rule in the crown colony of Hong Kong.

In 1917, the Jones Act, or the Organic Act for Puerto Rico, made Puerto Ricans citizens of the United States and made the island a US territory, still unincorporated.[55] However, this Jones Act was very different in purpose from the independence-minded bill of the same name passed for the Philippines a year earlier. According to its sponsor, Congressman William Jones, it was "framed upon the idea that Porto Rico is to remain a permanent possession of the United States." With part of their duty as citizens being to serve in a conscript army when called, 20,000 Puerto Ricans served in the US military during World War I and 55 died in the fighting on the western front in France.

Puerto Rico's future depended in large measure on the shape of its economic relationship to the US. Like the Philippines, the island was dominated by a small oligarchy whose status changed only marginally over time, thanks to the policy of *laissez faire* and free trade with the US that was established early on.[56] The effect of commercial policy was to tie the economy more closely to the United States and to change the nature of the island's agricultural economy. Before annexation, two-thirds of Puerto Rico's exports had gone to the US; by 1930, the figure was 90 percent.

Coffee had been the predominant export crop in 1898, but sugar planting quickly took over. Sugar exports increased from 57,000 tons in 1898 to 284,000 in 1910, 489,000 in 1917, and 606,000 in 1928. Coffee declined even further over time because of the depression and hurricanes of 1928 and 1932, so that by 1930, 53 percent of the island's export income came from sugar. The new crop was not as beneficial to the islanders as it might have been because they were prohibited by law from refining sugar, which left control in the hands of mainland US processors. In 1930, 58 percent of sugar production was controlled by four US corporations. By the end of the decade, 75 percent of the population was dependent, in one form or another, upon the sugar industry. The export of leaf tobacco and cigars also enjoyed a considerable growth, as did shipments of coconuts, pineapples and citrus fruits. A law passed in 1900 limiting corporate agricultural holdings to 500 acres was widely ignored. Ostensibly designed to protect small landholders, it is more likely that the legislation was designed to prevent Puerto Rican agriculture from becoming a threat to established US and Hawaiian producers.

For the first 30 years of American control, the standard of living failed to increase, thanks in large measure to rapid population growth.[57] Because of the depression, the sugar economy collapsed, leading to hardships and political protests. Agricultural employment had been low-wage and seasonal even in flush times, a wage rate of 70 cents per day being the norm in the late 1920s, but the 1930s were a particularly difficult decade for Puerto Rico. The plight of the islanders was worsened by their reliance upon relatively expensive food imports from the US, whose prices had been kept artificially high by New Deal anti-deflation programs. Making a bad situation worse, the Jones–Costigan Act of 1934 placed limits on the total amount of sugar that Puerto Rico was allowed to export to the United States. By 1933, 65 percent of the workforce of one-half million were unemployed and 42 percent of the population received some government relief.

In contrast to its neglect of the Philippines, Washington took major steps to deal with the depression on the island. The Puerto Rican Reconstruction Administration (PRRA), set up in 1935, was a New Deal organization whose bureaucracy of 53,000 was five times larger than that of the Puerto Rican government. The PRRA sought to promote land reform, eradicate monopoly, expand the base of small landholders, promote a more diverse agricultural economy, establish rural cooperatives as a way of combating monopolies, and encourage the growth of local industries. More controversially, it sought to find some way of dealing with the problem of overpopulation, which raised the hackles of the Roman Catholic church.

Despite energetic efforts by PRRA director Ernest Gruening, who hoped to make the island a regional showcase of American-sponsored development, progress was limited. The PRRA, like New Deal programs in the US, did little to pull the economy out of the depression. Matters were not helped by the tendency of Gruening to ride roughshod over the wishes of local political leaders. One of the island's mandarins, Luis Muñoz Marín said "the PRRA functions like a madhouse" – an accusation often brought against the New Deal by its critics in Washington.[58]

The 1930s also brought political turmoil to the island. Puerto Rican politics following annexation featured three basic positions: statehood and independence on the extremes, and an intermediate status of dominion or commonwealth as the mean. The Unionist Party, created in 1904, at first called for full constitutional rights and admission to statehood. As hopes for admission waned in the wake of the Jones Act, the Nationalist Party became the primary advocate of independence. Under the leadership of Pedro Albizu Campos, the Nationalists promoted a campaign of violence, including riots and demonstrations, that subsided only in 1936 after Albizu was sentenced along with others to 10 years in jail for seditious conspiracy following the assassination of the American chief of police.

The depression decade did produce a chance for independence, even though the US proposal incorporated a poison pill that was intended to kill the idea. The Tydings Bill, introduced in 1936, was prepared to grant independence in four years. However, its economic terms were far less generous than the Tydings–McDuffie Act passed for the Philippines. Because it provided for an abrupt end to tariff privileges, the economic divorce would have been extraordinarily painful, given Puerto Rico's high degree of economic dependence on the American market. Senator Millard Tydings proposed the measure because he wanted to end Puerto Rican immigration into the US and demonstrate forcefully to Puerto Ricans the economic advantages of access to the US market. PRRA director Ernest Gruening, on the other hand, welcomed the bill because of his belief that it would be defeated in a referendum, thus putting an end to charges of imperialism.

Having accomplished its anti-independence mission, the Tydings Bill never came to a vote. The measure split the Puerto Rican political elite, with victory in the next election going to anti-independence moderates. In response to grumbling from Puerto Rican politicians, Gruening said: "What do you expect? You can't have your cake and eat it too." Meanwhile, Luis Muñoz Marín formed the moderate Popular Democratic Party in 1938, which sought to put political issues on the back burner in the hope of first dealing with Puerto Rico's serious economic problems. Muñoz Marín became convinced that Puerto Rico could never choose "separate independence in a plebiscite except under conditions which would be disastrous to the welfare of the people of Puerto Rico and which would destroy any hope of continuing to improve their standard of living."[59] In his judgment, the bottom line was simple: the economic status quo was more favorable than the kind of treatment likely to be afforded in a system of sovereign equality with other nations. He decided that an intermediate status between independence and statehood was likely to offer the best solution.

Major economic changes took place under Muñoz Marín's Operation Bootstrap, which between 1945 and 1964 encouraged American firms to invest in the island. Lured by exemptions from federal and local taxes – enacted for the Philippines and Puerto Rico in 1921 – hundreds of firms invested to the tune of one-half billion dollars, but with mixed results. While economic conditions improved on the island, much of the investment was only temporary. Given the provision against repatriation of the tax-free profits, many firms ultimately closed down their operations and took back their profits once the tax-free grace period ended. Hoping to end this counterproductive kind of investment, in 1995 Congress voted to phase out the tax exemptions over a 10-year period.

Between 1953 and 1977, Puerto Rico experienced high rates of economic growth, an increase in real per capita personal income, and a tripling of consumption. During this period, what had been an overwhelmingly agrarian economy became more industrialized. Nevertheless, income inequality between the city and the countryside remained a problem. And despite the migration of one-quarter of the island's population to the United States, unemployment remained stubbornly high. The migration was circular, with much coming and going, but between 1947 and 1960, there was a net outflow of more than 500,000 Puerto Ricans to the US, primarily to the New York City area. By 1997, the number of Puerto Ricans living in the United States had grown to 3.1 million. Of the 800,000 who resided in New York City, 40 percent lived below the poverty line, a far higher poverty rate than that found among African-Americans or other Hispanics.[60]

During World War II, Puerto Rico's military importance to the United States further increased when the navy created Roosevelt Roads, one of the world's largest naval bases. In 1943, FDR, referring to the island shield in the Caribbean, said that "Puerto Rico is its center. Its possession or control by any foreign power – or even the remote threat of such possession – would be repugnant to the most elementary principles of national defense." With approximately 14 percent of Puerto Rico owned or controlled by the United States military at the end of the century, the island's military value continued to rank high. One of the more controversial issues surrounding the large military presence was the use of the island of Vieques as a large-scale test site for delivery of naval ordnance.

Agitation for independence resumed after the war. The Puerto Rican legislature passed a bill for a plebiscite that was eventually vetoed by President Harry Truman. Although Muñoz Marín continued to lobby for what he called a "Free Associated State," nationalists initiated a campaign of violence that included attacks against Muñoz and an assassination attempt against President Truman in 1950. In 1950, Congress agreed to grant free associated status to Puerto Rico, which was approved in a plebiscite in 1952. This allowed the islanders to draft their own constitution, by which Puerto Rico became something called a "commonwealth." The change may have been more apparent than real, for as one attorney general later pointed out, Puerto Rico remained "for constitutional purposes, a territory subject to Congress' authority under the Territory Clause."[61]

This solution remained in place. Even though violence resurfaced on occasion, most notably an unsuccessful 1954 attack on Congress by nationalist gunmen, independence remained a minority position. From the 1960s through the 1990s, parties advocating either statehood or "enhanced" commonwealth status with greater autonomy alternated in power. In 1993, voters agreed to retain the commonwealth and its continued exemption from federal income taxes. After Congress authorized public hearings on the future status of the island, another non-binding plebiscite held at the end of

1998 decided by a small majority against statehood. Less than 3 percent of the voters favored independence.

But framing the choice in this fashion failed to take into account the rather different perspective of American public opinion, which frowned upon the idea of statehood for Puerto Rico. For US conservatives, the only realistic choice for Puerto Rico was between independence and continued commonwealth status. Statehood was anathema to many Americans who could not accept the idea of incorporating a large non-English-speaking population of Hispanic culture. Some emphasized the vast difference in standards of living and the likely further drain on the federal treasury. As it was, the federal government was spending some 10 billion dollars annually on Puerto Rico. Others pointed out that the eight representatives to which Puerto Rico would be entitled in Congress – in all likelihood, Democrats – would outweigh the congressional representation of a number of mainland states. As the twentieth century came to a close, neither Americans nor the Puerto Ricans could agree on a future for the island.

Any assessment of America's impact on Puerto Rico depends on the yardstick one employs. If it is an American standard, economic progress in the twentieth century was slow. With an average per capita income of $8,300 per year, less than half that of the poorest state, Mississippi, two-thirds of the population lived below the federal poverty level. Unemployment was about 13 percent and at least half of Puerto Ricans received food stamps. In the last quarter of the century, the proportion of the workforce on the island employed in manufacturing actually decreased from 17 to 15 percent. Much of the economic growth was undercut by a rapidly growing population which, despite emigration, reached 3 million by the 1990s. Infrastructure, the environment, and education were all far below American standards. Drug-related murder was worse than New York or Washington, DC, and the incidence of AIDS was higher than anywhere in the United States.

On the other hand, Puerto Rico had attained the second highest standard of living in the Caribbean and Latin America, behind the Bahamas.[62] Over time, the economy had become less unbalanced. Sugar was surpassed by dairy production and other livestock products as the chief source of agricultural income, while agriculture had given way to a diverse industrial sector. With more than 4 million visitors annually, tourism had become a major source of income. But most Puerto Ricans measured their economic status by an American standard of living, not by the less fortunate conditions of other Caribbean and Latin societies.

Despite significant inroads by the English language, Puerto Rican culture remained resolutely Hispanic. Ubiquitous references to *los americanos* suggested that the United States continued to be viewed as a culturally alien presence, a view confirmed by the rabid fashion in which Puerto Rican fans rooted against American teams whenever they encountered Puerto Rican teams in international competition. Nevertheless, the huge Puerto Rican emigration to the US, with the large degree of travel back and forth, had created a hybrid, syncretic culture.

The American presence also had some positive social aspects. One can debate the merits of the American decision to abolish the lottery and cockfighting upon assuming control, but the elimination of barbaric punishments is not to be scoffed at. And though the legal system continued to be based on the Spanish civil code, the US imposed salutary aspects of its system such as relaxed divorce laws. Originally intended to import American codes of morality on to the island, the availability of divorce American-style allowed women some possibility of escaping from the patriarchal system of marriage sanctioned under the old Hispanic codes. Women also liberally took advantage of the legalization of abortion following the 1973 *Roe* v. *Wade* decision of the US Supreme Court.[63]

The Americans also imposed an American-style school system to deal with the 80 percent illiteracy rate and a school attendance rate of only 16.7 percent. Until 1949, English was the language of instruction. By the 1990s, about 90 percent of the population were literate, and school attendance stood at more than 95 percent, although the high school graduation rate was only 30 percent. A University of Puerto Rico was created in 1953, which expanded into eleven campuses with more than 30,000 students. Given the increasing importance of knowledge in the modern global economy, the island was much better situated than its West Indies neighbors for an economic take-off.

At the end of a century of American rule, Puerto Rico faced a dilemma. To satisfy its sense of distinctiveness by choosing a nationalist course would probably have required the acceptance of a degree of economic sacrifice that the islanders were not willing to endure. The ambivalence of Puerto Ricans reflected this understanding of costs and benefits. Muñoz Marín, when asked for a turning point, said: "When you are traveling in a circle, every point is a turning point."[64] Independence without subsidies would almost certainly have led to economic decline, whereas independence with subsidies would hardly be worth calling true independence.

The Occupation of Haiti, 1915–1934

What had become a pattern of American intervention received new justifications and took on new forms during the presidency of Woodrow Wilson (1913–21). The long-term military occupations of Haiti and the Dominican Republic, which occupied the western and eastern portions of the island of Hispaniola just east of Cuba, broke the pattern of exercising indirect control from the outside. Added to security concerns and economic motives was Wilson's desire to promote democracy in the region. In March 1913, in remarks originally aimed at Mexico, Wilson declared: "We can have no sympathy with those who seek to seize the power of government to advance their own personal interests or ambition." That lack of sympathy was expressed through some long-term occupations.

The intervention in Haiti, a nation independent since 1804 following a bloody revolt against France, took place in July 1915 following a revolutionary riot in which a Haitian president, after having arrested and executed hundreds of his political opponents, was dismembered by an angry mob inside the grounds of the French legation and his body parts thrown over the wall. This was only the most recent disturbance in a chronically turbulent political system in which revolution had become the preferred method of transferring power. Since 1911, seven Haitian presidents had been assassinated or forcibly removed from office, one of whom was blown to bits in the presidential palace.

Haiti's tumultuous politics evinced only disapproval from Washington. Some Americans attributed the island's problems to its political elite, a group of perhaps 5,000 people in a population of two million. "The people of Haiti are slaves," said one State Department memo, "their owners a lot of low politicians. The majority of the population desires to be free of the grafting generals and politicians."[65] Others, however, believed that the problem was rooted more deeply in the country's racial and cultural characteristics. Few Americans would have disagreed with Theodore Roosevelt's characterization of Haiti as "a land of savage negroes, who have reverted to voodooism and cannibalism."[66] Echoing this condescension, one State Department official contended that the unruliness of Haitian politics reflected "the failure of an inferior people to maintain the degree of civilization left them by the French."[67] Another described the Haitian people as "almost in a state of savagery and complete ignorance."[68]

There were also the by now familiar economic and strategic motives for intervention. Though Germany and France exercised considerable economic influence in the country, by 1910 the US controlled about 60 percent of the import market and a number of US firms had become involved in politically tangled railway construction projects. Increasingly, American interests gained managerial control over Haitian finances by virtue of a 50 percent partnership interest in the Banque Nationale. The bank was not bashful about defending its interests. By 1914, it was refusing to grant loans because of presumed fiscal irresponsibility on the part of the Haitian government. Its officials also informed the State Department that American interests would leave Haiti altogether unless a

customs receivership was installed to restore fiscal sanity to
the land. Given the unsettled conditions, there was also some
concern that the Germans might use the chaos as an excuse to
move in and appropriate the fine harbor of Môle St Nicholas.
In 1914, French and German suggestions for equal participation in a customs receivership raised warning flags in Washington.[69]

Despite some misgivings about sending in American troops
in the absence of any sound legal justification for doing so,
Wilson finally concluded that "there is nothing for it but to
take the bull by the horns and restore order." Even dyed-in-
the-wool anti-imperialists like Walter Weyl saw no other
choice. "In countries like Haiti, which show at present an in-
vincible distaste for orderly government, abstention is almost
impossible," said Weyl.[70] All things considered, as Wilson told
Congress, intervention seemed "the least of the evils in sight."
Because contingency plans were already in place, American
marines were landing even as the unfortunate Haitian president was meeting his Maker.

The ensuing occupation was a strange affair in which the
US attempted to force the Haitians to be free, as Americans
understood freedom, by imposing democracy upon a people
whom many Americans believed were racially unfitted to practice it. A Haitian–American treaty prepared before the invasion, signed in 1916 and extended for another 10 years in
1926, provided legal cover for the US presence in its new protectorate. Among other things, it sanctioned US control of the
customs houses on the Dominican model and allowed the US
to organize a constabulary to pacify the countryside.

Though the Haitians objected, they had little choice but to
go along. Only after they approved the treaty did the Banque
Nationale agree to release a 1.5 million dollar loan to the government. A new constitution, which FDR later bragged about
authoring, was imposed upon the Haitians in 1918 in the face
of resistance by their Congress. The Haitians, under pressure
from the Americans, were permitted to elect a new president,
Philippe Dartiguenave, but his authority was minimal and
cooperation was grudging (assured by occasional withhold-

ing of the president's paychecks). Military forces were disbanded and martial law, once declared, was not lifted until
1929.

The Americans engaged in numerous construction projects
with a view to modernizing the country's rudimentary infrastructure. A badly needed main road was built from Port-au-
Prince to Cap Haitien, 150 miles in all, by using very unpopular
corvée labor that was not abolished until 1918. Of course,
improved roads also helped the occupation by making it easier
to move and distribute troops quickly from point to point.
Sanitation and public health were not neglected. Newly created public health services struggled to eradicate malaria, hookworm, and yaws. By 1929, 12 hospitals and 147 rural clinics
had been created. School children were routinely vaccinated,
water supplies chlorinated, streets cleaned, trash collected,
slaughterhouses inspected, latrines constructed. Agricultural
modernization was fostered, as was fishing and forestry. Sixty-
five agricultural schools were created, in addition to a Central
School for Agriculture. Some leases for large-scale farms were
allowed in the hope of increasing agricultural efficiency. Light
industry was encouraged.

Despite this positive legacy, the occupation was always a
troubled one. A major handicap, though hardly the only one,
was race, a complicated subject in a country whose ruling class
spoke French, a tongue quite different from the creole patois
spoken by the masses, and considered itself to be white as a
result of much intermarriage with Europeans. But these kinds
of distinctions, all-important in Haiti, were lost on the Americans. In 1916, following the departure of Admiral William B.
Caperton, a man who had treated the Haitians graciously,
racial prejudices took over. The new military commander, a
Virginian, objected to "bowing and scraping to these coons."
Americans despised the upper-class Haitians for their aristocratic, privileged ways and scorned commoners and elite alike
for their blackness. All this came as a shock to the upper-class
Haitians, who were themselves prejudiced against their darker-
skinned countrymen.

Americans soon imported their notions of race by introducing racial segregation and discouraging mixing of the races. Sex being universally anarchic, American officers at first had consorted with Haitian women. However, with the routinization of the occupation and with the arrival of the white wives of American marine officers, Jim Crow was imposed. Diplomatic appointments to Haiti, once given only to blacks, were now given only to whites.

Although a civilian high commissioner for Haiti was eventually named in response to criticisms of the high-handed behavior of the American military, Haitians perceived little change in their situation. From the first, they wanted the Americans to leave. Despite the best efforts of American troops, Haiti was never pacified completely as guerrilla resistance movements, the so-called *cacos*, continued in the mountains. Some criticism circulated in the United States about southern officers committing atrocities against Haitian negroes, but a military court and subsequent Senate investigations recommended continuation of the occupation, though on a reorganized basis. In all, more than 3,200 Haitians were killed by Marines in a futile effort to stamp out the smoldering rebellion.

In 1929, strikes, demonstrations, and riots – including a violent confrontation between marines and a mob of protesters – brought home the widespread unpopularity of the occupation. The next year a commission of investigation, headed by former Philippine governor W. Cameron Forbes, was greeted by 6,000 demonstrators. President Herbert Hoover had told the commission that "the primary question is when and how we are to withdraw."[71] Realizing that the US had long overstayed its welcome, the commission decided that, following free elections, it would be best to end the occupation as soon as possible. One of its members, the progressive journalist William Allen White, concluded that the attempt to reform Haiti was futile. "We are in the 20th century looking toward the 21st," he said. "They are in the 18th century with the ideals of the Grand Louis always behind them as models."[72]

Despite nearly 15 years of occupation, the US high commissioner admitted that the Haitians were "little better suited for self-government than they were in 1915."[73] Notwithstanding such doubts about Haiti's capacity for self-rule, Herbert Hoover and his successor, FDR, felt it was time to go. After much dickering, the marines left in 1934. The Banque Nationale was sold to the Haitian government the following year and government offices were transferred gradually to the Haitians. But the customs receivership remained in force until 1941, when responsibility for servicing the foreign debt was transferred to the bank, which finally retired the debt some six years later.

In the end, the accomplishments were minimal: 1,000 miles of roads, a technical service, a public health service, and a national guard to maintain order. The US did open up avenues of social mobility for darker-skinned Haitians and for women, but the extended occupation came nowhere near to creating the country that Smedley Butler had imagined the Americans would leave behind them: "a first-class black man's country . . . [of] clean little towns, with tidy thatched-roof dwellings."[74] It would be too much to say that the Americans left in frustration, given the low expectations with which they entered the country in the first place. If anything, it was the expectations of the skeptics that were fulfilled. Within a short period of time, Haiti's politics reverted to the traditional, disorderly norm, except for the calm of the cemetery imposed by occasional dictatorships. As for the Haitian masses, their country continued to be the poorest nation in the hemisphere, specializing in the production of surplus numbers of people rather than goods.[75]

The Dominican Occupation, 1916–1924

After a period in which the financial situation in the Dominican Republic had begun to look up, the sky once again darkened as the government engaged in fiscal excess, thereby endangering the customs receivership. Although the convention of 1907 focused on matters of fiscal control, the US had begun to interfere in Dominican politics as well. President Taft and his secretary of state, Philander Knox, insisted that the Dominicans pursue financial and military reforms and conduct their elections under American rules. Upon coming to office, Wilson was even more concerned to break them of their insurrectionary habit, the product of a political system in which loyalty was given to strong men capable of organizing private armies in their pursuit of power.

When a government brought into office through American-supervised elections in 1914 failed to maintain order (largely the result of the perception that it was caving in to further American demands for reform), troops were landed in 1916 to quell riots and to prevent an undesirable presidential candidate from seizing power. Martial law was declared immediately and a decree forbade the carrying of firearms – a bitter pill to swallow for many Dominicans, for whom owning a gun was a rite of passage to manhood. Dominican politicians protested and left the government, but this only provided a convenient excuse for the US to suspend elections to the National Assembly in 1917. Thereafter nothing appeared to stand in the way of a complete reconstruction of Dominican society by the Yankees.

The Americans were a bit more enthusiastic about their redemptive mission in the Dominican Republic than they were in next-door Haiti. As one diplomat said, the Dominicans at least had "a preponderance of white blood and culture," whereas the negro Haitians were "almost in a state of savagery and complete ignorance."[76] Still, there was much to redeem. Although the convention of 1907 stipulated the creation of a Department of Public Works, the Dominicans had neglected it. There was no public sanitation to speak of; disease, especially venereal disease, was epidemic; the illiteracy rate stood at 90 percent; there were only 40 miles of good roads, the remaining thoroughfares being primarily wagon trails.

Occupation policy was made by the American proconsuls on the scene. Though largely left to their own devices, they conscientiously resorted to the full panoply of measures that were, by now, standard operating procedure. Law and order being the chief priority of any occupation, the Americans invested much time and money in creating a new national guard, a constabulary designed to deal with the chronic problem of banditry in the countryside. Officered mainly by Americans, the guard took up fully 25 percent of the occupation budget by 1919. Americans viewed the guard as something of a social experiment that provided an avenue of upward mobility for poor youths from the villages. And so it proved to be, though not in the way intended. Instead of being kept at arm's length from politics, the guard became the basis of political power. One of the first graduates of the American-created military academies was Rafael Trujillo, who would use the national guard to become dictator shortly after the Americans departed.

More successful was the occupation's ambitious public works program, which was made possible by revenues deriving from the wartime prosperity. By 1921, 90 miles of macadam roads and 260 miles of second- and third-class roads were in existence. A bankrupt railroad was repaired and revived. Port facilities were improved, including repairs to docks and customs houses. A new national penitentiary was built, as was a leprosaurium. A national telephone system was created out of a patchwork of formerly private companies. Though these infrastructural improvements stimulated economic activity, they did not change the economic system and, according to one account, "primarily advanced the fortunes of the country's existing planter and merchant elite."[77]

Education, as usual, was another area of concentration for the occupation. There were only 18,000 students in the school system at the beginning of the occupation out of a school-age population of 200,000. Rather than build public schoolhouses, the Dominican government had instead rented private houses. The curriculum failed to inculcate basic skills of literacy and numeracy. Seven hundred primary schools were opened on the American model, and attendance between the ages of 7–13 was made compulsory. Two public high schools were created and two normal schools to train teachers. Of the "two so-called universities," as described by the navy's military governor, one was closed down and the Central University was modernized to provide training in law, medicine, pharmacy, math, dentistry, obstetrics, and so on.

Although the Americans constructed schoolhouses and enrolled 100,000 students in primary education, the effort was hampered by a serious shortage of adequately trained teachers, which meant that "very little learning was accomplished in many schools."[78] But even this measure of progress was later undermined by a shaky tax structure that was unable to provide continuing levels of support for the educational system when the economy turned downward.

American health and sanitation efforts focused chiefly on the countryside, but war was also waged on filth and disease in the towns and cities. The occupation provided for such basic civic services as street cleaning, garbage removal, and installation of latrines. Waste disposal facilities were inspected. Food, drink, and drugs were regulated in the name of public health. All public dwellings needed to be approved for habitation. Vaccination was required. Prostitution was outlawed. Health councils and sanitary brigades were created for enforcement of all these measures. Unfortunately, the health efforts were hampered by a serious shortage of medical personnel and the usual financial stringencies, while the sanitation regime was disliked for its imperious style and peremptory enforcement methods.

As usual, restoring the soundness of the public finances ranked high in American priorities. Claims against the former government were settled by the sale of bonds in 1918. The budget was balanced, though this achievement was made very difficult by a post-World War I depression, which necessitated firing a full 60 percent of government employees. However, some later budgets were deliberately unbalanced in order to allow for the completion of major public works projects.

Occupations, by their nature, operate under a law of diminishing returns, all the more so when they are military in character. Armies excel at waging wars, but they are poor instruments for creating modern societies. As time went on, the occupation, never popular to begin with, began to grate even more on the Dominicans. Though there were some collaborators, overall public sentiment remained hostile and was reflected in low-level guerrilla activity in the countryside which continued until 1922. According to a report by Ernest Gruening in 1922: "In ten days' diligent inquiry in the Dominican Republic I could not find a single native who did not want the American Occupation to get out, bag and baggage, at the earliest possible moment."[79] Military censorship, a thin-skinned response to barbed criticism of the American presence, boomeranged by becoming the subject of increasingly vocal opposition among Dominicans, not to mention a growing chorus of domestic critics of the occupation.

More importantly, sentiment changed within the United States. By 1920, the navy and State Department had begun to quarrel about continuing the occupation, with the navy arguing that rehabilitation should continue. One admiral argued that "the only hope of those negroes is wise white guidance," and prophesied catastrophe if the US should withdraw. But the Wilson administration was prepared to concede that the usefulness of the occupation was nearing its end. The Harding and Coolidge administrations, which felt similarly, also had to face growing public criticism of the occupation from within the United States.

Dominicans rejected a 1922 proposal for US withdrawal, which restored fiscal sovereignty in return for legitimizing all the acts of the military government. But within the next year a deal was worked out in which the Dominicans agreed to continue the customs receivership and American troops were out by 1924. By 1930, Trujillo had seized power, beginning a ruthless 31-year reign. Altogether, the results were not inspiring. If it is true, as one historian has argued, that "the intervention was an example of anti-colonialism and anti-imperialism at its best,"[80] one shudders to think what it was at its worst.

The Decline of the Caribbean Empire

In the 1920s, the tide of American interventionism in the hemisphere began to recede from its high-water mark. By the end of the decade, the US had already withdrawn from the Dominican Republic and was on the verge of pulling out of Nicaragua and Haiti. A potentially serious confrontation with Mexico over the expropriation of American property was defused with the agreement to use some ambiguous words rather than guns to settle their differences. By the administration of Herbert Hoover (1929–33), the floodwaters of interventionism were in retreat. "True democracy cannot be imperialistic," Hoover said in 1928. In his inaugural address, he insisted that "we have no desire for territorial expansion, for economic or other domination of peoples." That sort of thing had been said before, most notably by Wilson prior to his interventions, but this time the United States was willing to act accordingly.

The State Department's publication in 1930 of the Clark Memorandum, written two years earlier, made clear that the infamous Roosevelt Corollary to the Monroe Doctrine was now being "de-corollated." The memorandum argued that the Monrovian creed "states a case of United States vs. Europe, and not of the United States vs. Latin America." But this was not a revivalist return to first principles. The growing reluctance of the United States to intervene in the banana republics was due not only to the jettisoning of the Roosevelt Corollary, but to a weakening of the doctrine itself. According to one historian, the Monroe Doctrine as a whole "effectively became an anachronism" in the postwar years.[81] Of course, the Doctrine retained an aura of sacredness that insulated it from criticism. But, as is true with many objects of worship, people could no longer say with certainty why it was worthy of veneration.

On the thesis that idealism grows with distance, American behavior in the Caribbean is often described as an example of the United States hypocritically failing to practice what it preached in Europe and Asia. Speaking of the Caribbean, one author wrote in 1918 that "America is still a world within a world."[82] But geographical variation should not be confused with geographical difference. US policy was in fact logically articulated with its policies in other regions. Having been nurtured in one kind of ideological soil, imperialism withered as perceptions of the world shifted in the wake of the Great War.

Most of the interests that stood to benefit from empire were still around and in some cases had grown more potent, but these interests were overshadowed by an ideological shift in which a powerful new global perspective began to dominate the thinking of policy-makers.

The result was that imperialism fell out of fashion. The Republican administrations of the 1920s reasoned along the following lines. If Europe was no longer an "alien" system, if the same rules of conduct held good throughout the world, and if the great powers were all engaged in a more or less cooperative project to promote global peace and prosperity, then it was pointless to engage in pre-emptive imperialism. The assumption that the world was a peaceful whole removed the struts of defensiveness that had propped up the two Monroe Doctrines. With the diplomacy of imperialism increasingly perceived as a dangerous feature of international relations in the wake of World War I, anti-imperialism became an integral feature of US foreign policy (see chapter 5). There seemed, in any case, no geopolitical need for defensive imperialism, as the probability of European intervention in the western hemisphere in the 1920s approached zero. Not least, as the Sandinistas in Nicaragua showed, imperialism, formerly a nearly effortless exercise, was becoming militarily frustrating and costly to boot.

There was, however, relatively little change in the underlying belief in the inferiority of Latin American peoples, a condition that was usually attributed to a combination of climatic, racial, and cultural handicaps. Nevertheless, during the decade a sizable number of intellectuals, scientists, and radical journalists took issue with traditional explanations for underdevelopment by pointing to the role played by disease and unfavorable distribution of natural resources.[83] This critical approach to old platitudes was supplemented by a growing appreciation of the attractive features of Latin cultures. But while the net result was growing pressure against Caribbean interventionism, the civilizing impulse remained strong. Direct imperial control was replaced by a growing liberal emphasis on cultural relations to do the work of civilization, "to define Pan-American relations along cultural rather than strategic or economic lines," as one historian has put it.[84]

The administration of Franklin D. Roosevelt (1933–45) institutionalized the anti-interventionist approach that came to be known as the "good neighbor policy." After a shaky start in which the administration came close to intervening militarily in Cuba to deal with the political aftermath of Machado's downfall, the Platt amendment was finally abrogated. As the right of intervention had already been publicly renounced the year before at the Montevideo Inter-American Conference, US forces soon left Haiti and Nicaragua. Despite a good deal of tension, a dispute with Mexico in 1938 over the expropriation of American-owned oil properties was peacefully resolved. American diplomats, formerly proconsuls in the American empire, now refused to signal thumbs-up or thumbs-down to contending political factions. Though opportunities to meddle were not in short supply, the Roosevelt administration steadfastly refused to send in troops.

Anti-interventionism was, on the whole, an improvement over the naked imperialism of the preceding generation. Nevertheless, even though formal relations with Latin America had never been better, the situation was far from ideal. For one thing, despite the New Deal's ideological sympathy for left-of-center reformist regimes, there were few such governments to be found in the region, in part because non-interventionism gave authoritarian governments license to flourish without fear of incurring Washington's wrath. Ironically, on occasion this situation evoked interventionist pleas from some veteran anti-imperialists who, undaunted by the miserable failure of Wilsonian attempts at implanting democracy through compulsion, believed that these regimes were so repulsive that they ought to be forcibly removed, if necessary. If nothing else, this showed how easily the justification of intervention for reasons of civilization, which was long a part of the rhetoric of imperialism, could enter the anti-imperialist vocabulary. And despite the more healthful climate of cultural relations, Americans continued to adhere to powerful negative stereotypes of their southern neighbors.[85]

Other critics who claimed to see through the good neighbor policy's pieties maintained that overt control had merely been replaced by a more subtle, but equally potent, economic imperialism. The 1934 Reciprocal Trade Agreements Act was a good example. In the attempt to re-start foreign trade stalled by the great depression, this measure sought, on a case-by-case basis, to bring about a general lowering of tariffs. Most of the agreements were signed with Latin American nations. But according to the anti-imperialist critic Carlton Beals, this promotion of free trade resulted in a *de facto* economic imperialism imposed by the superior strength of the American economy. In his words, the agreements demanded that Latin Americans "remain dutiful little colonies under Uncle Sam's tutelage."[86] By this reckoning, outright military control had been replaced by an economic and political hegemony that maintained a status quo favorable to American interests that curbed more radical options for development. "In the end nonintervention served the same purpose as intervention," says one historian.[87]

Cold War Geopolitics and After

But the good neighbor policy proved to be only a non-interventionist intermission. Although the economic stake in Latin America continued to grow, overall it remained a small proportion of America's global trade. Thus, as in the past, global developments rather than specific regional interests were decisive in shaping American policy in the region. After 1945, with the Cold War now providing the international backdrop for US policy in the region, the fear of communist expansion became an all-consuming preoccupation for American policymakers. Despite the acknowledgment by both the US and USSR that imperialism was no longer legitimate, each side insisted on painting the other in imperialist colors. As an extraordinarily vivid fear of Soviet imperialism replaced older fancies of European expansionism, American policy in the region took on a geopolitical seriousness that prompted a return to pre-emptive interventionism and a resurrection of developmental concerns.

Cold War interventionism in the region was reminiscent of Teddy Roosevelt's "big stick," but it was intervention with qualitative and quantitative differences that suggested the nation was now playing for higher stakes. The signature of the Rio pact in 1948, which created the Organization of American States (OAS), meant that intervention would require the multilateral sanction of a regional collective security organization. Even though the US was the dominant power in this body, it meant that at least a fig leaf of international approval would be required to make virtuous an otherwise offensive exercise of American power.

In any case, covert means of intervention were always available when formal approval was too troublesome to obtain. In 1954, the CIA financed a rebel army to overthrow a left-leaning government in Guatemala after John Foster Dulles had obtained a resolution condemning communism at a meeting of the OAS. In response to Soviet complaints in the United Nations about American high-handedness, US ambassador Henry Cabot Lodge Jr, told the Russians to "get out of this hemisphere." Shortly thereafter, to demonstrate that the United States was interested more in hemispheric security than in profits, the Department of Justice filed suit against the United Fruit Company, long the corporate symbol of American imperialism in the region, for monopolistic practices.[88]

Until the late 1950s, Latin American affairs were generally buried in the back pages of newspapers. American foreign aid, much of it in the form of military hardware and internal security training, seemed to be doing a good job. But then two events pushed the region into the headlines. One was the 1958 goodwill tour of Vice President Richard Nixon to South America in which he was greeted by breathtakingly hostile mobs. In Caracas his car was stoned and nearly overturned by howling demonstrators. The other was the success of Fidel Castro's revolution in Cuba in 1959.

In the course of two eventful years, Castro went from Robin Hood to public enemy number one as he drifted into the Soviet camp. In April 1961, the CIA sought to repeat its former successes by training an exile army of Cubans to invade the island in the hope of overthrowing him, but an invasion at the Bay of Pigs turned into a propaganda fiasco for the United States when all the planning went wrong. Only the following year, in the wake of the crisis caused by the Soviet emplacement of nuclear-tipped missiles on the island, did the United States provide a binding non-invasion pledge.

But no such pledges were offered for other countries. As presidential adviser McGeorge Bundy wrote: "We have to live on the same world with the Soviet Union, but we do not have to accept Communist subversion in this hemisphere."[89] In 1965, President Lyndon Johnson authorized the use of force in the Dominican Republic when he scented another Cuba being created there. In 1983, US forces invaded the tiny island of Grenada when its prime minister appeared to be leading it in a Castroite direction. Most notably, Ronald Reagan authorized covert intervention in Nicaragua in an attempt to oust the leftist Sandinista regime that came to power in 1978. So determined was the administration to aid the so-called "contra" guerrillas that it illegally used profits from secret arms sales to Iran to finance the anti-Sandinista freedom fighters. The revelations of such hanky-panky created a wave of scandal that nearly capsized the Reagan administration in its closing years.

The Cold War also brought a renewed emphasis on modernization in Latin America. With the survival of the American way of life thought to depend on proving the global superiority of the American system, foreign aid became a major instrument of American foreign policy. As an optimistic social scientific "modernization theory" began to emerge in American universities in the 1950s, American policy-makers developed a new-found confidence in their ability to generate economic growth in underdeveloped societies. "The tricks of growth are not all that difficult," claimed Walt W. Rostow in his seminal work, *The Stages of Economic Growth*.[90]

The Kennedy administration's Alliance for Progress was the most ambitious example of this marriage of geopolitical necessity and can-do social science. Kennedy called for "a vast cooperative effort, unparalleled in magnitude and nobility of purpose," to promote development throughout Latin America. The Alliance would make available what American military occupations earlier in the century had refused to supply: large sums of American dollars. In return, the recipients were supposed to supply a missing ingredient of their own: the will to meaningful reform and regional economic integration.

Conceived in the wake of Fidel Castro's shocking takeover of Cuba (Latin politicians referred to the funding as "Fidel's money"), the Alliance was a breathtakingly ambitious program that was supposed to promote a whole series of modernizing goals: industrialization, democratization, improved agricultural productivity, tax reform, and land reform, among other things. To target land reform was especially audacious for a region where 5–10 percent of the population owned anywhere from 70 to 90 percent of the land.[91] Exuding optimism, one US official predicted that "within a decade the direction and results of centuries of Latin American history are to be changed."[92] Kennedy and his advisers were banking on a new generation of left-of-center Latin politicians – Venezuela's Romulo Betancourt was the poster boy – to lead the way in this revolution from above. If successful, American-stimulated modernization would put an end equally to right-wing military rule and to the threat of violent socialist revolutions.

An outside power can prevent development, but no nation can impose it. This was as true of the Alliance for Progress as it was of dollar diplomacy or the modernizing American military interventions earlier in the century. Although funding for the Alliance continued to flow as promised throughout much of the 1960s, this ambitious program was, in the end, a failure. Despite its revolutionary pretensions, the US was reluctant to risk funding agrarian reforms that might turn truly radical.[93] Instead of spawning democrats, the region produced more despots in a series of right-wing military takeovers. Though these coups had not been encouraged by Washington, the underlying security rationale of the Alliance meant that the new military rulers were ultimately accepted as a lesser evil than radical regimes.

Not surprisingly, then, programs were turned to the purposes of the ruling elites, thus reinforcing the very socioeconomic patterns that the Alliance was intended to overturn. Understandably, frustration set in among American officials. "What is wrong," said one administrator in trying to explain Guatemala's lack of progress, "is that you are dealing with a society here that has a concept of mankind opposed to that of Western civilization."[94] In a region where the tradition of the middle way was weak, the dilemma was that neither conservatives nor radicals wanted the kind of reform being promoted by Washington.

A change of sentiment about the Alliance among Kennedy's successors contributed to the disappointing outcome. Lyndon Johnson refused to make the Alliance a tool for opposing right-wing dictatorships. His director of the Alliance, Thomas Mann, saw the colonels and generals as being "on the whole, a pretty decent group of people."[95] With the election of the more conservative Richard Nixon to the presidency in 1968, the Alliance was written off as yet another symptom of Great Society excesses. Reinforcing the president's gut instinct was the report of a committee headed by Nelson Rockefeller, which criticized "well-intentioned but unrealistic rhetoric" and noted the distortions that resulted when aid programs and trade policies were bureaucratically reshaped with a view to benefiting American special interests.[96] Although the Rockefeller Commission advocated ambitious new programs of its own, it was unable to recapture the sense of urgency that had inspired Kennedy's New Frontier.

While the end of the Cold War eliminated security rationales for intervention, arguments for civilization continued to justify American military involvement in the internal affairs of other countries in the region. The Panamanian dictator, Manuel Noriega, was given ample opportunity to reflect upon the continuing willingness of the US to extend its power into the Caribbean as he languished in an American prison. And in 1994, the United States orchestrated a United Nations inter-

vention in Haiti to rid the country of a stifling military dictatorship in the hope that a more progressive regime might create the improved conditions that would discourage desperate
Haitian boat people from landing on American shores and
claiming political asylum. Despite this hope, in the years following the introduction of troops, it was hard to claim that
any improvement had taken place in Haiti, which remained
one of the most impoverished places in the hemisphere.

Over the course of the century, US-influenced changes in the
political weather in the Caribbean basin were repeatedly shaped
by shifts in the global political climate. At different times, considerations such as security, anti-imperialism, protection of
economic interests, political stability, democracy, and development took turns to dominate US policy thinking. As a result
of these changes in the political environment, there is no simple, single judgment to be made about this intricate history.
To the extent that the American imperial presence contributed
to the goal of preserving American security in the Caribbean
region by preventing European powers from interfering, by
protecting the approaches to the Panama Canal and by forestalling the spread of communism, American policy was quite
clearly a success – despite the painful Cuban stone in Uncle
Sam's shoe. In addition, by the end of the twentieth century,
democracy had taken root in much of the region, though more
so in the Caribbean islands than in Central America.[97]

In other ways, however, the United States failed to meet its
objectives. With the qualified exception of Puerto Rico, the
American imperial presence failed to jump-start the economic
development that policy-makers liked so much to talk about
and it failed to plant the roots of political democracy. Moreover, the activist legacy of "Yanquí imperialism" in the Caribbean – with 17 separate military interventions between 1901
and 1933 – did more harm to America's international image
than its behavior in any other area of the world. In no other
region was the gap between America's self-image as a progressive and benign nation so at variance with the perceptions
of the nations who were forced to deal with it. And, as always

with imperious behavior, its morality leaves much to be desired.

But morality is a poor substitute for complex and often nuanced historical judgments. One example of simplistic reasoning is the tendency to blame the US for built-in problems in the region. One historian, for example, insists that intervention in Cuba produced "debased political institutions, deformed social formations, and dependent economic relationships."[98] It is true that the US wound up fostering, sometimes by inadvertence, at other times by choice, some nasty dictatorial regimes, and it is also clear that the concern with stability has worked against the kind of progressive change that Americans believed would result naturally from law and order. But it takes a stretch of the imagination to suppose that the Latin American republics would have been free and prosperous without American intervention.

No doubt the Haitians, for example, would have been ecstatic to see the Americans depart post-haste, but would they have been politically the better for it, except in some hazy psychological sense? And would the region as a whole really have made better progress if the United States had not intervened? If the United States had not been there politically, is it not likely that the Europeans would have stepped in? Without an American cultural presence, would not European cultural influences have moved in to fill their shoes? And is it not possible that the pursuit of sovereign equality sometimes makes for international inequality? The questions simply overwhelm the hard answers available to us.

Criticisms of American commercial and cultural imperialism also need to be taken with a grain of salt. The American economic presence, which changed significantly over time as it shifted from agricultural to industrial investment, had varying impacts in different countries. While it stimulated the appetite for modern consumerism and individual freedom among certain professional and working segments, at the same time it often led to political unrest and anti-Americanism among groups who failed to benefit from the introduction of new economic patterns.[99] Conceivably, without American financial and corporate interference the region might have experienced breathtaking economic growth. But while American-directed attempts at economic modernization made only very limited headway, Ernest May's judgment that without the American presence the region would have been like Africa, undeveloped rather than underdeveloped, seems more plausible.[100] In an imperfect world, the best-case alternative to uneven development may have been an egalitarian non-development, an equitable sharing of poverty, along the lines of Castro's Cuba. One cannot rule out the possibility of a happier outcome, but it is hard to see how it could have come about.

Similarly, criticism of American cultural imperialism exaggerates the extent of informal cultural influence when, in fact, the American cultural imprint was rather shallow. Even where the US exercised direct control over the fate of societies, it failed to transform their cultures and their basic institutions. If anything, the effect was to stimulate a stronger sense of cultural identity in which anti-Americanism was a prominent feature. A greater modernizing effort would have required a cultural imperialism far more ruthless than anything the Americans were willing to contemplate and more transformative than the occupied peoples were willing to tolerate.[101] What is amazing, in retrospect, is that the United States bothered to try.

4

The Modernization of China and the Diplomacy of Imperialism

America's two-century-long encounter with China showed yet another facet of its many-sided imperial experience. To over-simplify, US policy in China stood midway conceptually between "pure" imperialism in the Philippines and pre-emptive interventionism in the Caribbean. Whereas the civilizing mission dominated in the Philippines and an opposition to the diplomacy of imperialism was the chief concern in the Caribbean, America's China policy contained both elements to a heightened degree. The prospect of bringing western civilization to China fired the imaginations of modernizers much more so than in other imperial venues, at the same time that relations with other imperial powers, conducted in a distinctive policy framework known as treaty port imperialism, were more intense and continuing. In short, China was a prime site for testing the American yearning to modernize pre-industrial societies while promoting great power cooperation.

Historians of all stripes agree that Americans were attracted by the dream of the China market. Indeed, the vision of a China market was for a long time just that – a dream, an illusion. Given the absence, until very recently, of any substantial economic interests in China, hard profit motives were peripheral to the relationship. But the dream was none the less compelling because it appealed to America's image of its global self, to its sense of international identity. It tapped into a larger

vision of world history in which China was to be Christian-
ized, industrialized, and democratized under American tutelage as part of a noble experiment in transferring civilization.
Indeed, the vision was grander still, for China was viewed as a
field in which the great powers were supposed to cooperate
with one another in a peaceful project of modernization that
would benefit all involved. By the middle of the twentieth century, China became a symbol of the vision's failure and a focal point of fears for another world war, only to see the
optimistic vision experience a surprising revival in the 1970s.

Whatever one thinks of them, the dreams in which China
figured were far from abstract reveries. Like no other place in
the world, China offered Americans an open field for the full
exercise of their historical imaginations.

Commercial and Cultural Origins of
the Modernization Policy

Though the two nations were situated on opposite sides of the
earth, the cultural distance between them seemed greater still.
China was a land in which men wore gowns and pigtails and
women wore pants, in which red was worn at weddings and
white at funerals. It was a country in which people ate dogs
and hated milk, used strange eating utensils, served the soup
course at the end of the meal, wrote with a strange script that
was read in an up-and-down direction, stapled their papers
on the wrong side, and where a smile was often a token not of
pleasure but of embarrassment and trouble. Of course, the
Chinese were equally perplexed by the strange and often offensive practices of westerners, who were viewed as rank "barbarians" with disgusting customs. The vast civilizational
distance between the two societies made the American cultural relationship with China an unlikely union.[1]

Originally, the terms of the trading relationship were dictated by China under the so-called "tribute system," which
was an application to foreign affairs of the Confucian sense of
hierarchical superiority from which Chinese emperors had long

viewed the outside world. Since China's position as the Middle Kingdom made her the pivot of all earthly affairs, it was her duty to introduce civilization to adjoining areas – not by conquest, but by demonstration of Confucian moral superiority. From this ethnocentric point of view, westerners as clear inferiors were permitted to trade with China only on terms that reflected the unequal status of the two civilizations. Commercial access was granted as a matter of imperial benevolence, but only following appropriate expressions of humble submission on the part of western supplicants.

The kowtow, the series of ritual prostrations performed on the occasion of a rare audience with the emperor, was a ceremonial that "left no doubt in anyone's mind, least of all in the performer's, as to who was inferior and who superior."[2] The hierarchical relationship was further skewed by the absence in historically self-contained China of any need for foreign goods. As one Chinese emperor famously wrote to England's King George III in 1793: "Strange and costly objects do not interest me . . . I have no use for your country's manufactures . . . it behooves you, O King, to respect my sentiments and to display even greater devotion and loyalty in the future, so that by perpetual submission to our throne, you may enjoy peace and security for your country thereafter . . ."

This assumption of Chinese superiority was the conceptual basis for trade under the "Canton system," which remained in place from 1760 to 1840. At first, the Chinese threw up all kinds of obstacles in their effort to limit the western presence. Western traders were limited to the southern port city of Canton, which was intentionally far removed from the center of imperial power, and were permitted to deal only with specified middlemen or "hongs." Foreigners were not allowed in the city proper, but were restricted to certain areas outside its walls. Essentially, it was a system of trade on Chinese conditions, designed to limit the impact of the foreign presence on the Chinese way of life. The terms of trade were initially in China's favor, with westerners paying in silver when they lacked desirable goods to exchange.

American trade with China began in the 1780s in the shadow

of the British East India Company. The first US vessel bound for China left in 1785, seeking to purchase silks and cotton cloths, porcelains, and, the most prized commodity, Chinese tea. Americans at first had difficulty finding saleable commodities to offer in exchange and could do no better than sea otter and seal skins, sandalwood, and ginseng, a herb said to increase sexual potency. Until the 1830s, this miscellaneous assortment of goods was never sufficient to cover the cost of desired Chinese products, which meant that the balance had to be made up in scarce hard currency.

The end of the tribute system came as a result of the large-scale smuggling of opium into China, mostly by the British, but also by American merchants. Opium, which the British produced from poppies grown in India, became the basis of an enormous illegal trade that was connived at by everyone with much corruption. Because of the great demand in China, the trade was hugely profitable, providing for approximately one-seventh of the revenues of British India. It was the opium trade that helped to finance the growing British appetite for Chinese tea. In 1839, Great Britain exported 30,000 chests of the drug, each weighing 133 pounds. One historian estimates that the American trade in opium, which had to be transported from Turkey, amounted to one-fifth of the British commerce, a not insignificant level of participation.[3] Whatever its morality, this explosive growth of the international narcotics trade solved, in a most satisfactory fashion, the problem of finding a saleable product to export to China.

By 1839, corruption among Chinese officials had become so rampant and the social consequences of widespread addiction so horrendous that the emperor finally attempted to suppress the trade. The British, liberally aided by the opium merchants, objected and sent a small expeditionary force that defeated China in the Opium War (1839–42). The justification was that no civilized state had the right to refuse to trade. Kibitzing from the sidelines, John Quincy Adams asserted that the Chinese refusal to trade openly had been "an enormous outrage upon the rights of human nature."

To this point in time, the west had been incapable of defeating China militarily. Given their contrasting land and sea orientations and China's sheer mass, the likelihood of combat between the two has been likened to the difficulty of an elephant and a whale coming to grips. But the Opium War coincided with the beginning of the industrialization of warfare, a development that enabled the west to mass produce weaponry that other societies had no hope of replicating unless they themselves had industrialized. In this case, the British were able to use shallow draft, steam-driven gunboats to force their way up the Yangtze river, capturing tribute junks along the way. If the Chinese had not sued for peace, the British would have been able to steam invincibly up the Grand Canal all the way to the capital city of Beijing.

The war ended with the Treaty of Nanjing, which inaugurated the "treaty port system" of western imperialism in China. This new arrangement was an extension and elaboration of the tribute system, except that the former power relationships were turned upside-down. Its principal elements were the treaty ports, which expanded the number of ports from which foreigners were entitled to trade – from five at first to more than 80 eventually. Each port had a new, privileged foreign section (typically dominated by the British consulate because, throughout the nineteenth century, Great Britain was the dominant foreign power in China). The treaty ports became states within a state that were governed by foreigners, by virtue of another feature of the new system, extraterritoriality, which made foreigners, and often those in their immediate employ, exempt from Chinese law.

This crippling of Chinese sovereignty also had precedents in earlier Chinese practices that allowed foreigners to govern themselves according to their own laws on the theory that they were too benighted to be expected to conform to China's enlightened ways. In principle, western law was supposed to be enforced by the consuls. But all too often, extraterritoriality became a virtual license for foreigners to behave in an outrageous manner against the Chinese and get away with it. Extraterritoriality eventually grew to quite sizable dimensions because it could be transferred to employees, land, and institutions. For the Chinese, this "treaty port system" became known as the "unequal treaties," whose removal became the abiding object of a century of Chinese diplomacy.

The economic linchpin of the new system was the treaty tariff, in which the Chinese were limited to charging a duty on imports of about 5 percent *ad valorem*.[4] By the 1850s, the imperial customs were being expertly administered by Sir Robert Hart's mainly British staff. Setting taxes on imports is, of course, a normal element of sovereignty. It was especially important in the late nineteenth century because of the growing reliance upon protective tariffs as a basic tool of industrialization. The United States, for example, resorted to protectionism during the Civil War as a way of sheltering its "infant industries" from potentially disastrous foreign competition. The treaty tariff effectively prevented China from adopting a protective strategy.

The United States became a participant in treaty port imperialism in 1844. In July of that year, Caleb Cushing, an envoy sent by President John Tyler to formalize diplomatic relations with the Celestial Empire, signed the Treaty of Wanghia. This agreement not only secured for the US all the advantages enjoyed by the British but, thanks to the inclusion of a most-favored-nation clause, made Americans automatically eligible for any additional treaty benefits that the Chinese might bestow in future upon other nations. This was such an impressive modification that the other powers soon felt compelled to include it in their revised treaties with China. The Chinese, employing the ancient principle of "using barbarians to control barbarians," were taking a chance on the Americans in the hope that they might prove useful in the future. Thus did the United States become involved in a form of "hitchhiking imperialism," having thumbed a ride with the British navy on its way to becoming one of the imperialist treaty powers in China.

Over the years, extraterritoriality became a corrupt practice and, for the Chinese, an infuriating symbol of their weakness and inferiority *vis-à-vis* the west. In the case of the Americans, the absence of jails in China in the early days was indicative not only of the reluctance of consuls to prosecute fellow-countrymen, but of the inability of a weak state to discipline its nationals. Thus for a time all blue-eyed prostitutes claimed to be American. All sorts of western riff-raff came to China, including a sizable number of ladies of ill repute who found a new frontier there after the American west lost its wildness. A few of these ladies, as well as some saloon-keepers and others engaged in marginal callings, made sizable fortunes. Until 1906, when a US District Court for Shanghai was created and the consular system was reformed, most American consuls stayed in their posts for only a few years, trailing clouds of corruption behind them as they departed.[5]

For the commercial houses engaged in the China trade, business was for some years extremely lucrative and some large fortunes were made. That began to change after the Civil War, however, as the industrial revolution made higher rates of return available in other types of investments. As the locus of opportunity shifted, the fortunes made by American merchants in China were later applied to domestic ventures. Consequently, as a percentage of the nation's total foreign commerce, the China trade actually began to decline in the 1840s.

Only in the 1890s did exports, primarily kerosene and cotton products, begin to climb upwards, multiplying five-fold in the course of the decade to a total of 15 million dollars per year. Investments enjoyed a spurt as well, swelling to 20 million dollars by 1900.[6] A revived sense of commercial promise was reflected in the formation in 1898 of a commercial pressure group, the American Asiatic Association, whose mission was to promote commercial opportunity in China. "The wants of these four hundred million are increasing every year," said one journal. "What a market!"[7] "There are 400,000,000 active stomachs in China, and each cries out for food three times a day," said a newspaper in 1900.[8] But this was mostly hype. The truth was that China was a minor market for American goods and capital, comprising only 2 percent of all US foreign trade and 3 percent of all US foreign investments, while the spurt of growth during the 1890s was no greater for China than for other regions of the world.

American imperialism in China entered under a commercial passport, but it was not long before it acquired idealistic and developmentalist credentials.[9] In a burst of evangelical energy in the early nineteenth century, American mission societies, especially the American Board of Commissioners for Foreign Missions, sent missionaries to preach the gospel throughout the world. Under the terms of the Canton system, western missionaries had been shut out of China. But in the aftermath of the Opium War, they received extraterritorial protection and, following a further expansion in the number of treaty ports extorted from the Chinese, were allowed to penetrate into the interior of the country in their quest to spread the gospel to the "heathen Chinee."

Viewed simply in terms of the number of converts, the missionary enterprise had disappointing results. It gained fewer than 200,000 converts by 1905, and another 300,000 by the mid-1930s, a period that some have called the "golden age" of the mission. The cultural soil for planting the seeds of Christianity was stony given the wide gap between the missionaries and the Chinese. For the missionaries, the Chinese had their admirable qualities, such as their stress on education, the family, and moral behavior. At the same time, they were seen as depraved: by their addiction to gambling, their harsh treatment of women, and their superstitious religious and philosophical beliefs.[10] One traveler described them as "morally, the most debased people on the face of the earth."[11] For their part, the Chinese viewed the missionaries with great suspicion, and with good cause. As one missionary sympathetically described the situation of a potential convert, Christianity demanded "so complete a surrender to all that belonged to his education, his theory of government, and society, his views of nature, his ancestral worship, his domestic relations, and his modes of life, that it is a wonder that a convert is made."[12]

Small wonder, then, as one historian has noted, that "Protestant missionaries and the local Chinese elite were as natural enemies as cats and dogs."[13] Western missionaries were suspected of boiling infants in oil, of capturing the spirits of ancestors, of upsetting the ancient order of things by requiring attendance of men and women in church services, and so on. Not surprisingly, conversion tended to be limited at first to the immediate household staffs of the missionaries and to so-called "rice bowl Christians," individuals who accepted the gospels less out of conviction than in the assurance of getting three square meals daily in a land increasingly beset by over-population and other disasters, both natural and man-made.[14]

With their congregations back home eager to hear news of success, the missionaries resorted increasingly to an indirect approach in which they shifted their emphasis to education and to the provision of medical services. The Chinese had them-selves experimented with education by sending the famous Yung Wing mission to the United States in 1871. Organized by the first Chinese to graduate from Yale in 1854, this mission re-sulted in the dispatch of 120 Chinese youths, complete with pigtails and gowns, to the Connecticut river valley. A decade later a Chinese envoy was horrified to see that these young men were being Americanized, i.e. becoming barbarians, and the educational experiment, for the time being, was at an end.

For American missionaries in China, however, the hope was that education and medicine would attract clients and, over time, help make the Chinese more receptive to their religious message. In theory, the demonstration through science of the wonders of natural law would point with greater clarity to its ultimate source in divine law. In this way, secular education became indispensable to the success of the missionary enter-prise. "It is Western education that the Chinese are clamoring for, and will have," said John R. Mott of the YMCA. "If the Church can give it to them, plus Christianity, they will take it; otherwise, they will get it elsewhere, without Christianity."[15] By targeting the future elites of China, education also prom-ised to provide greater bang for the buck in the long run. The Manchurian warlord Jiang Tso-Lin's practice of baptizing his troops with a fire hose was a comical illustration of large-scale conversion, but it was a splendid example of the multi-plier effect. And, of course, education was also necessary for training Chinese Christian ministers to carry on the work of evangelization.

By the 1890s, the United States, though one of the weaker treaty powers in China, commanded the strongest foreign cultural presence in the land. The number of Protestant mission workers peaked at about 5,000 by 1925. In that year, the missions had 301 hospitals and 500 dispensaries scattered throughout the land. There were in addition more than 300 Protestant middle schools and 16 colleges and universities.[16] The number of American schools and hospitals and the sizable missionary establishment easily outstripped that of the other China powers. Other secular educational institutions and American social reformers also flocked to China. The YMCA established itself in the main cities in 1899. American feminists moved in to combat foot-binding, the custom whereby the feet of women were permanently deformed at an early age for reasons of esthetics and social status, and concubinage, the practice of keeping multiple wives. As one suffragette said, "All workers in reform realize the advance in civilization is relative to the status of women."[17]

Missionary work was not necessarily inconsistent with commercial visions. As one minister to China remarked: "As the condition of the Chinese improves, his wants will increase. Fancy what would happen to the cotton trade if every Chinese wore a shirt! Well, the missionaries are teaching them to wear shirts."[18] "Missionaries are the pioneers of trade and commerce," said Charles Denby in 1895. "Civilization, learning, instruction breed new wants which commerce supplies."[19]

Education, though seemingly altruistic, was an important component of the seductive vision of a rejuvenated China in a modernizing world that Americans increasingly began to carry around inside their heads. In combination with Christianization, education would provide new, forward-looking elites to guide the country in place of the discredited Confucian mandarins. Some of the American beliefs were quite naïve. For example, one journal predicted that "the people of the nation acting as teachers of China will win a popularity which will help to advance all relations between the two peoples – diplomatic, commercial, industrial, and social."[20]

From the Chinese perspective, things looked very different.

The United States was, after all, one of the imperial powers in China. Though rightly suspicious of the missionary threat to their way of life, many none the less took advantage of western education with a view to using it against the foreign presence. On the whole, these western-educated Chinese combined a fierce Chinese nationalism with a sense that China would have to westernize in order to overcome its backwardness and political impotence at the hands of the treaty powers. The desire to modernize while preserving China's essence created something of a paradox that China today is still attempting to resolve.

Eventually, the missionary influence was complemented and even supplanted by more secular voices. By 1910, significant figures within the new and well-endowed philanthropic foundations were urging assisting the Chinese "to develop their educational, social and political institutions . . . without regard to the result of such effort either upon the spread of right ideas among the non-Christian community or of development in numbers and strength of the Christian community."[21] In other words, modernization was superseding Christianization, a development that would eventually make for a better fit between public policy and private initiatives.

The newly incorporated Rockefeller Foundation made a daring move when it decided to fund a world-class medical school in the capital city of Beijing. "If science and education are the brain and nervous system of civilization, health is its heart," said one Foundation executive in 1913.[22] The goal in creating this school was only incidentally the saving of lives; if that had been the primary purpose, it would have made more sense to invest in public health programs, which would have been more cost-effective. Instead, the Rockefeller trustees were more fired by the prospect of developing "the circumstances under which Science flourishes." By introducing first-rate western science into China, they hoped to insert a powerful lever for modernization into a country that had long resisted western claims to having a superior kind of knowledge.

The Open Door Policy as Modernization

The foreign-policy crisis of the 1890s eventually pushed the American government to define a China policy that emphasized the promotion of modernization. The US government was stimulated to catch up with and surpass the busy private sector by the worrying consequences of the Sino-Japanese War of 1894–5. Like China, Japan had been forcibly opened up to western commerce in the 1850s. But the comparison stopped there. Whereas China's leadership continued to believe in the sufficiency of the classical order of things and saw no need for fundamental reforms, following the Meiji Restoration of 1868 the Japanese leadership mounted a concerted effort to modernize and industrialize their country with a view to ending foreign control of their land. As the slogan had it, they sought to develop a rich country and a strong army. By the 1890s, Japanese leaders believed that they were in a position to demonstrate their equality with western nations. A key indication of their new status would be their ability to become a player in the diplomacy of imperialism in China.

Following some jockeying for position in Korea, Japan defeated the Chinese empire in a short war in 1894–5 and exacted treaty rights and territory of its own from China. Shocked by the Japanese victory, the western powers decided to bring them up short. The Triple Intervention, concerted by Germany, France, and Russia, forced Tokyo to give back some of the concessions that it had won in the war. More importantly for the United States, this European initiative touched off a new scramble for privileges and concessions known as "spheres of influence" that, if left unchecked, might well do away with the treaty port system. If this movement gained momentum, Chinese sovereignty might disappear altogether and the United States would lose its position in China.

The specter re-emerged in 1900 in the wake of the so-called Boxer Rebellion, an anti-foreign outbreak that led to western military intervention. With 200 missionaries dead and thousands of converts slaughtered, the intervention was aimed nominally at rescuing westerners besieged by the Boxer rebels, including the western legations in the capital city of Beijing. However, the US, which contributed 2,500 soldiers to the allied expeditionary force, worried that some of the powers would use the occasion as an opportunity to press new imperialist demands upon China. The massive foreign military presence threatened to trigger a collapse of China as a political unit.

Out of these circumstances was born the "open door" policy, which has long been celebrated – and denigrated – as the centerpiece not only of America's China policy, but of US foreign policy as a whole. The open door notes were themselves the formalization of a policy, implicit in the treaty port system, that had been pursued *ad hoc* for a half-century. So long as it was widely understood and adhered to by the China powers in practice, there had been no need to declare a policy. But by the late 1890s, the dream of commercial and cultural advances in China was in danger of being killed off by a predatory diplomacy of imperialism that threatened to end in outright colonialism with a partition of China. Thus the initial impulse of American diplomacy was to restore the old treaty port status quo in China.

After ruling out a joint declaration with the British, Secretary of State John Hay issued his first open door note in September 1899. This message, addressed to the other treaty powers in China, asked that the principle of equal commercial opportunity be respected and that foreign nationals not be given preference in spheres controlled by their governments. The second open door note, sent in the midst of the Boxer uprising the following year, stated the principle that China should not disappear in a wave of colonial annexations – China's "administrative entity" ought to be preserved. The two notes were complementary, since there could be no equal commercial opportunity without a China to which the unequal treaties could be applied.

Inasmuch as there were no outright rejections of Hay's notes, Americans behaved as if they had been accepted – and not without reason, for the other powers, though certainly not averse to expanding their influence, were not keen on starting a war to do so. Indeed, over the next decade, the principle was affirmed by a number of treaties and agreements signed by non-American powers in China.[23] The reception of the notes, however grudging, was a reminder that maintaining the treaty port status quo, when compared to the alternative of igniting a much more explosive diplomacy of imperialism, was by far the more preferable course. Like many Victorian marriages, this union of the powers was held together by mutual convenience, not love.

But it soon became clear that there would be no return to the stability of the old treaty port relationships. Anticipating stormy seas ahead, the Japanese and the British signed an alliance in 1902. In the years that followed, American diplomats in Manchuria complained about Russia's exclusionary practices in that province. In 1904, after a period of growing tension, Japan and Russia went to war over Korea. As Japan's power continued to grow in the region in the wake of its striking military successes, Roosevelt's reaction was to draw back. While he did not abandon the open door in principle, he took care not to suggest an American challenge to Japan's dominant position in north-east Asia.

The relationship with China also changed for the worse as the open door policy did little to dispel tensions between the two nations over the issue of immigration. Though Americans long had the ambition of westernizing China, they refused to allow Chinese to emigrate freely to the United States. The relationship had started tolerantly enough with the Burlingame treaty of 1868, which encouraged the entrance of Chinese laborers to help construct the transcontinental railroads. But by the 1870s, violent anti-Chinese sentiment developed on the west coast, fueled by the belief that the Chinese were taking jobs away from American laborers and depressing their wages. Congress responded by enacting immigration restriction in 1882.

Following the passage of yet another anti-Chinese immigration statute in 1904, Chinese merchants in major cities, generously supported by Chinese residing in the United States, launched a boycott movement against American goods and services. The boycott had consequences apart from its impact on trade. Americans, particularly missionaries and educators in China, lived through some tense and worrying days. The number of students coming to the US was declining, while the number going to Japan enjoyed a remarkable increase to 5,000, a number so large, the chargé in Japan darkly suggested, "as to have some effect upon the relations of these two peoples."[24] In dealing with the situation, Roosevelt vacillated between offering the carrot and threatening the big stick, but the chief force in resolving the crisis was the Chinese imperial government, which realized that it stood to alienate the lone international champion of China's territorial integrity if the US should turn hostile. By 1906, thanks in large measure to Beijing's discouragement of the boycotters, the movement faded away.

TR had little respect for the Chinese and, unlike many of his contemporaries, did not believe that the United States was the natural mentor for China. As one historian described his views of China, he:

> Regarded her leaders with disdain and would not consider working through them to protect American and Chinese rights in Manchuria. As he saw it, their policy was one of inertia. They respected strength, not justice. They lacked patriotism and the martial virtues – serious deficiencies in Roosevelt's scale of values. Indecisive, face-saving behavior was typical of them. The very term 'Chinese' meant for him an inability to see things clearly, to face facts and act accordingly. Roosevelt saw the Chinese as an uncivilized people, a prey to the vigorous countries of the West.[25]

As for the commercial side of the open door, Roosevelt was never one to turn handsprings of excitement at the mention of money-making prospects. In sum, he showed little desire to cultivate the goodwill of China or to assert the open door in China against powers like Japan. Faced with two basic options, retreat or transformation of the China situation, Roosevelt chose to backtrack.

But TR's indifference to commercial and cultural relations with China turned out to be only a temporary setback to the further advance and evolution of an open door policy that was given a new life with William Howard Taft's victory in the 1908 elections. Unlike his mentor TR, Taft was willing to attempt a transformation of both the diplomacy of imperialism and the old approach to China. Taft, who possessed considerable diplomatic experience with East Asia, was more enthusiastic about the missionary enterprise than Roosevelt and had higher hopes for an expanded commerce with China. In addition, he was more optimistic than Roosevelt about the possibility of working out a cooperative China policy with the other powers in which the United States would play a major role. Consequently, Taft's China policy made a conceptual leap forward in which, ideally, commerce would be replaced by modernization and the treaty port system would be supplanted by cooperation among the great powers, not only in China but across the globe.

Hitherto China had been viewed as a country in an anesthetized state; a drugged giant with little chance of regaining full consciousness. It was, as one social scientist put it, "a fossilized representative of an antique system, physically active but mentally inert."[26] Another described the Chinese as "a fine example of a people of great natural ability, letting their intelligence run to waste from lack of a scientific standpoint."[27] Its ruling elite, the famed scholar–bureaucrats, had been selected on the basis of a mastery of the literary classics, a system that ensured that the country would be run by backward-looking types. By comparison with the amazing progress made by Japan, China seemed hopeless.

In the wake of the reforms of 1905, however, which abolished the old examination system, the American image of China underwent a profound reversal. Now more and more Americans began to see China as a nation on the verge of a cultural renaissance akin to that experienced by Europe 500 years earlier. William Jennings Bryan, after a 1906 tour of East Asia, talked of the "great awakening of the flowering kingdom" and suggested that "the sleeping giantess, whose drowsy eyes have so long shut out the ray of the morning sun, is showing unmistakable signs of awakening."[28] Should such a cultural rebirth take place, democratization, modernization, and the much-talked-about China market might actually become realities.

An official expression of this cultural optimism came with the remission of 11 million dollars of the Boxer indemnity, the excess remaining after payment of damage claims arising from rebel actions against western "foreign devils" in the summer of 1900. The US might have pocketed the entire indemnity, but instead it chose to earmark some 18 million dollars in all for the education of Chinese students. Tsing Hua College was opened in Beijing to prepare them for advanced study in American colleges and universities. Though the Chinese government sought persistently to have the money channeled to other uses, principally railway development in Manchuria, in the end it was spent in accordance with American desires. By 1925, some 1,000 Chinese students had taken part in the program. These numbers did not include the many students turned out by the impressive American educational system in China. Many top-flight US universities had created Chinese affiliates, such as Harvard-Yenching and Yale-in-China.

By mid-century, more than 20,000 Chinese students had pursued advanced studies in American educational institutions of one kind or another.[29] These American-educated Chinese were seen as a powerful force for modernization and for strengthening the American position in China. For example, in 1908, William Howard Taft gave credit for China's reforms to "the guidance of the Chinese graduates of American universities who have forged to the front in politics in that Empire."[30] A year earlier, Taft, then secretary of war, looked forward to China being "guided by the young Christian students and scholars that either learn English or some foreign language at home or are sent abroad to be instructed, and who come back and whose words are listened to by those who exercise influence at the head of the government."[31]

He believed that the relationship with China had improved considerably in the aftermath of the boycott thanks to consular reforms, a more relaxed administration of immigration statutes, and the remission of the Boxer indemnity. He took pride in the description of the United States as "the one western country which can look China in the face without a blush of shame."[32] Importantly, Taft understood that before America could sell substantial quantities of goods to China and before China could provide the "almost boundless possibilities of absorption" for America's trade surpluses that visionaries like Brooks Adams talked about, China had first to industrialize. "The more civilized they become, the more active their industries, the wealthier they become, and the better market they will become for us," he said. America's best markets, he pointed out, were "those countries in which there is the greatest prosperity and the greatest advance."[33] It followed that the quest for markets and the promotion of modernization abroad went hand in hand.

Herein lies the significance of Taft's "dollar diplomacy," which shifted the open door from a concern with trade in goods to a focus on capital investment, whose emphasis was much more on modernization. Taft's most daring maneuver was a proposal floated by his secretary of state, Philander Knox, to internationalize Manchuria's railroads. It was an audacious move because foreign-owned railroads, which had the right to post garrison troops and build foreign company towns, were among the most potent agencies of imperialism in China. In Manchuria, control of that frontier region's railways was the object of a three-way competition among Japan, Russia, and Chinese nationalists. Taft and Knox reasoned that if the Manchurian railways were "neutralized" by being turned over to an international syndicate or consortium composed of the major China powers, they would become useful instruments of Chinese modernization rather than agencies of foreign penetration. At some distant point, when the bonds were retired, the railways would be turned over to China.

In this way, the open door policy became a dual-pronged modernization strategy that aimed at reforming China and harmonizing great power behavior in the region. Actually, Taft had even larger ambitions for his policy, hoping eventually to cement great power cooperation in *all* matters. Knox's initiative failed, largely because Japan and Russia instantly sensed what was afoot. Their resistance, combined with British indifference to the scheme, condemned it to oblivion. Though historians have been quick to condemn Taft and Knox for their naïveté in Manchuria, they usually fail to mention that the attempt to rein in the diplomacy of imperialism was more successful when applied to China proper. Thus, when the question of lending money to the Chinese central government arose in 1911, a new six-power consortium was formed as a way of preventing competition from getting out of hand.

At first, it appeared as if the forces of modernity within China were moving in tandem with the trend to great power cooperation. In 1912, a revolution against the Qing dynasty succeeded in dethroning the last emperor and creating a Republic of China. Despite a sizable number of doubters in the business community and among old China hands, the general public seemed thrilled by the possibility of a rapid transformation and modernization of Chinese society. As one enthusiast put it, this seemed "the brightest time for striking at the roots of superstition."[34] A concurrent resolution of Congress noted that "the people of China, after centuries of oppression, are reclaiming their inherent right to self-government."[35] A newspaper cartoon showed a young China in western dress, driving a car, forcing the old China in traditional garb off the road.[36] The progressive journal *Outlook* concluded that "China means to become a nation in the western sense of the word."[37]

A combination of internal and external developments conspired to frustrate these hopes. Internally, the former Qing bureaucrat Yuan Shi-kai assumed the presidency and in the course of a few years seemed bent on establishing another dynasty with himself as the new Son of Heaven. His death in 1916 foreclosed that possibility, but it also threw China into turmoil, kicking off a 10-year period of internal division known as "the warlord period" in which portions of the country were dominated by various generals and their followers.

China also faced growing pressure from Japan. With the Great War in Europe consuming the attention of most of the treaty powers, the expansionist Japanese saw an opportunity to strengthen their position in China. In 1915, they imposed the so-called Twenty-one Demands on China, which if accepted would have gone far toward making China a protectorate of Tokyo. The only power not then preoccupied in Europe that was capable of stopping the Japanese was the United States. After some acrimonious bickering, the Lansing-Ishii accord of 1917 papered over the two countries' differences of opinion over China, at least for the time being. The Japanese ritually acknowledged once again the principle of the open door, whereas the US confirmed the special Japanese position in Manchuria on the basis of "territorial propinquity."

Woodrow Wilson introduced some significant modifications to Taft's policy that clarified American priorities. In 1913, he forced American banks, who had been dragged into the scheme by the government only with great reluctance, to withdraw from American participation in the consortium on the grounds that the restrictive conditions of a proposed loan to China, with its demands for oversight, seemed to "touch very nearly the administrative independence of China itself." But Wilson eventually reversed himself and agreed to rejoin the consortium in 1919 as he came to understand its usefulness as an institutional tool for checking the diplomacy of imperialism. As for China, he was quite enthusiastic about the prospect of democratization, which he called "the most significant, if not the most momentous, event of our generation."

By the time his presidency ended in 1921, the pattern had become clear. The United States gave priority to checking the diplomacy of imperialism over China's modernization. The tendency of anti-imperialist cooperation to work against modernization was symbolized by the failure of the consortium to issue another loan until its legal dissolution in 1946. To the extent that the US did concern itself with China, it tended, at the diplomatic level, to focus on political modernization to the neglect of economic issues. Though it is possible to see this as a case of misplaced priorities, the reasons behind this policy emphasis are hardly mysterious. The imperialist symptoms were clearly much easier to treat with diplomatic remedies than the underlying disease of Chinese backwardness and lack of unity, for which no sure-fire cure existed.

Fruition and Failure of the Open Door

With the apparent triumph of President Woodrow Wilson's liberal peace program in 1918, it appeared for a brief moment that the diplomacy of imperialism would soon come to an end and China would be allowed to westernize of its own accord. Wilson's emphasis on the principle of national self-determination was avidly seized upon by the Chinese, who hoped that the peace conference at Paris would put an end to the unequal treaties and affirm the equality of the races – the latter point being pressed with equal fervor by the Japanese in Paris. Coupled with the enthusiasm for "Mr. Science" and "Mr. Democracy," the prospects for the success of western liberal democracy were, on the face of things, never so bright as at this moment. As one scholar put it, "the scientific spirit was replacing the Confucian spirit, and science was thought to supply a new philosophy of life."[38] For the western-educated scholar Hu Shih, the New Thought would "recreate civilization."

But the Chinese were badly disappointed by Wilson's performance in Paris. Wilson did suggest, quite tentatively, "that China might be put on the same footing as other nations, as sooner or later she certainly must be," but failed to press the matter.[39] Largely because an affirmation of racial equality would have cut the racialist underpinnings out from under the justification for British imperialism, the Paris peace conference refused to acknowledge this principle. Just as importantly, Wilson gave in to Japanese demands to succeed to the German sphere of influence in Shantung province, the previously agreed-upon payoff for Japan's joining the war on the side of the Entente powers. If denied, Wilson feared that the Japanese might quit the conference. Without Japan as a member, his League of Nations, the organization that was supposed to prevent another great power war from breaking out, would be severely hobbled from the start. Wilson chose the League in the belief that, through its mediation, "all extraordinary foreign rights in China and all spheres of influence should be abrogated by the common consent of all the nations concerned."[40]

Despite America's failure to join the League, some steps toward reordering China's external and internal affairs were taken in the Washington treaties of 1922. One of the most significant was the nine-power treaty, which finally made the open door policy in China, in its updated Taftian version, part of international law. The treaty also agreed, without setting a specific date, to do away eventually with the treaty tariff and with extraterritoriality. Separate treaties also pledged cooperation among the powers and instituted a program of naval disarmament. American policy finally appeared to have realized, by peaceful means, the ambitious goals first set out in the Taft administration. Recalling these achievements a few years later, Secretary of State Charles Evans Hughes described the treaties as "a record of a change of heart" by the great powers in China.

However, the Washington treaties had succeeded only in suppressing the imperialist symptoms of great power competition instead of attending to the underlying disease of colonialism in China.[41] They failed to satisfy an increasingly nationalist opinion in China that wanted an immediate end to the treaty system. The Wilsonian moment was quickly replaced by the student-led May 4th movement, many of whose disillusioned supporters now embraced communism and anti-western nationalism. The newly founded Chinese Communist Party, operating on Leninist principles, excoriated western imperialism in the country. From the conservative side, the National Peoples Party or Kuomintang, under the leadership of Jiang Kai-shek undertook to reunify the country by force. Its successful Northern Expedition (1925–7) caused grave concern because of the many anti-foreign incidents that it spawned and because it threatened the vested interests of treaty powers like Japan, which had a major economic stake in China and in Manchuria.

Despite a good deal of exasperation with Jiang and the nationalists during this period, there was little the United States was prepared to do by way of coercion. The US preferred to use honey rather than vinegar by being the first power to recognize the Nationalist regime and by agreeing to restore tariff autonomy in 1928. Though the abolition of extraterritoriality was agreed to in principle, it would have to wait another 15 years. In 1929, Henry Stimson, now Hoover's secretary of state, announced that the Nationalist government was "the beginning of a permanent change in the Chinese government and character." With the successful conclusion of the Northern Expedition, the political storms surrounding the diplomacy of imperialism and the domestic disturbances within China seemed finally to have abated.

At long last China had a breathing spell during which it could turn its attention to development. Although the Kuomintang's nationalism had a pronounced anti-missionary inflection, America's cultural influence in China was still considerable. Jiang, though he spoke no English, claimed to be a devout Methodist, which certainly helped the missionary societies to loosen their aid purse strings. His charismatic and attractive wife, born to the powerful Soong family, was a graduate of Wellesley College who spoke English better than most Americans. Within the Nationalist elite, an astounding number of professors, governmental ministers, and diplomatic envoys were American-educated. The western-educated returned students, epitomized by the scholar-diplomat Hu Shih, appeared to be dedicated to promoting a Chinese renaissance that took its bearings from western conceptions of learning.

These were also good years for westerners within China. One American remembered the period that ended with the 1920s as follows:

> In my time everybody loved China. The white man was respected to a high degree. We loved the way of life. Business was good. The white man was master. It was a cheap place to live. There were varying views of the Chinese, but generally people were pretty fond of them.[42]

One sees here the kind of "sentimental" attitude toward China that was entertained by many Americans. "China became our favorite charity," said John King Fairbank, with only little exaggeration.[43] But sentimentalism is a poor word to describe an approach to China that was grounded in a larger historical perspective.[44] And there was, as usual, another and less edifying side to the story, as gangsterism and corruption flourished in the treaty ports under the umbrella of the extraterritoriality regime.

The favorable view of events in China was due to the apparent taming of imperialism and the seeming assent by the Chinese Nationalists to a program of westernization. Over the next 10 years, the so-called "Nanjing decade," Americans became involved in numerous modernization efforts aimed at promoting this cultural revolution from above. They helped to create Chinese counterparts of the National Education Association, the American Library Association, and other kinds of non-governmental organizations integral to a modern civil society. Agronomists sought to transmit the best of western agricultural and farming know-how. The Rockefeller Foundation became involved in rural reconstruction programs in China in the hope of raising the standard of living of the impoverished peasantry. In part because of American educational influence, English had easily become the second language of China.

The formal study of China also had its beginnings in the postwar years. The American Council of Learned Societies, shortly after its establishment in 1920, began to promote the study of Asian cultures and history. Later in the decade, organizations like the Institute of Pacific Relations and the Harvard–Yenching Institute provided even greater impetus to a scholarly understanding of the Orient. Even in the fields of art collecting and interpretation of Chinese and Asian art, the 1920s saw the emergence of a deeper, professional understanding.[45] Young scholars like John King Fairbank cut their teeth in the inter-war years and would later provide the intellectual leadership for a greatly expanded and professionalized China scholarship.

Although the Chinese government, jealous of its prerogatives, imposed various restrictions on American educational institutions operating in the country, private initiatives continued to flourish. Americans were active in famine relief, agricultural extension work, the promotion of rural reconstruction with a heavy emphasis on mass literacy, and the introduction of modern technology into the farms and villages. Westerners helped to build roads and tame rivers and build irrigation networks. "All this work," said one adviser, "is necessary before China will be the neighbor we hope she will be – one with living standards sufficiently high so that she may partake in a large way of all our own country has to offer."[46]

The work of outsiders was always dependent, especially in the Nanjing decade, upon a close connection with the Kuomintang, which showed little enthusiasm for pushing fundamental changes that might improve the abysmal conditions of the Chinese peasantry.[47] For all the reforms, experiments, and ambitious schemes of economic expansion, the economy stagnated. Culturally, too, the Kuomintang seemed less interested in importing western liberalism than in continuing to refurbish traditionalist values as ideological props for its authoritarian rule. Much was accomplished, but it was still only a drop in the bucket, and in the end China was left to its own resources.

Whether the Kuomintang would have been able to modernize China had it been given a longer grace period can never be known with certainty, for it was soon confronted with a "double malaise," a combination of domestic and foreign military threats that was made all the more dangerous by its own inefficiency and unpopularity.[48] Domestically, Jiang's regime was challenged by the Chinese communists. The communists had been allies of Jiang until 1927, when he double-crossed them and nearly wiped them out in a bloody purge. After reconstituting their forces and finding a new base area in north China in Yenan province following the heroic "long march" of 1934–5, the communists under the leadership of Mao Zedong built up their strength and became increasingly formidable foes in a resumed civil war.

More serious, for the time being, was a renewed imperialist thrust from Japan. Throughout much of the 1920s, the Japanese had accepted many of the peaceful liberal internationalist assumptions that underlay the Washington treaties. Western observers commonly assumed that Japan, during this decade, was transforming itself from an authoritarian society into a western-style liberal democracy based on mass suffrage. However, the emergence of a strident Chinese nationalism in the late 1920s, coupled with the collapse of the world economy upon which the export-based Japanese economy depended, led to a revival of military influence in the Japanese government and a return to the expansionist principles that had guided Japanese policy prior to World War I.

The unity of the China powers had already broken down in the late 1920s, but the Japanese invasion and conquest of Manchuria beginning in September 1931 was a forceful announcement of the re-emergence of the diplomacy of imperialism in China. In July 1937, the antagonism flared into a full-scale war between Japan and China. By the end of 1941, the United States, as a result of the connection between the crises in the Far East and in Europe, found itself at war with Japan and a formal ally of China.

The concern with China's modernization and development was not put on hold by World War II. On the contrary, America's entanglement in China's internal affairs grew by leaps and bounds as the exigencies of fighting and winning the war led growing numbers of Americans to demand greater efficiency from Jiang. At first, Washington pursued a policy of "unconditional support" for Jiang in the belief that he would prosecute a vigorous war effort against Japan and create what one of FDR's advisers called "a modern, democratic and powerful state." On the surface, this policy appeared to be well conceived. *Time* and *Life*, influential magazines controlled by a China-born son of missionaries, Henry Luce, placed Jiang on their covers six times during the war. Stories reaching the US chronicled a heroic Chinese war effort in the face of massive obstacles.

The reality was quite different. Reporters and diplomats witnessed incredible corruption, mismanagement and outright dereliction in fighting the war. Despite a massive famine in Hunan in 1942–3, the government did nothing for the peasants; in fact, it continued to extract heavy taxes, which went into the pockets of corrupt officials. Jiang was both unwilling and unable to reform the system of corruption because he derived his authority from it. With his power base rooted in the support of the landlords and rural gentry and military chiefs – to agree to American calls for domestic reform would have been to reform himself out of existence. The growth of a powerful communist insurgency in the north further disinclined Jiang to seriously prosecute the war. All his demands for aid to build up his army had postwar objectives in mind, particularly a decisive showdown with the communists. For Jiang, it was the Americans who would have to bear the brunt of fighting Japan.

Thus, even as China was being officially promoted as an equal partner in the war against Japan and a future mainstay of the planned United Nations Organization, old patron–client tensions reasserted themselves when the United States became involved in a tug-of-war with Jiang Kai-shek over the future political and cultural direction of his country. The most spectacular collision between Chinese and American sensibilities was the attempt by General Joseph Stilwell, who had been appointed chief of staff to Jiang, to undermine his superior in favor of someone more committed to fighting the Japanese. Stilwell was the US army's most knowledgeable expert on China. He spoke Chinese, having picked up the language in the 1920s and 1930s while serving as a military attaché. In 1942, he was appointed commander in chief of US forces in China and adviser to Jiang, with the aim of building up Chinese armies for an offensive against Japan.

Stilwell, whose interest was "in what China could turn *into*," was appalled by the corruption and inefficiency of the Chinese army.[49] He was also highly upset by Jiang's decision to deploy his best troops to the north in Yenan, where they could keep an eye on Mao's communist army, rather than use them to fight the Japanese. Well aware of Stilwell's hostility, Jiang played up his military rival in China, General Clair Chennault, who advocated air power as a way of winning the war and of cutting the ground out from under Stilwell's plans. For a time in 1944, FDR threatened a cut-off in aid to China unless Stilwell were given complete command, in which case his troop train-ing program and preference for engaging the Japanese would have been put into effect.

The struggle to control military decision-making in China was only the tip of the iceberg, however. Many Americans were more ambitious still, hoping to pressure Jiang into re-forming the corrupt, inefficient, and inegalitarian political sys-tem to which he owed his authority. Jiang's fondness for reactionary ideas that supported his rule had to go, particu-larly his promotion of "pernicious and antiquated views in regard to the process of intellectual adjustment to the modern world which China must sooner or later make."[50] As the war ground on, more and more officials began to look favorably upon expanding recently inaugurated cultural programs with China in a humanistic direction with a view to exposing China to western liberal values. Private American organizations pro-tested what seemed to be intolerable authoritarian behavior by a major ally. Reformist demands were being made by other American officials in China who were disturbed by the suffer-ing of the peasants and by the undemocratic, and for some, fascist-like nature of the hopelessly corrupt and inefficient Kuomintang. John King Fairbank saw "little hope in the present regime because it cannot trust the mass of the people emotionally and is too inefficient to help them much practi-cally."[51]

Fed up with the Kuomintang, some Americans even went so far as to flirt with the idea of making common cause, at least militarily, with the communists, the only political force in China that seemed capable of organizing effective military resistance against Japan. Stilwell had long since thought about it. "Something ought to be done to clean up this stinking gang and put some real people at the head of things," he had writ-ten.[52] After being given such a powerful kick in the pants, one foreign service officer believed "that the Kuomintang would be forced to reform its policies" and "change its present reac-tionary leadership."[53] Others, looking to the future, took it for granted that the communists would win the civil war and hoped to cement a workable relationship while the time was ripe. "How might we draw them away from future reliance on the Soviet Union and into dependence on the United States?" asked John Paton Davies.[54]

These ideas did not seem far-fetched at the time, given that Stalin's USSR was already a principal partner in the Grand Alliance against Nazi Germany and a core member of the projected United Nations Organization. The Office of Strategic Services even sent a group of observers, the Dixie mission, behind communist "rebel" lines to gauge the suitability of the communists as a potential coalition partner. In the end, convinced that the strategic situation was not serious enough to warrant dumping an ally, FDR sided with Jiang. Stilwell was dismissed and all the calls from Americans within China for reform were ignored. The new ambassador, Patrick Hurley, sided openly with the Generalissimo and took it as a sign of personal disloyalty to him when his staff members criticized the Chinese government.

The De-Americanization of China

With the end of hostilities against Japan in August 1945, the suspended civil war resumed in China. Although technically neutral, the United States in effect chose sides when it ferried Jiang's troops to northern cities, enabling them, rather than Mao's communists, to accept the surrender of Japanese forces and equipment. After spending a year in fruitless negotiations as a go-between trying to bring the two sides together, President Truman's personal representative, General George C. Marshall, packed his bags and returned home. With neither Jiang nor Mao willing to surrender control of their military forces in any new governmental arrangement, the civil war would have to be fought to a finish.

Marshall's decision to throw in the towel was made easier by the realization that the Soviets were withdrawing their forces from Manchuria. Thus disconnected from the burgeoning Cold War, China became, as one historian put it, "a backwater of marginal geopolitical importance,"[55] a status that allowed the

Truman administration to accept with relative equanimity a communist victory. By 1947 the communists had gained the upper hand and confidential intelligence assessments in Washington were predicting victory for Mao's forces. The Truman administration believed that Jiang was incapable of modernizing China. "The Chinese Communists had succeeded," Secretary of State Dean Acheson later acknowledged, "to a considerable extent in identifying their movement with the popular demand for change."[56] Were it not for some strong domestic political pressure exercised on Jiang's behalf by a "China lobby," Truman would probably have thrown in the towel and conceded victory to the communists. Despite his belief that the Kuomintang leaders "were all thieves, every last one of them," the political heat on Capitol Hill was so high that he reluctantly approved the largely symbolic China Aid Act of 1948.

The long-anticipated communist victory finally came in 1949, when Mao Zedong triumphantly proclaimed the People's Republic of China (PRC) in Beijing. Everyone, including the administration in Washington, assumed that it was only a matter of time before Mao's forces mounted a successful invasion of the island of Taiwan, to which Jiang's reeling forces had retreated, and restored a unity to China that had been lacking since the revolution of 1911. Then, after a seemly period of "waiting for the dust to settle," as Acheson put it, the Truman administration anticipated opening diplomatic relations with the People's Republic. The expectation was that the regime, though communist, would also be strongly nationalist in persuasion. And that might be enough to turn the PRC against Soviet imperialism in Asia and keep China disconnected from the germinating Cold War geopolitical crisis.

It did not turn out that way, as events at home and abroad made a normal relationship impossible. Relations with the PRC grew ever more tense as time went on. A number of American diplomats were held virtually hostage within their legations and embassies. It was clear, too, that the large number of American missionaries, doctors, and educators who had come to China with the intention of modernizing the country had worn out their welcomes, as they were now being treated as cultural imperialists by the new regime. In a taunting farewell to the China-born American ambassador, Mao openly accused the United States of having committed "spiritual and cultural aggression." One article referred to America's cultural investments as "fertilizer for America's trade with China."[57] From the looks of it, the new regime seemed bent on ripping out every last plank of American influence from the cultural flooring that had been installed so laboriously over the years.

Thus, one of the chief developments of the late 1940s was what one historian has called "the de-Americanization of Chinese life"[58] as the American cultural presence in China was effectively put out business. Having cast his lot with Moscow in the Cold War, Mao defined world politics as a struggle between imperialists and anti-imperialists in which China had no choice but to "lean to one side." Anti-imperialism was his first foreign policy principle, but it was anti-imperialism with a difference. Although defined in Marxist terms, Mao sensed accurately that the United States had been seeking more than profits in China. Despite its anti-imperialist labors, the United States was now seen, because of its cultural presence and Americanizing ambitions, as the greatest imperialist power of all.

On the domestic side, the fall of China demonstrated the degree to which the idea of a democratic, modernizing China had taken hold in the American collective imagination, which found it hard to come to terms with the recent turn of events. One heartbroken seer predicted that historians 100 years hence would agree that "the death knell of western civilization was sounded in China in the autumn of 1948."[59] The churches who supported the missionaries still believed in the dual mission of conversion and enlightenment. The China lobby continued energetically to promote aid to Jiang, however ineffective though it might prove to be in practice. Republican Senator Kenneth Wherry of Nebraska, sometime known as "the merry mortician," could still dream of lifting "Shanghai up and up, ever up, until it is just like Kansas City."

The bad news from Beijing gave rise to a phantom limb

syndrome in the body politic when it touched off a ferocious debate in the United States over the question of "who lost China?" Republican "Asia-firsters" accused the Truman administration of having sold Jiang down the river. Suspecting the State Department of harboring communist sympathizers, critics pointed to the recommendations made during World War II by "China hands" who had advocated dumping Jiang for Mao as a way of getting Chinese troops into battle against Japan. The administration, for its part, released a controversial "White Paper" which argued that the fault was Jiang's and suggested a happier outcome had his regime only been more efficient, democratic, and honest. Republicans refused to swallow this line, however. The White Paper was criticized as "a 1,054 page whitewash of a wishful, do-nothing policy which has succeeded only in placing Asia in danger of Soviet conquest."[60]

Had the "loss" of China been the concern only of the China-lobby special interest group, its foreign-policy consequences would have been relatively mild. This commercial and cultural separation, though painful, was accompanied by a growing sense that America's half-century-long opposition to the diplomacy of imperialism had ended in a stunning failure. In other words, *all* the pillars that had historically sustained America's China policy – commercial, cultural, anti-imperialist – had collapsed. In addition, the geopolitical disaster that the United States had sought to prevent when taking on Japan, beginning in 1938, had finally come to pass, but this time with the USSR replacing Germany and China replacing Japan. From a global perspective, the stunning success of Moscow's diplomacy of imperialism, coupled with its empire in eastern Europe, produced a threat that resembled the German-Japanese combine in its implications for the breakdown of modern liberal civilization. Indeed, in one major respect it was even worse. At least with Japan, which had long been associated with the "yellow peril," there had been nothing to lose. Japan had never become a repository of accumulated hopes of the sort that had been invested in China.

Whereas the PRC used imperialism to define its relationship with the US, American policy-makers also talked in terms of imperialism, but from a different perspective that was also informed by the past. The close relationship between Beijing and Moscow, confirmed by the signature of treaties in Moscow in February 1950, meant that the diplomacy of imperialism had succeeded. Thus Assistant Secretary of State Dean Rusk described the PRC as "a colonial Russian government – a Slavic Manchukuo on a larger scale." Secretary of State Dean Acheson attempted to put his finger on the deeper historical roots of the problem. "Communism is the most subtle influence of Soviet foreign policy that has ever been devised," he argued. "It is really the spearhead of Russian imperialism." He insisted that "the attitude and interest of the Russians in north China . . . long antedates communism. That is not something that has come out of communism at all."[61] On another occasion he pointed out that "foreign domination has been masked behind the façade of a vast crusading movement."[62] Thus China's decision to side with the Soviet Union was seen as an updated and even more dangerous version of the diplomacy of imperialism in Asia on account of its linkage to the crisis in Europe.[63]

The breaking point with the PRC came in June 1950 when Truman, following the invasion of South Korea by communist North Korean troops, made it clear that US naval forces would not allow the communists to cross the Taiwan straits and end the civil war once and for all. To defend Korea, a country with few historical ties to the United States, while abandoning the now-mythical image of friendship with China, would have been difficult to sell to the American public. Having re-intervened in the Chinese civil war, the US soon found itself in a war with the PRC. The situation reached crisis proportions when Chinese "volunteers" crossed *en masse* into Korea in October 1950 and began to engage American troops near the Manchurian border. The Korean War ended after three years of stalemate with the signature of an armistice in June 1953, but only after the US had suffered more than 33,000 combat deaths, while Chinese and North Korean losses totaled some one and a half million. Thus, as one historian put it,

"the Chinese heroes of the 1940s became the Chinese mon-
sters of the 1950s."[64]

One way of interpreting the situation would have been to
acknowledge that China had become a great power. Instead,
the relationship continued to be formulated in traditional terms
that harked back to the bad old days of the diplomacy of imperialism in China. In Dean Rusk's opinion, "the continued
inroads of Soviet power into Manchuria under the cloak of
the Korean aggression mean[s] in fact that China is losing its
great northern areas to the European empire that has stretched
out its greedy hands for them for at least a century."[65] By the
end of 1950, Americans believed overwhelmingly that China
was taking orders from Moscow. The global Sino-Soviet
"monolith" was thus seen as an amalgam composed of one
part European power politics and a lesser part of imperial
domination in East Asia. Americans still hoped eventually to
break up this combination, but the tactic adopted was to lean
on the Chinese with a view to showing them that their Soviet
allies could not be relied upon in the crunch.

During the 1950s, a number of crises emerged in which talk
of all-out war, including the use of nuclear weapons, was in
the air. The Eisenhower administration seemed hard pressed
at times to rein in a hawkish military that seemed eager to
vent its Cold War frustrations on the Chinese.[66] Despite the
relatively cautious and occasionally flexible behavior of Chinese policy-makers, the combination of fire-breathing Maoist
rhetoric, the Korean War, and some tense confrontations over
Taiwan in 1955 and 1958, in which the storm clouds of nuclear war hung heavy in the air, produced a frightening image
of China in the United States. Culturally, American descriptions of the Chinese seemed more appropriate to the nineteenth century than to the twentieth. As historian Gordon
Chang has pointed out, "the dreaded Yellow Peril had con-
verged with the detested Red Peril."[67]

After Korea, the transformation was complete. China, once
thought to be the nation's closest friend in Asia, had become
its most hated foe, a nation that the US refused to recognize or
allow to occupy China's seat in the UN Security Council. The

Eisenhower administration felt compelled to deal with China as "an evil fact."[68] In a discussion with Indian Prime Minister Jawaharlal Nehru, Eisenhower reported that Americans rated Red China "at the bottom of the list, even below Russia." Secretary of State John Foster Dulles told reporters that the Chinese communists were "much more violent and fanatical, more addicted to the use of force than the Russians."[69]

Many Americans came to believe that the "life is cheap among Orientals" stereotype applied to the communist Chinese and their willingness to run enormous risks. President Eisenhower, for example, told Winston Churchill that the communist Chinese "can pay any price in manpower, with complete indifference to the amount."[70] That frightening perception was reinforced by accounts of Mao's cavalier dismissal of the bomb. As early as 1946, Mao had insisted that "the atom bomb is a paper tiger which the US reactionaries use to scare people. It looks terrible, but in fact it isn't."[71] For Mao, the United States would be the clear loser in a nuclear war. This same line was invoked again in 1964, when the Chinese government officially announced the detonation of its first nuclear device. The bad atomic news set off alarm bells, not only in Washington but in Moscow.[72] The Soviets were even more nervous than Americans at hearing wild talk that even if 400 million Chinese died in a war, 300 million would remain.[73]

Amazingly, for a few years in the 1960s, China was promoted from subaltern status as a lackey of the USSR to the chief threat facing the United States. As the focal point of Cold War confrontation shifted to the Third World, China became not only a power but for a time the chief geopolitical threat in what seemed truly an east–west contest. Following the Cuban missile crisis of October 1962, it became clear that the USSR wanted to turn down the ideological volume of the Cold War, while the Chinese, by contrast, were furiously cranking it up. Strangely, peripheral issues became central as Washington became obsessed with countering the "wars of national liberation" that China so vociferously supported. The tail of imperialism was now wagging the geopolitical dog.

Unlike Korea, which carried a "made in Moscow" label,

the Vietnam War was perceived as a Chinese export. While explaining America's role in Vietnam to some Congressmen, Secretary of State Dean Rusk pointed to "the militant brand of the world revolution announced by Peiping, subscribed to by Hanoi, and given effect in action."[74] A victory by Hanoi would "stimulate the expansionist ambitions of Communist China."[75] He pointed to the specter of "one billion Chinese armed with atomic weapons."[76] "Behind the government of Ho Chi Minh is the very larger specter of an expansionist red China," said Under-secretary of State George Ball.[77] More than any other reason, it was the fear of massive Red Chinese intervention that prompted the Johnson administration to fight a war of attrition with distinct limits on its willingness to escalate.

The ideological low-point of the relationship was reached in the mid-1960s. The outbreak of the Great Proletarian Cultural Revolution in 1966, a decade-long domestic upheaval inspired by Mao as a way of reinstilling communist fervor into his people, further confirmed the image in the west of the PRC as a country led by menacing ideological fanatics. This purification ritual, a planned civil war led by youthful "red guards" who spouted slogans from Mao's Red Book, threatened to end in utter chaos. By turning inward as a way of mobilizing itself against the west, China seemed to be reverting to a xenophobia extreme even by its historical standards. Ominous anti-imperialist rhetoric from Mao's heir-apparent, Lin Piao, about the world "countryside" surrounding and swallowing up the "cities" stirred old fears of the "yellow peril" and added to the estrangement.

The Rebirth of Modernization

The situation finally began to turn around in 1969 following the outbreak of hostilities between the Soviet Union and the PRC along their 4,100 miles of common border. For a time, the Soviets even toyed with the idea of launching massive pre-emptive nuclear strikes against the PRC on the theory that it was better to deal with the problem sooner rather than later. The prospect of war with the USSR redirected China's attention from global Cold War issues to more pressing problems of survival and made possible a radical change in relations with the United States. Chairman Mao and Premier Zhou Enlai made overtures to the Nixon administration, the most spectacular being a spur-of-the-moment invitation in April 1971 to an American table-tennis team then touring Asia to visit the PRC. In fact, though, it was a low-risk move since Nixon had already signaled his willingness to re-think the relationship.[78]

Nixon's sensational trip to China in February 1972 ended with the signature of the Shanghai communiqué, in which both countries stated their opposition to "hegemony" in Asia, i.e. Soviet domination, and looked forward to the "normalization" of relations between the two countries once the Taiwan issue was satisfactorily resolved. The opening to China was supposed to set the stage for a global "triangular diplomacy" in which the Soviet Union would have a greater incentive to moderate its behavior by playing the Nixon–Kissinger game of *détente*, or relaxation of tensions. But this geopolitical conception assumed that the global competition was realistically based when, in fact, it was an ideologically rooted fear that had created China's image as a global ogre. Thus, as soon as the deafening ideological volume was turned down, the international conversation took on a new meaning altogether.

Whatever the short-term benefits, over the longer term it became apparent that the value of the "China card" in the global poker game between the superpowers was greatly overblown.[79] Far from creating a new global balance of power, playing the China card had the reverse effect of decoupling East Asia from global politics. Although relations between the PRC and the USSR would not improve substantially until the 1980s, the Sino-Soviet dispute, which began as an in-house ideological rivalry, was defined increasingly in traditional political rather than ideological terms. As ideological noise was pushed into the background, events in the East Asia region were no longer blown up to global proportions and China was reduced to a regional power. One striking example was the Chinese punitive invasion of Vietnam, a Soviet client state, which indicated a return to a regional balance of power. By the 1980s, it was clear that Sino-American political relations had exited the global superhighway and turned on to the slower local lanes of regional politics, even as Moscow and Washington were once again stepping on the gas in their Cold War competition following the collapse of *détente*.[80]

There was little complaining heard among Americans at the miscarriage of Nixon's grand design because the re-opening of a dialogue with the PRC had satisfied a deeper historical yearning. Beneath its power political aspects, Nixon's announcement had a modernizing, civilizational dimension that acknowledged, implicitly, a partial return to the point of view that had dominated American thinking earlier in the century: that a truly global society could not be built in the absence of China. "Mainland China, outside the world community, completely isolated, with its leaders not in communication with world leaders, would be a danger to the whole world that would be unacceptable," said the president.[81] "They were a billion people," recalled Gerald Ford, then Republican leader in the House. "We couldn't ignore them in perpetuity."[82] Comments like these suggested that the United States, by turning China into a pariah, had been defeating its own larger purposes. Oblivious to geopolitical abstractions, Americans once again became excited by the prospect of China's modernization and integration into the developmental mainstream of international life.

Slowly but surely, Sino-American relations reverted to themes that in some ways recalled the days of treaty port imperialism: trade and standards of behavior. China itself encouraged that interpretation following Mao's death in 1976. After a brief intra-party struggle, developmentalists took control of the country under the leadership of Deng Xiao Ping. Early in the 1960s, Deng had nonchalantly insisted that "It doesn't matter if a cat is black or white, as long as it catches mice." In December 1978 he persuaded the party to adopt a program of "reform and opening up to the outside world" in which ideological consistency was thrown to the winds in a mind-boggling way by loosening the socialist command economy and encouraging the hothouse growth of capitalist market forces. This new course was necessary, Deng believed, if China was at last to achieve the "four modernizations" – military, scientific, agricultural, and industrial – that had eluded the country in a series of false starts since the middle of the nineteenth century.

Early in 1979, the administration of Jimmy Carter re-established diplomatic relations with the PRC and the process of "normalization" appeared to be on track. But what was "normal" with China? Though there were some hopes that the pre-1949 pattern would be restored after a Maoist interregnum, a host of problems plagued the relationship, most formidable being the future of Taiwan. For the time being, the problem of Taiwan's status was finessed through diplomatic ingenuity (sometimes thought to be an oxymoron). At Beijing's insistence, Taiwan was de-recognized, but only through some lexical sleight-of-hand: the US embassy in Taipei was, overnight, magically transformed into the American Institute in Taiwan, after which it continued to provide diplomatic representation in everything but name. One year's notice was also given of termination of the Mutual Defense Treaty (the PRC agreed that the Taiwan situation would be handled peacefully, though it refused to pledge not to use force). To make sure that Beijing would not be tempted to intervene if Taiwan could not be cajoled back into the fold, Congress declared in the Taiwan Relations Act that use of force would be of "grave concern" to the United States.

But Taiwan could not be abandoned. Over the years, the island had become a successful "created interest" with close connections to the US. By the late 1970s, Taiwan was coming to exemplify the kind of social and cultural transformation that the US had long been striving to set into motion in mainland China. In combination with some astute economic planning, the appropriation of 2.5 billion dollars in aid to Taiwan between 1951 and 1965 had helped its economy to become one of the key success stories in Asia's "economic miracle."

Politically, too, Taiwan had made significant progress. Following Jiang's death in 1975, his son and successor, Jiang Ching-Kuo, began gingerly to turn the Kuomintang-dominated system in the direction of political liberalization. Taiwan was thus a token of the China that might have been and, for many Americans, the China that might yet be. This idea had been present from the beginning in America's support for Taiwan, which John King Fairbank had called "an investment for a happier day."[83] The modernization of China that had succeeded in microcosm on Taiwan would not easily be given up.[84]

But Taiwan was not allowed, at least not at first, to stand in the way of a transformation of American perceptions that was nothing short of miraculous in the comprehensive way it seemed to redefine relations between the two countries. Within the space of a few years, the cultural contacts between the United States and China, which for two decades had been almost entirely cut off, were resumed with a vengeance. It was clear that private American organizations that formerly had China programs were prepared to pick up where they had left off – indeed, in anticipation of eventual normalization, many of the programs had been "mothballed" rather than eliminated.

During the period of enmity, China studies in the United States had taken off as an academic field, thanks in part to the generous funding of university programs by the Ford Foundation. As a result, a new generation of China experts was on hand to provide leadership in the post-thaw period. Importantly, much of the educational effort was aimed at increasing American understanding of China, a change that one scholar has called "a stunning reversal of the one-way flow of the previous one hundred years."[85] Meanwhile, exchanges had been continued with Taiwan. According to one estimate, "more Chinese were trained in the United States in the 1960s than in all Chinese universities combined."[86] In 1966, a Committee on Cultural Communications with the People's Republic was formed to promote contacts even as the Vietnam War was entering its most intense phase. As was the case a century earlier, private developments anticipated changes in public policy.

In a spurt of educational ardor that far outstripped the educational initiatives earlier in the century, Chinese students flocked to the United States to study in American graduate schools. In the US, a severe case of "China fever" and "Marco Poloitis" set in, as swarms of American scholars, tourists, and businessmen journeyed to China to learn, to sight-see, and to make a buck. The magnitude and intensity of this interaction was startling, all the more so when compared with the pitifully few exchanges then taking place between the US and the Soviet Union. It was a strange situation: two countries from the same civilization had almost no contact, whereas, by contrast, the relationship between the United States and China, where the cultural distance was about as great as one could imagine, was pulsing with transcultural energy. The cultural investments of the past, once thought to be symptomatic of a hopeless self-delusion and idealism among Americans, appeared finally to be paying some enormous deferred dividends.

At first, the reports of the returned visitors tended to be glowingly, almost ecstatically positive about the achievements of the communist system. Accepting as a given the fact of China's ideological and cultural uniqueness, the People's Republic was described as a peaceful country that was preoccupied with questions of internal development and social justice. China was breathlessly praised for the economic successes of communism and for its egalitarianism, wise social policies, and idealism. However, by the 1980s, the bloom was off the rose, and the comments began to turn critical. Complementing the deflation of China's image as a geopolitical giant was the growing realization that it was first and foremost an underdeveloped country. China was still poor, authoritarian, inefficient, corrupt and much more elitist than starry-eyed first visitors had realized.

Occupying the middle ground between these extremes was the policy that came to be known as "engagement," an approach whose encouragement of economic modernization in the hope that democratization would follow clearly harked back to old open door ideas. Modernization, which had been a theme of American policy since the Taft administration, had been frustrated by the diplomacy of imperialism and by turbulence in China. But now that China had disconnected itself from the Soviet model and the Cold War, it had taken a course compatible with the traditional American vision. For all the negative views of the communist regime that emerged once disillusionment with the romantic image of the PRC set in, the fact remained that Deng's regime was dramatically changing the economic system in such a way that the slogan of Louis Philippe's France, "get rich," was not out of place. Thus the management of modernization finally moved to center stage.

But the 1980s and 1990s brought further twists and turns to the relationship that gave the strategy of engagement a problematic course. The relationship settled into one reminiscent of the early twentieth century, with the US promoting an internationalist version of development, while the Chinese clung to a more self-centered course. There was an enormous difference, however, this time around: China's status as a regional power precluded any possibility of reviving, even in vestigial form, the diplomacy of imperialism. The winds of Chinese nationalism that refilled the ideological sails left slack by communism assured that commercial, cultural, political, and strategic problems that emerged in the relationship would all be colored by the legacy of imperialism.

To begin with, the economic relationship with China never fulfilled the expectations that Americans brought to it. In the early 1970s, some people wondered whether trade was not already "approaching some sort of upper limit in virtue of China's ability to pay for further purchases from the United States." US exports to China in 1973 were only 65 million dollars, while imports were over 700 million.[87] When Coca-Cola announced in 1979 that it was entering the China market, it looked to be the beginning of a stampede of American investment that would finally realize the dream that emerged in the nineteenth century.

China did in fact become a huge trading partner of the United States, but the terms of trade were not exactly what China-market visionaries had hoped for one hundred years earlier.

Over the next 25 years the terms of trade shifted lop-sidedly in China's favor as annual US trade deficits with China began to approach 50 billion dollars, thanks to the vast array of inexpensive Chinese products that poured into the US market. In an ironic role reversal, the United States had become the fulfillment of China's dreams of commercial expansion, while for the US China remained an "emerging market." Meanwhile, American investors and manufacturers in China were hamstrung by all kinds of bureaucratic restrictions, while US exports were admitted on sufferance. Accusations of intellectual piracy of inventions covered by patents and failure to conform to copyright rules added to US dissatisfactions. Some observers wondered whether the international economy and environment could withstand the strain of a neo-mercantilist economy like China's.

Economic modernization without integration into the world economy was fundamentally at odds with America's liberal approach to international economics. Even when China sought to get on the right side of the issues, political complications continued to frustrate mutual accord. The 1999 visit to the United States of Chinese Prime Minister Zhu Rongji failed to resolve disagreements about China's membership of the new World Trade Organization, mainly due to congressional pique at China's human rights record. And, despite China's professed desire to join, it was clear that membership was hugely unpopular with sizable segments of the PRC's bureaucracy, for whom admission would mean having to compromise China's nationalist approach to trade. Nevertheless, a new trade agreement was finally reached at the year's end. Thus, China was modernizing according to market principles and American policy-makers in the George Bush and Bill Clinton administrations were betting that economic liberalization would become a powerful engine of democratization in China. As Clinton's national security adviser said, hopefully, "it is difficult to tell people to be economically creative and politically repressed."[88]

Despite the assorted speed bumps, the economic relationship was less troubled than the political and cultural interactions. The most divisive incident – one that Secretary of State

James Baker feared could derail the relationship – was a spectacular series of pro-democracy demonstrations, involving as many as a million protesters, in Beijing's Tiananmen Square in 1989. Fed up with the repressive leadership of a party that no longer possessed ideological legitimacy, the student leaders hoped to spark nationwide protests that would transform the Chinese political system. Their construction of a papier mâché goddess of liberty, which bore a striking resemblance to the Statue of Liberty in New York harbor, seemed to many Americans the symbolic vindication of the long-held belief that the Chinese, like people everywhere, had a deep yearning for freedom.

The regime, however, thought differently, and ordered troops and tanks to disperse the demonstrators. In another example of how disconnected China was, Tiananmen showed that China was dramatically out of phase with the democratic ideology that was sweeping triumphantly through the rest of the world. The Cold War was clearly on the verge of ending in Europe in 1989 and, by the end of 1991, the Soviet union had collapsed. In China, however, the communist regime continued, despite calls for sanctions from some Americans and pressure from Congress for action against the "butchers of Beijing."

Human rights issues also continued to vex the relationship as China's treatment of dissidents came in for persistent criticism from American activists. The regime's reliance upon convict labor to produce some export goods also came in for negative comment, as did issues like freedom of religion and forced abortions. A host of other human rights issues roiled the waters. The Chinese takeover of Tibet in 1959 continued to be an irritant, thanks in large measure to the amazingly good press enjoyed by the Dalai Lama in the US. Even environmental concerns, particularly worry about the harmful effects of the massive Three Gorges Dam project, added to the tensions.

Although the regime was practicing a "kinder, gentler politics" in China by shifting from massive to selective repression, this counted for little among western critics who took up the cause of the most celebrated dissidents.[89] Despite the determination of the Bush and Clinton administrations to emphasize economic development in a world-market economy over political democracy, relations between the US and China worsened dramatically over the course of the next decade. As Secretary of State James Baker recalled, "the relationship was on the verge of sliding into an abyss."[90]

Another reason for the darkening skies was the continued failure to resolve the Taiwan issue, which was the political equivalent of a low-pressure system off China's coast. Taiwan became more important to Beijing as nationalism began to replace an exhausted communism as the party's ideological instrument for controlling the masses. For their part, by the 1990s the Taiwanese had grown much cooler toward the idea of "one country, two systems" that Beijing was proposing as a basis for eventual reunification. As more and more people warmed to the idea of Taiwan becoming the chief force for modernization in the PRC, it became clear that the civil war had taken on an economic and cultural dimension that made it even more difficult to contemplate abandonment of the island regime. As the rhetoric heated up, President Clinton dispatched US naval units to the Taiwan straits to prevent military posturing from escalating into outright conflict.

This upsurge of Chinese nationalism did not fit easily into the post-Cold War notions of great power cooperation. In fact, the demise of the USSR hurt US–Chinese relations by eliminating a common enemy. China showed no enthusiasm for various US-led interventions in other parts of the world. While it did not veto measures in the United Nations Security Council, neither did it give its approval. The inadvertent bombing of the Chinese embassy in Belgrade by NATO planes in June 1998 during NATO's war with Serbia ignited a firestorm of anti-American outrage among Chinese. The American embassy in Beijing was pelted with rocks and other missiles and American diplomats were virtually besieged for several days. Quite clearly, in Chinese minds the United States had replaced the USSR as the region's – and the world's – hegemonic power. Thus, after all the ups and downs of the relationship over the past half-century, the US was still viewed as an imperialist power and hopeful talk of a "strategic partnership" was silenced.

The Chinese also remained as wary as ever about the large-scale importation of western culture, which they believed would result in the breakdown of traditional values and social cohesion. Apart from the opposition to US human rights initiatives, which were thought to be potentially damaging to the party's control, sporadic campaigns broke out against "anti-spiritual pollution" and "anti-bourgeois liberalization." Western pornography was seen as an insidious element of a decadent morality that could only corrode basic values. The animosity toward the United States was based not on the fear that it would bring back the imperialism of treaty port days, but that it might succeed in re-introducing the American way of life. Even many Chinese who were sympathetic to modernization and eventual liberalization believed that it would be better to concentrate for the time being on economic liberalization and leave politics and culture to the future.

Despite their unhappiness with China's human rights record, American policy-makers tended to agree. The future democratization of China in the long term, if it was to happen at all, would have to follow a path that emphasized economic growth here and now. Speaking from Beijing during a 1998 visit, President Clinton observed: "Never before have so many Chinese had the opportunity to start businesses, lift their families out of poverty, choose where to live, work, and travel, and enjoy the fruits of their labors." While he also noted "resistance to change,"[91] it was clear that further development was his prescription. "Our task is to encourage China to become a full and fully constructive participant in the international system," said his secretary of state, Madeleine Albright.[92]

Clinton's statement neatly summarized the basic standpoints of the two nations. The United States was following the internationalist commercial and cultural path originally laid out in the first decade of the twentieth century. The Chinese, by contrast, were using their global connections to pursue the nationalist goal of attaining wealth and power that had begun to stir their souls a century earlier. Though they pursued modernization, they remained at the same time wary of its internationalizing consequences and defined their identity in opposition to the world. In Washington, the concern was less with Chinese expansionism – there was little evidence of that – than with China's failure to adopt wholeheartedly the western vision of China's global destiny.

The story of America's relationship to imperialism in China is therefore a complex one. By the end of the twentieth century, it had gone through a variety of phases – imperialist, commercial, cultural, anti-imperialist, and geopolitical – before returning rather unexpectedly to developmental themes that had taken root a century earlier. With no other country, perhaps, have the variations on the theme of imperialism been so elaborately played out over such a long period of time. The relationship has been complex in its historical ups and downs and its ironic outcomes.

The story is all the more dramatic because of the lack of any powerful interests that obliged the US to play such a large role in China. The absence of such interests has led many historians to describe the open door policy and the goal of creating a strong and democratic China as an American fantasy. In the words of one prominent chronicler of Sino-American relations, the American role needs to be understood "in terms of the vision that both drew from and fed back into the national fantasies of redemption and dominion."[93]

While it is true that America's China policy cannot be understood in terms of interests, it does not necessarily follow that visions are fantasies. The test of a vision is in its application. Despite the many ups and downs in relations between the two societies, the web of commercial and cultural connections spun over the course of two centuries has come to bind the two societies together. The focus on economic modernization by both sides assured domestic and international tranquility for the time being, but at the price of deferring potentially explosive political and cultural issues to the future. Whether all this is sufficient to provide the basis for a stable long-range relationship is open to question. The best judgment is the same as the response provided by a twentieth-century Chinese historian when asked his opinion of the French Revolution: "It's too early to say."

5

Imperialism and Anti-imperialism in America's World Policies

For a number of reasons, any study of the United States and imperialism that fails to take anti-imperialism into account is incomplete. At the very least, in the aftermath of the failure of the Mugwump anti-imperialists to reverse the decisions of 1898, the emergence of new forms of anti-imperialism helps to explain why the enthusiasm for empire was so short-lived. Anti-imperialism also matters because it was a key ingredient of America's imperial adventures. As the record of American involvement in Latin America and China makes clear, powerful anti-imperialist motives coexisted with the country's entanglements in those areas. Finally – and this shall be the central theme of this chapter – a recognition of the part played by anti-imperialism is indispensable to an understanding of American globalism in the twentieth century.

At first, American anti-imperialism was directed more against the horizontal than the vertical aspects of imperialism; that is, the problem had less to do with colonial rule than with the diplomacy of imperialism that came as part of the package. The new opposition to imperialism did not emerge out of a moral condemnation of colonialism and the civilizing mission. Though that kind of disapproval would eventually become a powerful argument against imperial pretensions, it did not surface fully until World War II, when American policy-makers finally began to acknowledge openly that colonial rule was deeply inconsistent with their desire to create a harmonious world based on liberal principles. Until then, the new anti-imperialism was inspired primarily by the dangers posed by the great powers and their diplomacy of imperialism. Ironically, because these imperialist rivalries were perceived as growing threats to the ideal of civilization, following the trail of anti-imperialism brings us in the end to a better understanding of the outlook that motivated American imperialism in the first place.

Where do imperialism and anti-imperialism fit into the larger scheme of things? Unfortunately, their place in the historical panorama of US foreign relations is not very well understood. Consider, for example, the assertion found in many US history textbooks that imperialism announced the arrival of the United States as a world power.[1] Describing the dramatic change in public opinion in the wake of the Spanish-American War, Archibald Cary Coolidge claimed that "Now all at once, [the American people] were willing to give up their isolation and plunge into the fray."[2] This is the conventional wisdom, but does the claim, which is usually left unexamined, hold up?

It is true that the springboard of empire launched the United States into the deep waters of modern international relations. But as soon as one factors anti-imperialism into the equation, things begin to look rather different, for it quickly becomes apparent that the US encounter with the diplomacy of imperialism was the beginning of America's *opposition* to power politics. Thus, to be more precise about it, imperialism did not make the United States a world power like all the others; it was, rather, an aversion to the diplomacy of imperialism that first entangled the nation in some unwelcome geopolitical complications.

Over time, Americans evolved three distinct kinds of anti-imperialism: cooperative, Wilsonian, and progressive. The first to emerge was a natural outgrowth of quite traditional policies like the "open door" and the Monroe Doctrine. In China, when other powers refused to check their expansionist ambitions, American policy-makers were faced with the question of how to respond. The answer, which was quite consistent with a half-century's adherence to open door ideas, was to oppose it in principle in the hope of securing a reaffirmation of the principle of partnership. The result was a distinctive and innovative kind of diplomacy in East Asia, an open-door anti-imperialism. In the Caribbean, a more assertive pre-emptive imperialism emerged in the shadow of the Roosevelt Corollary. In each case, US anti-imperialism presupposed, as a condition of its effectiveness, an absence of fundamental conflicts of interest among the great powers.

The two other varieties of anti-imperialism arose as interpretive responses to the upheavals of the Great War in Europe. The more dominant of the two, at least in the long run, was Wilsonian anti-imperialism, which laid the blame for modern great power conflict partly, though by no means exclusively, at the feet of imperialist competition. First articulated and championed in only a tentative way by President Woodrow Wilson, this variety of anti-imperialism, once it was fleshed out and institutionalized, became part of the reigning ideological view of US policy-makers for the remainder of the twentieth century. The other outlook was progressive anti-imperialism. Unlike Wilsonianism, it attributed the causes of the war almost entirely to imperialism, perceived little danger to the United States from other powers, and counted the US among the guilty parties. Though this point of view never attained official status, its underlying assumptions continued to inspire some powerful critiques of US foreign policy throughout the twentieth century.

Although advocates of these three types of anti-imperialism would have felt uncomfortable had they found themselves placed in the same room, their views had a common source: they all developed out of a growing concern for the increasingly ominous trend of international politics. Each, in its own way, was a reaction to globalization gone wrong, to the dark side of international modernity. Each form of anti-imperialism was the product of an occasionally grim, though still fundamentally optimistic, interpretation of the direction being taken by this larger global process.

In this chapter, I shall trace the rise and decline of these three varieties of anti-imperialism with a view to outlining their place in the broader sweep of US foreign relations in the twentieth century.

Cooperative Anti-imperialism

In a classic study of international politics at the end of the nineteenth century, William Langer wrote that "The main theme in the history of international relations in this period is the clash of imperialisms."[3] Opponents of empire like Andrew Carnegie, who on one occasion warned that "the Far East is a mine of dynamite, always liable to explode," would have agreed with Langer's Darwinian emphasis,[4] but most American imperialists took a more optimistic view of the situation. For example, General Arthur MacArthur, commanding general in the Philippines, chose to argue that America's thrust into Asia was a contribution to a "stage of progressive social evolution that may reasonably be expected to result in the unity of the race and the brotherhood of man."[5] If anything, the late nineteenth-century rhetoric of imperialism spoke not the language of competition and conflict, but the communal idiom of reform Darwinism, with its emphasis on combination, cooperation, social control, and the rational management of conflict. The progressive "search for order" applied equally to international relations and domestic politics.[6]

According to this outlook, the civilizing process was a common project of the so-called "civilized powers." As Theodore Roosevelt later pointed out when discussing America's role in the Philippines, "there are points of resemblance in our work to the work which is being done by the British in India and Egypt, by the French in Algiers, by the Dutch in Java, by the Russians in Turkestan, by the Japanese in Formosa."[7] On another occasion, he noted that "it was a good thing for Egypt and the Sudan, and for the world, when England took Egypt and the Sudan."[8] Along the same lines, Robert E. Spear, the head of the Board of Foreign Missions of the Presbyterian

Church, claimed in one of his speeches that "the civilized nations are beginning to perceive that they have a duty, which is often contemptuously spoken of, to police the world."[9]

The argument from civilization not only suggested, but positively required, great power cooperation in the global management of imperialism. According to the Reverend Josiah Strong (often cited incorrectly as an exponent of dog-eat-dog international social Darwinism), a modern world community required that "the world Powers . . . assume responsibility for the world's order."[10] By one new reading, even Alfred Thayer Mahan, long identified as the paragon of expansionist navalism, was less concerned with asserting national power than with promoting the idea of multinational naval cooperation as a means of protecting international trade.[11]

Though for a time the idea of civilized cooperation pointed in a colonial direction, it took an anti-imperialist turn after 1900 when Americans discovered that their expectations of great power harmony had been too optimistic. Although the Mugwump anti-imperialists issued the noisiest warnings of geopolitical complications, all sides to the debate had been wary about steering into the maelstrom of imperialist politics. Even the most steroidal advocates of the Large Policy, however much they may have been pumped up with visions of national greatness, feared that European imperialism would infect the Caribbean. Nevertheless, it is indicative of the prevailing optimism of these years that whenever imperialism's harmful side-effects became obvious, Americans saw opportunities to promote great power cooperation.

The American desire to substitute cooperative colonial management for the diplomacy of imperialism faced its clearest and most challenging test in East Asia. For all the hurly-burly, imperialist rivalries among the great powers had been handled without major incident until the late 1890s. But, as it happened, the competition in East Asia began to heat up just as the United States was acquiring a regional position in the Philippines, and Americans soon felt the pull of the vortex. John Hay's observation that "the storm center of world politics has gradually shifted to China" succinctly expressed the significance that many Americans ascribed to the diplomacy of imperialism. Hay even went so far as to assert that "the world's peace rests with China."

Hay's remarks seem altogether gloomy and portentous at first sight, but they were remarkably optimistic in one vital respect. In their assumption that China was the most serious problem facing the great powers they implied that other great power issues – the European balance of power, for example – were well under control and scarcely worth bothering about. Otherwise, given China's relative unimportance in the larger scheme of things, Hay's comments have an air of the ridiculous about them. From this perspective, the shifting of the geopolitical spotlight to China, far from suggesting that a global calamity was in the making, was an indication that the powers had little else to squabble about.

To be sure, for East Asian powers like Russia and Japan who competed for control of territory as well as trade, the stakes were higher than for other contestants. But in the United States the prevailing sensibility, shared across the political spectrum by conservatives and progressives alike, was a sense of optimism that war among the civilized powers was growing less likely. As the relatively pessimistic Mugwump anti-imperialists went into decline, the burgeoning peace movement, with its sanguine views on international cooperation, became more representative of American thinking about great power relations during these years.[12]

What military trouble spots there were appeared to be located in the non-civilized areas of the world. In his presidential message of December 3, 1912, Taft pointed out that "only the failure of small nations to maintain internal stability could affect the peace of the world." Or take, for example, Roosevelt's considered views on the subject:

> If China became civilized like Japan, if the Turkish Empire were abolished, and all of uncivilized Africa and Asia held by England or France or Russia and Germany, then I believe we should be within sight of a time when a general international agreement could be made by which armies and navies could be reduced so as to meet merely the needs of internal and international police work.[13]

This observation suggested that international violence in the contemporary world was likely to arise in one of two ways. Its central thrust was to emphasize the continued danger of conflict between the great powers and the "barbaric" peoples, hence Roosevelt's well-known assertion that "warlike intervention by the civilized powers would contribute directly to the peace of the world." But in its reference to the Ottoman empire and to China – the "sick man of Europe" and the "sick man of Asia" – it also hinted at a more ominous possibility: great power rivalry over the carcasses of dying empires.

If, as many Americans believed, imperialism was the last arena of competition among the great powers, it was also a logical place to promote their cooperation. And China, where the diplomacy of imperialism burned with a new intensity after 1900, provided ample opportunity, as well as numerous incentives, for Americans to try to douse its flames. Besides impeding the open door objective of assuring the principle of equal commercial opportunity, which was essential to maintaining America's access to the China market, imperialist rivalries were also a barrier to China's development and modernization, upon which the success of the open door ultimately depended. Not least, imperialist contention in China was a standing reproach to the dream of great power cooperation that Americans assumed would be one of the fruits of global modernization. On the eve of World War I, the progressive Walter Weyl provided perhaps the best description of America's stake in China. "Our interest," said Weyl, "apart from a share of the trade and investment chances, lies in contributing to the world's peace by removing that vast territory from the field of international political competition." China, he insisted, was "a world, rather than a national, interest."[14]

The chief obstacles to the open door in China were Russia and Japan, nations who in the first decade of the century became imperialist arch-villains on whom a good deal of heated rhetoric was expended. The Russians, suspected of conniving at creating an exclusive sphere of influence in Manchuria, were, according to Hay, "a strange race" of whom anything could be expected "except straightforwardness."[15] "Russia's objective," said Frederick Wells Williams, "is international monopoly. There is no place in her scheme for countries that her garrisons do not occupy."[16] By 1903 Roosevelt was telling Hay that he was "thoroughly aroused and irritated" at Russia's exclusionary policies in Manchuria and found their behavior "most annoying."[17] Writing to his ambassador in St Petersburg, TR recalled that "for years Russia has pursued a policy of consistent opposition to us in the East, and of literally fathomless mendacity. She has felt a profound contempt for England and Japan and the United States, all three, separately or together. It has been impossible to trust any promise she has made."[18] Many State Department officials on the scene were, if anything, even more outraged.

Although Japan seemed at first to be a more benign power, that perception changed in the wake of the Russo-Japanese war of 1904–5. Despite an early sympathy for Japan's cause, the striking successes of its army and navy, coupled with growing suspicions that it was driven by an expansionist chauvinism, caused TR to have second thoughts about Japanese power in East Asia. At first, the Japanese, who "played the game of civilized mankind" by taking on the perfidious Russians, seemed an ideal team to cheer on from the sidelines. But Roosevelt soon changed his mind and began privately to voice his suspicion that the Japanese, deep down, viewed westerners "as white devils inferior to themselves not only in what they regard as the essentials of civilization, but in courage and forethought." TR was not alone in his doubts, as attested to by the fact that US contingency planning for military conflict with Japan dates to these years.

But American antipathies were never allowed to proceed to the point of war. As John King Fairbank has observed of the China scene, "[The United States] was not engaging in power politics there. It was present only on a me-too basis."[19] Like a teetotaler in a saloon, the US was unwilling to enter into arrangements like the Anglo-Japanese alliance of 1902 to preserve its interests in China, nor was it willing to defend those interests unilaterally against other powers. John Hay explained the predicament in this way: "we do not want to rob China

ourselves, and our public opinion will not allow us to interfere, with an army, to prevent others from robbing her."[20]
American abstinence was not due solely to a constraining public
opinion, however. However reprehensible the diplomacy of
imperialism in China, it posed no threat to American security
or to the American way of life that warranted fully fledged
entry into the power struggles over that nation's future.

If one views the situation in China at the time as a struggle
of power politics, the refusal of the United States to shove
military chips into the pot suggests that it was, effectively,
impotent. But the standard of civilization that American policy-
makers used to judge events in China led to a far more upbeat
assessment. Because an aggressive approach would have been
a confession of ideological bankruptcy, it was never a serious
option. Instead, the policy menu listed only different forms of
cooperation from which to choose. American policy-makers
selected two ways of preserving the idea of cooperation in
China: a regional approach to accommodation as adopted by
Roosevelt, and a more outspoken universal course championed by the Taft administration. Although these contrasting positions have often been painted as black-and-white
opposites, the struggle between the two is better understood
as a family feud in which both sides shared the common values of civilization.

A clear example of cooperation defined as a regional division of labor was the Roosevelt Corollary that announced
the customs receivership in the Dominican Republic. Its cooperative side comes into view as soon as it is realized that this
so-called corollary to the Monroe Doctrine was, in fact, a significant deviation from the principles of that venerable dogma.
The Monroe Doctrine had been based on the assumption that
the world was separated into watertight political compartments, each with separate "systems" of politics. The point
was to keep the American system separate, especially from
the European balance of power. As Thomas Jefferson had
observed, "The European nations constitute a separate division of the globe; their localities make them part of a distinct
system; they have a set of interests of their own." Hoping to

make this view stick, the doctrine announced that the Americas were "henceforth not to be considered as subjects of future colonization by a European power."

Roosevelt's pronouncement, however, was made not from a regional standpoint of hemispheric isolation, but from a universal frame of reference in which "civilization" had conferred upon the United States "an international police power." From Roosevelt's perspective, the United States was *cooperating* with the Europeans; indeed, it claimed to be acting as their proxy. Henry Adams held a similar conception of America's duty in the Caribbean. "Whatever the American people might think or say about it," he wrote, "they would sooner or later have to police those islands, not against Europe, but for Europe."[21]

On its face the Roosevelt Corollary was rather simple, but its ideological clockwork was rather complex. Though it was an imperialist doctrine, it was prompted by a hostility to the diplomacy of imperialism and, in yet another twist, it was justified by a global process that legitimized imperialism for all the great powers. Though this was tricky logic, it was not sophistical. The mainspring of Roosevelt's thinking about international relations was his belief in a global process of civilization, a "world movement" that advanced great power cooperation and promoted imperialism, even as he entertained a healthy suspicion of the diplomacy of imperialism in the western hemisphere. There was simply too much consistency in his various attempts to juggle these sometimes conflicting factors to conclude that the internationalist rhetoric of the corollary was nothing but smoke and mirrors.[22]

Civilization provided a point of linkage connecting Roosevelt's policies in the Caribbean to his thinking about China. In an ideal world, he would have preferred that "the same policy could be pursued in China" as the United States was pursuing in the Caribbean.[23] Because civilization mattered to Roosevelt in East Asia, he had long been on the lookout for a single power to protect the interests of civilization in the region much in the same way as the US was doing in the Caribbean. For TR, the problem with East Asia's politics was that there were too many imperialist cooks in a kitchen where the diplomatic cuisine would have been far more savory had China's affairs been organized by the guiding hand of a single chef. Years later, he reaffirmed his long-standing belief that there had been war in China "precisely because there has been no Asiatic Monroe Doctrine."[24]

Unfortunately, TR concluded that the selfish national traits of Russia and Japan meant that they were not up to the task of serving as responsible regional trustees. In his mediation of the Russo-Japanese War, a service for which he later received the Nobel Peace Prize, TR later wrote of his desire to create a "balanced antagonism" between the two contestants in the Treaty of Portsmouth. But if that was his goal, he failed rather strikingly to achieve it. It soon became clear that Japan's power was still rising in China, particularly in Manchuria; this in addition to the potential threat that it already posed to the Philippines.

Japan's good behavior could be purchased, not by balancing, but only at the price of disavowing any intention of interfering with its exclusive interests in China. Although the usual genuflections before the open door principle were inserted into the Root–Takahira agreement of 1908, Roosevelt deferred to the Japanese position in Manchuria in return for Tokyo's acknowledgment of US paramountcy in the islands. According to historian Raymond Esthus, Roosevelt was so apprehensive about Japan's increasing power in the region that he was "willing to sacrifice the open door and the integrity of China in favor of the economic and strategic interests of Japan in Manchuria."[25]

The Rough Rider's retreat from America's vocal antagonism to the diplomacy of imperialism was not surprising because, when it came down to hard issues of military security, he cared far more about the Caribbean than about China or the open door. As Charles Neu has argued, an accommodationist Roosevelt "was willing to see Japan's expansionist thrust absorbed on the mainland of Asia where there was little friction with the United States. It was Japan's task, not America's, to lead China along the road to modernization."[26] He had, in any case, never been an enthusiast for the open door or America's mission in China. As he saw it, the only "radical cause of friction" between the US and Japan was the immigration issue, not China.[27]

Still, TR refused to retreat to a monastic seclusion within the western hemisphere. He was a cosmopolitan internationalist who believed in international cooperation.[28] And, despite his willingness to compromise the open door in practice, he never abandoned it in principle. By backpedaling, he at least preserved the idea of an international division of labor along regional lines among the imperialist powers, an idea that was hardly as far-fetched at the time as it seems today.[29] One must not forget that, in Roosevelt's day, the image of Japan was still unsettled. For everyone who purported to see a "yellow peril," there was someone else who saw Japan as a civilized power. For his part, TR hoped that Japan's belligerence was "only a passing phase and that when Japan settles down she will feel a desire to enter more and more into the circle of the great civilized nations as one of their number."[30]

One of the puzzles of America's diplomacy in China during these years is that the energetic and forceful Roosevelt came out looking uncharacteristically wimpy in comparison with the torpid and peace-loving Taft, whose East Asian policy has been seen as rather aggressive. But just as TR did not see his retreat as appeasement, Taft did not view his policies as belligerent. The difference between Roosevelt's view of regional cooperation as a division of labor and Taft's pursuit of global cooperation in joint association with other great powers came down to this: TR viewed the world as a condominium apartment building, where individual ownership still played a large role, whereas Taft saw it as a co-op dwelling, where communal management was the dominant principle.

Thus, while TR opted to sit out the diplomacy of imperialism, his global-minded successor, Taft, decided to play what cards he had in an attempt to dismantle competition in China. Unlike TR, who smelled trouble in such an initiative, Taft believed that opposition to the diplomacy of imperialism, far from risking war, was actually a way of promoting great power harmony. "The tendency of modern times is manifestly toward international unity," said his secretary of state, Philander Knox.[31] In its international involvements, Taft insisted that the United States was simply attempting to do its part "in keeping the house of the world in order."[32]

Taft's most celebrated step in this direction was his attempt to create a cooperative framework for the administration of Manchuria's railways. This was in keeping with his administration's larger approach to world politics, "dollar diplomacy," which assumed that modern industrial civilization, no longer dominated by predatory militarism, had created a built-in disposition to cooperate among the developed industrial nations of the world. Though most closely identified with China, the open door had always been much broader in scope, witness America's attendance at international conferences in the 1880s that assured the principle in Morocco and the Belgian Congo. To this point in time, the United States had only the theory of the open door, which Knox correctly noted had "not really been tested in a concrete way."[33] So long as it remained an abstract generality, Taft told Roosevelt, "no one will take us seriously and consequently no one will take offense." But it seemed preferable to Taft "to try to bring Japan's policy in China up to the level of ours . . . than to lower the policy to the level of hers."[34] Thus, in the absence of willingness to threaten force against the other powers, Taft's dollar diplomacy was the *only* possible way of advancing the American cause in China.

While Roosevelt backed away from the diplomacy of imperialism, Taft refused to be scared off by it, believing that the race could still be run according to open door rules. He agreed with TR that China was not worth fighting over and that the United States could not have forced the issue in any case, but he was also convinced that an attempt to undermine the diplomacy of imperialism by peaceful means was worth the effort.[35] In so doing, his dollar diplomacy at least sustained the open door idea in China and kept alive the ideal of great power cooperation. But, at the same time, as a necessary condition it also endorsed the principle of great power oversight of a China that was not considered to be fully civilized. Not surprisingly, then, Chinese nationalists found it hard to view the open door policy in the altruistic light in which Americans habitually bathed it.

The refusal of the other powers to go along with Knox's scheme produced plenty of carping about a "pin-pricking policy toward Japan and Russia" that "brought results of a boomerang nature."[36] When chastised by TR for having irritated the Japanese, Taft's response was to assert that war with Japan over China was unthinkable. As Knox insisted, even "the heartiest competitors in business may yet be the firmest friends."[37] Taft's position assumed that the great powers had no irreconcilable conflicts of interest among themselves and that their differences over how to deal with underdeveloped areas like China should not be allowed to get out of hand. As one historian has reminded us, the peaceful character of the open door policy was "as much an accepted fact to John Hay's contemporaries as it is a forgotten one to Americans several Asian wars later."[38]

Dollar diplomacy failed in Manchuria – as many historians have noted, it had the quite unintended effect of driving Japan and Russia closer together for a time – but the setback was only temporary. The revolution of 1911 in China provided the occasion for the creation of a six-power financial consortium, which included Japan and Russia, to manage foreign developmental lending to China. As one newspaper put it, Japan and Russia were "likely to cause less trouble inside than outside the group."[39] Imperialism appeared thereby to have been put in its place and the to-do with Japan was waved off as only a "temporary misunderstanding."[40]

In taking stock of its joust with the diplomacy of imperialism, the Taft administration patted itself on the back by insisting that the "motives and results of our international action have tended to advance the brotherhood of nations."[41] This was, to be sure, self-serving praise, but it was not entirely fanciful. The threads of Taft's China policy would be picked up in the 1920s and applied with greater immediate success. If the events of the 1930s had not derailed a peaceful outcome to the China problem, Taft's open door diplomacy – "a great diplomatic conception" in Knox's immodest words – might well have been hailed as a work of genius by historians.[42] Of course, things did not work out in this gratifying way because the United States failed, in the short run, to moderate the diplomacy of imperialism or to successfully promote China's modernization.

If nothing else, these developments underscored the extraordinary lack of foresight in the debate over empire that took place a decade earlier. Relations as they actually developed among the great powers in China were nowhere near as dire as the anti-imperialist Cassandras had warned, but neither were they as amicable as the optimists had expected. Optimism was still possible when Taft handed over the reins of the presidency to Woodrow Wilson. But with the outbreak of World War I, a very different and far more gloomy assessment of the foreign-policy implications of imperialism was about to emerge.

World War I and the Emergence of Geopolitical Anti-imperialism

World War I (1914–18) was a watershed event in the history of US foreign policy. In contrast to the false start of 1898, it marked the true beginning of America's career as a world power. But it is also important to our story, for it was the point in time when new and more enduring forms of anti-imperialism became part of the ideological fabric of American foreign policy. By the time the United States entered the war in 1917, anti-imperialism had become an important aspect of a distinctive new critique of power politics. Many Americans had already come to dislike what they had seen of the diplomacy of imperialism in China, but the world war prompted a dramatic upward revision of its dangers. Formerly little more than an annoyance, imperialism now became a danger to the national security that threatened to destroy the underpinnings of modern global civilization.

The new anti-imperialism was made up of distinct ideologi-

cal shoots that sprouted from the ashes of the original conservative anti-imperialist impulse of 1898. "The Gilded Age
anti-imperialist coalition made its final stand in opposition to
McKinley's decision to annex the Philippines," says one historian.[43] Frustrated by their inability to influence policy and
distressed at having been forced to abandon their natural political home in the Republican Party, many conservative anti-
imperialists began to trim their sails by adjusting their views
to the prevailing winds of Republican Party positions. Soon
they stopped advocating independence for the Philippines in
favor of the kind of protectorate established by the Platt amendment in Cuba.

These conservative anti-imperialists were gradually supplanted by progressives and liberals who made a remarkable
about-face from their support for imperialism at the turn of
the century. Only a few years earlier, progressives had generally favored annexation of the Philippines and on the whole
had applauded Theodore Roosevelt's application of the "big
stick" in the Caribbean. For example, Woodrow Wilson, then
the reform president of Princeton University, insisted that the
Filipinos "are children and we are men in these deep matters
of government and justice."[44] Even Taft's "dollar diplomacy,"
a policy that almost begged to be branded as a tool of the
corporate interests that progressives so loved to hate, aroused
little complaint.[45]

Progressives had supported imperialism for many reasons.
Obeying the herd instinct, many had simply traced without
question the path first laid out by their charismatic leader,
Theodore Roosevelt. But the enthusiasm for the colonial mission was the product of more than a matter of irrational at-
tachment to a dynamic personality. Most progressives backed
imperialism because it seemed to be an enlightened program,
a way of transferring civilization to backward peoples and
promoting international cooperation among the civilized powers. In other words, it seemed the right thing to do. As Willard
Range has explained it, "the humanitarian, paternalistic, missionary spirit of the imperialism of the liberals of the Progressive Era kept their imperialism from being sordid."[46]

Imperialism was also attractive from the standpoint of world peace. As long as imperialism seemed a reliable way of promoting a peaceful, modernizing global society, it was enthusiastically accepted. But progressivism also had a pessimistic side that lived in dread of a collapse of modern civilization unless its negative tendencies were reigned in. The progressive turn to anti-imperialism can be seen as a reaction to some of the flawed features of that civilization. As imperialism became aligned with the forces of darkness, progressives came to reject it with a degree of dislike that surpassed the enthusiasm they had formerly displayed on its behalf. Both imperialism and anti-imperialism, then, were elements of a broader progressive outlook on international politics in an era of rapid globalization.

During the Great War, anti-imperialism crystallized into two distinct outlooks: progressive and Wilsonian liberal. In Christopher Lasch's terms, the division was among those who believed that the war was a conflict between autocracy and democracy and those who believed that it was the product of rival imperialisms.[47] For many progressives, imperialism was *the* factor explaining the outbreak of World War I. One of the more articulate among them was the young journalist Walter Lippmann. "The weak spots of the world are the arenas of friction," he said. "The arena where the European powers really measure their strength against each other is in the Balkans, in Africa, and in Asia." Given the raw intensity of the diplomacy of imperialism, Lippmann concluded that "the accumulated irritations of it have produced the great war."[48]

For progressives like Lippmann, this was a conflict in which neither side was completely free of sin. From his point of view, one of the chief problems facing the United States as it stood on the doorstep of intervention in the Great War in 1917 was the imperialism of its allies, who had signed treaties among themselves in which anticipated territorial acquisitions were lavishly parceled out. Economically, too, Americans feared that the British and the French were seeking to divide up the world into exclusive zones at the war's end. Thus Lippmann described the country as searching for a policy "which associates us with the Allied democracies and still acts as a moderating influence on their imperialism."

Imperialist wars were attributed to what Walter Weyl called "the omnipresent economic motive." "Remove the economic factors leading to war, give men more than enough, and the chief incentive to war disappears," he argued. But this anti-imperialism was also a domestic critique, since the same economic forces making for imperialism in other nations were also active in the United States. Combining the global and the local, the progressives argued that, ultimately, "internationalism begins at home." To make sure that capital was gainfully employed in the domestic economy, they typically called, as did Weyl, "for creating a better distribution of wealth, a wider consumption and therefore a larger employment of capital in industries for home consumption."[49] Progressive anti-imperialism was thus part of a wide-ranging critique that targeted US foreign policy, the domestic distribution of wealth, and the system of international relations as a whole. By comparison, the earlier generation of anti-imperialists had found far less to criticize in domestic affairs.

Many progressives were understandably thrilled, therefore, to hear Wilson condemn imperialism as one of the deadly sins of the "old diplomacy." Wilson explained the role of economic interests and imperialism as aspects of the German danger to one audience, in 1918:

> Their purpose is undoubtedly to make all the Slavic peoples, all the free and ambitious nations of the Baltic peninsula, all the lands that Turkey has dominated and misruled, subject to their will and ambition and build upon that dominion an empire of force upon which they fancy that they can then erect an empire of gain and commercial supremacy, an empire as hostile to the Americas as to the Europe which it will overawe, an empire which will ultimately master Persia, India, and the peoples of the Far East.[50]

Despite some obvious affinities, however, Wilson's perspective on imperialism diverged in some rather dramatic ways from the progressive point of view. The chief difference was that he disagreed with the progressive insistence on the centrality of imperialism. For Wilson, imperialism was a peripheral affair. It was as if the European powers, who were already rolling the dice in a high-stakes game of power politics on the continent, were at the same time engaging in imperialist side bets.

While most progressives explained the war almost wholly in narrow economic terms, Wilson saw economics as only a contributing factor, not as the decisive cause. For Wilson, the ultimate source of great power competition was archaic social and political systems dominated by anti-democratic castes who held fast to outmoded conceptions of war and genuflected slavishly before age-old balance of power precepts – the "old diplomacy," for short. It was these atavistic groups that promoted the mindless piling up of armaments and the use of trade as an instrument of aggression. Thus, whereas the progressive anti-imperialists saw World War I as a wholly modern war, a conflict brought about by a dysfunctional capitalism, Wilson saw it as a conflict between the past and the present, between antiquated social systems that represented the past and democratically controlled nations that stood for the future. "At bottom," concluded one of Wilson's advisers, "the whole trouble was militarism."[51]

This struggle between the remnants of the feudal past and the forces of the modernizing present was being played out in a global conflict of such immense scale that Wilson came to believe that modern war had become too widespread, too violent, and too revolutionary to be employed as a routine instrument of foreign policy. The periodic reconstitution of the balance of power by military means had clearly become too expensive and dangerous a method to apply on a constant basis. As if that were not bad enough, the worst-case outcome of the struggle could be world domination by a single reactionary power. Thus Wilsonianism saw an unprecedented threat to national security posed by the old diplomacy. To the extent that imperialism was implicated, it was not only a bad thing in the abstract, but a factor in a much broader and more dangerous crisis of western civilization. In this way, imperialism, which had formerly been associated with a benign vision of "normal internationalism," had shifted meanings to become a part of Wilsonian "crisis internationalism."[52]

In the famous Fourteen Points speech, in which he outlined the terms of a lasting peace, Wilson gave prominent mention to the problem of imperialism. "We feel ourselves to be intimate partners of all the governments and peoples associated together against the Imperialists," he declared. His fifth point spoke of the need to manage colonial rivalries through "a free, open-minded, and absolutely impartial adjustment of colonial claims" with equal weight being given to "the interests of the populations concerned."[53] If this formulation was quite vague, it took no mind-reader to divine why ambiguity was in order. America's wartime partners were among the leading imperialist nations in the world and some important segments of their publics entertained further grandiose dreams of territorial expansion. To oppose imperialism outright – and there is no evidence that Wilson wished to go that far – would have been to undo the coalition.

Wilson fought hard at the Paris peace conference to keep imperialism in check. The colonies of Germany and former Ottoman possessions were parceled out as mandates under the League of Nations. Most of the territorial ambitions of the allies remained unrealized, particularly Italy's quest for territory in the Adriatic. Indeed, so poorly did his nation eat from the table of wartime spoils that at one point the Italian premier walked out. But Wilson could go only so far without wrecking the conference. Despite impassioned pleadings from the president, the Japanese insisted on obtaining Germany's former privileges in China's Shantung province. Wilson argued strongly for a cooperative approach in which "by pooling their interest the several nations that had gained a foothold in China ... might forego the special position they had acquired."[54] To no avail. Fearing that a Japanese walk-out over Shantung would cripple the League of Nations at birth and make another world war likely, Wilson gave Japan what her treaty rights entitled her to get.

Clearly, for Wilson, the need to cement great power cooperation was more important than the desire to end the diplomacy of imperialism. Bad as imperialism was, for Wilson it was the lesser evil. "The defection of Japan might not only break up the Peace Conference but destroy the League of Nations," wrote Wilson's confidant, Ray Stannard Baker, in his diary.[55] Better to have Japan in the League with Shantung than beyond the civilized pale. As the League became a going concern, Wilson hoped that the Japanese would be persuaded, over time, to drop their claims to special privileges. While not proud of the Shantung decision, Wilson believed above all that "he *must* work for world order and organization against anarchy and a return to militarism."[56]

Wilson's opposition to imperialism was impure in another respect: its racialism. Had the diplomacy of imperialism not been dangerous to the great powers, it is quite possible that Wilson might not have placed anti-imperialism on his diplomatic agenda at all. Though he was willing to contemplate an eventual return of China's sovereignty, it was only "sooner or later." Wilson still believed (as did most scientists of his day) in the racial inferiority of non-white peoples. He presided over the meeting in Paris that quashed a Japanese motion for a declaration of racial equality. No doubt he realized that this motion, without Great Britain's support, could go nowhere, but its defeat accorded with his own thinking on race.

His willingness to employ force in Mexico, Haiti, and the Dominican Republic on behalf of democracy had exhibited few scruples about cultural or racial equality. In the case of the latter two, Wilson, like other Americans, assumed that "they have African racial traits. That is why they differ completely from all the other republics."[57] Viewed in context, however, Wilson's views were not particularly retrograde. His outlook accepted a "higher imperialism," advanced for its time, in which the racial and/or cultural inferiority of non-white peoples was taken for granted. According to this view, it was not imperialism *per se* that was bad, for some peoples were clearly incapable of self-government; rather, competitive imperialism was the evil to be guarded against. Such ideas formed the conceptual underpinnings of the mandate system adopted by the League of Nations.

Consistent with this view, Wilson did make an attempt at Paris to adopt a higher international standard of colonial governance. The American delegation hoped that the peace conference would "write a code of conduct binding upon all colonial powers."[58] At Paris, Wilson and his advisers pressed the trusteeship principle, by which the imperial powers, serving as guardians in the name of civilization, were not free to do as they pleased. According to one interpretation of Wilson's views, the implication was "that a colonial power acts not as owner of its colonies, but as trustee for the natives and for the interests of the society of nations." This effort bore fruit in article 22 of the League of Nations Covenant, which stated that "the well-being and development" of the former German colonies formed "a sacred trust of civilization." In article 23, moreover, the signatories agreed to "undertake to secure just treatment of the native inhabitants of territories under their control." Enforcement mechanisms, however, were lacking.

The Shantung decision was a grievous disappointment to the many Chinese who had hoped that Wilson would deal a death blow to the unequal treaties. The decision struck a raw nerve in China, touching off demonstrations and launching a nationalist revival that would come to be known as the May 4th movement. Wilson's cave-in on Shantung also disillusioned many American progressives and liberals, who interpreted the decision as a complete sell-out by Wilson to the "old diplomacy," not realizing that it was consistent with his hierarchy of priorities. Their repudiation of Wilson's leadership added yet another ally to the diverse coalition that defeated the peace treaty in the Senate, and ended any possibility of the United States joining the League of Nations.

In the immediate postwar years, neither Wilsonianism nor progressive anti-imperialism became the governing outlook. Instead, the cooperative version of anti-imperialism that had first been applied by the Taft administration was revitalized in the foreign policy of the 1920s, this time with much more heartening results. Abandoning Wilsonianism in favor of a new and improved version of dollar diplomacy, a string of Republican administrations launched a series of anti-imperialist initiatives in the belief that the China powers were now, at long last, ready to cooperate with each other. Foremost among them was the Washington conference of 1921–2, which is best known for the landmark naval disarmament treaty that produced proportional reductions in the number of battleships and heavy cruisers in the world's leading navies.

Important as this agreement was, the other treaties signed in Washington were more striking in their impact on imperialism. A nine-power treaty validated the Taftian version of the open door and looked forward to the eventual abandonment of the treaty port system in China. Until that unspecified day arrived, great power competition would be tamed by ending the Anglo-Japanese alliance, which since 1902 had served as the centerpiece of the Far Eastern balance. In its place was substituted a rather vague four-power treaty that looked forward to consultation among the signatories in the event that peace was disturbed in the East Asia region. The conference thus drove a stake through the heart of the diplomacy of imperialism, or so it was widely believed at the time.

Although open door anti-imperialism dominated official policy in the 1920s, progressive anti-imperialism enjoyed something of a golden age in that decade. It had both intellectual and political dimensions. Its most visible political work was done in the US Senate, where a small band of progressive anti-imperialists managed, on occasion, to successfully press the Republican administrations for the withdrawal of American troops from lands then under occupation in the Caribbean.[59] Not satisfied with the official triumphs against the diplomacy of imperialism, these critics propounded a more comprehensive, politically isolationist anti-imperialism that sought to subvert the open-door approach. But while there were quite clearly tensions between anti-imperialist critics of US foreign policy and Republican policy-makers, there were also large areas of overlap that allowed for dialogue between the two. In many cases the critics were trying to break down a door that was already beginning to swing open.

The politicians were backed by the work of scholars, intellectuals, liberal journalists, African-Americans, and women peace crusaders. In searching for basic explanations of American behavior abroad, radical and progressive scholars sought to do for foreign relations what Charles Beard had done a decade earlier in his path-breaking interpretation of the Constitution: to expose and demystify the self-seeking economic interests that led the US to intervene in obscure places for reasons that had little to do with the national interest, broadly conceived. In a best-selling work of history, Beard and his wife Mary explained American imperialism in the Caribbean: "As the needle the magnet, so public policy followed the course of economic events . . ."[60] Many progressives like John Dewey accepted the thesis that imperialism sprang from domestic economic determinants. "The natural movement of business enterprise," Dewey argued, "combined with Anglo-American legalistic notions of contracts and their sanctity, and the international custom which obtains as to the duty of a nation to protect the property of its nationals, suffices to bring about imperialistic undertakings."[61] More radical analyses like those of Scott Nearing argued that American imperialism was generic to capitalism, that "economic expansion and the development of financial imperialism were not confined to Europe."[62]

Progressive anti-imperialism had a number of features that are worthy of mention. First, it was an oppositional point of view that, despite moments of influence, never managed to become embedded as an official foreign-policy doctrine. Second, it was an internalist critique that defined imperialism as a home-grown problem that stemmed from the expansionist needs of the free-market economy. Available in either high-cholesterol Marxist formulas or low-calorie progressive versions, the view that *American* foreign policy was, at bottom, an imperialistic project rooted in economic expansion continues to occupy a good deal of shelf space in intellectual supermarkets even today. Given this domestic preoccupation, the progressive critique of imperialism was focused primarily on American imperialism, particularly in the Caribbean.

Third, in their live-and-let-live advocacy of cultural pluralism, these critiques appeared to be hostile to the commercial and cultural internationalism that lies at the core of global modernization. And yet, their advocacy of cultural relations with Latin America bore the unmistakable imprint of the continued belief in the civilizing mission. For many, it was clear that gentler cultural methods were intended to produce the cultural transformation of Latin America that political power had failed to achieve. Thus one supporter of cultural relations admitted his underlying desire to "see to it that the republics of Tropical America behave like citizens of the world rather than like pirates or members of savage head-hunting tribes."[63]

Lastly, despite a principled concern with the imperialism of nations other than the United States, this anti-imperialism was even less politically engaged than the kind then being promoted by the Republican administrations of the 1920s. Official Washington, at least, saw the United States as having a stake in a peaceful, cooperative internationalism and was willing to undertake a variety of multilateral initiatives. But the critique of American open door expansion and cultural imperialism pooh-poohed foreign dangers and suggested instead that America's problems, which were thought to be home-grown, could be solved domestically. In consequence, anti-imperialism lacked the element of fear that was so prominent a part of Wilsonianism, its underlying assumption being that neither American security nor identity was at risk from crises abroad.

The howling political winds of the 1930s swept away the stagnant anti-imperialist outlooks of the 1920s. When Japan decided to resume a course of military expansion in China with the invasion of Manchuria in 1931, the inherited attitude of non-interventionist hostility toward the diplomacy of imperialism was still the dominant outlook. After the dispute had been submitted to a dithering and ultimately impotent League of Nations, the United States adopted a widely imitated policy of non-recognition, in which President Hoover and his secretary of state, Henry Stimson, refused to accord diplomatic recognition to the new "state" of Manchukuo, i.e. the former Chinese province of Manchuria, which was in fact a thinly disguised colony of Japan run by bureaucrats in Tokyo. This action was justified on the grounds that Japanese aggression had violated the Kellogg–Briand pact of 1928, which presumably had outlawed war, and the nine-power treaty of 1922.

Stimson had a Wilsonian sense of foreboding about the potentially catastrophic implications of Japanese imperialism. As he put it, "at any moment an accident might occur which would set the whole world on fire."[64] He would have preferred sterner measures, but not so his chief, Hoover, who had been trained in the old school of cooperative anti-imperialism in which it was unthinkable for the United States to hector the Japanese about their treaty violations. That might produce a danger of a war that Hoover did not believe was worth fighting, as Japanese imperialism in China posed no serious threat to the United States nor placed any fundamental American interests at risk. In any case, he was convinced that the Japanese, by taking on China, were attempting to swallow more than they could successfully digest. His successor, Franklin D. Roosevelt, had a more pessimistic view of the situation, but the deepening of the great depression at home, coupled with growing public concern at becoming involved in another world war, forced him to concentrate on domestic affairs well into his second presidential term. Thus, as one historian described the policy, "the United States would acquiesce in, but not assent to, Japanese expansion already undertaken at the expense of China."[65]

The Hoover–Stimson non-recognition doctrine, by finessing a dangerous confrontation with Japan, exposed to the full light of day the long-standing unwillingness of the United States to take tough measures on behalf of the open door policy. In retrospect, however, it was a significant departure from past practice, because the refusal to legitimize Japan's actions put an end to the policy of cooperative anti-imperialism in whose name the US had always been able to strike deals, even if those agreements had only papered over the many contradictions between principle and practice. The policy menu that produced a compromise between the traditionalist Hoover and the Wilsonian Stimson was far different from the variations on the theme of cooperation that Theodore Roosevelt and Taft had to choose from.

Until this point in time, as one historian has noted, "imperialism in China was fundamentally a cooperative venture."[66] But Japan's action pretty much destroyed any lingering hopes for cooperation. Thus, after articulating its point of view, the US government placed the cooperative, hortatory, and optimistic open door sensibility in storage in the years to come.[67] Tucked away in the attic of diplomacy, it was largely forgotten and left to molder. The Roosevelt administration continued to emphasize cooperation, but, tellingly, in geographically and legally broader terms of international law and order that went well beyond a concern for China. When the fear of confronting Japan ceased to govern policy toward the end of the decade, the cooperative approach was not restored, but replaced.

As for the progressive anti-imperialists, the decade's brewing geopolitical storms pushed many of them into the ranks of isolationists who wanted as little as possible to do with events abroad in the belief that foreign wars were none of America's business. This tendency of many progressive anti-imperialist butterflies to change into isolationist caterpillars in the 1930s exposed a core belief that differentiated them from the soon-to-be-resurgent Wilsonians: though convinced that imperialism was a bad thing, morally, they did not believe that the diplomacy of imperialism threatened American security. Their chief fear was of military involvement that might result from imprudent, principled opposition. The great depression and the fear of another world war – the unhappy consequences of the Great War had left a sour taste in the mouths of many – had led many to conclude that the United States should tend its own garden.

Even in the western hemisphere, anti-imperialism went temporarily into eclipse in the 1930s. This was because the good neighbor policy, with the abrogation of the Platt amendment in 1934 and the renunciation of the right to intervene at the Montevideo Conference a year earlier, cut the ground out from many of the criticisms of US policy. But for internationalists like FDR, the good neighbor policy was intended to be a standing reproach to the diplomacy of imperialism. It was, he understood, less an example of power than an expression of the power of example, but he hoped nevertheless that it would have "at least some *moral* repercussions in Europe."[68]

By the end of the 1930s, the progressive and open-door forms of anti-imperialism – one dormant, the other extinct – were overtaken by a revival of Wilsonian anti-imperialist thinking. As the decade wore on, America's isolationist reticence began to dissolve. The change was most noticeable in a new toughness in the US approach toward China, which marked a further evolution in America's policy in East Asia. Having begun with a narrow commercial interest in the nineteenth century, the open door had taken a developmental turn in the first decade of the twentieth century. While anti-imperialism had been a feature of the open door since 1899, it had traditionally been rooted in the ground of great power cooperation and did not envision American intervention against imperialist rogue states. By the late 1930s, however, US anti-imperialism in East Asia took on a geopolitical form as American policy-makers began to act on the assumption, first articulated by Wilsonians during the Great War, that imperialism was an extraordinarily dangerous phenomenon. Far from being guided by the same old open door outlook, policy toward Japan would henceforth be shaped by a new anti-imperialist framework.

Following the outbreak of the Sino-Japanese War in July 1937, the US began to exert pressure on Japan by degrees. By 1938, the US started to take serious anti-Japanese measures at a time when it was still acting gingerly toward Adolf Hitler's Germany. After a series of modest economic steps helpful to China, FDR's government began to turn the screws by imposing increasingly harsh economic sanctions against Japan. In July 1939, the State Department gave six-months' notice of its intention to terminate the 1911 commercial treaty between the two countries. To have no treaty meant that transactions would be *ad hoc* and subject to sudden governmental mood swings. Following the Japanese occupation of southern Indochina in July 1941, the US froze Japanese assets in the United States. Without approval from the government to release their dollar assets in US banks, the Japanese were unable to purchase oil. Thus the freezing of assets order turned into a *de facto* oil embargo, which left the Japanese with the choice of either submitting to US demands that they back off in China, or to go to war before their oil reserves ran down. They chose war.

As presidential adviser Adolf Berle remarked, with some wonderment: "It is a curious fact that the United States, which bolts like a frightened rabbit from remote contact with Europe, will enthusiastically take a step which might very well be a material day's march on the road to a Far Eastern war."[69] It was all the more curious given the axiomatic assumption in Washington that Japan was less of a threat to the US than Nazi Germany. If that was the case, why, then, this get-tough approach to Japan?

In the absence of more persuasive answers, America's fixation with China has long been the default historical explanation of why the United States became involved in the Pacific War. In part, the outbreak of war was related to the collapse of the twin pillars of America's China policy. Had the US been successful in holding up only one of the supports – either by keeping the diplomacy of imperialism in check or by more effectively promoting the modernization of a China that would not easily be made the object of expansion – the war in the Pacific would not have taken place. But while it is obvious that China was an important part of the equation, the belief that there was an obsession with China remains the chief stumbling block in explaining America's entry into World War II. Citing the new-found eagerness to support China and the open door as the primary cause of the conflict makes sense only if one isolates the part – the diplomacy of imperialism – from the civilizational whole that gave it meaning.

If one looks at the hard numbers, there is not much to be said for the China argument. Economically and historically, China was a long way from being a vital interest. Japan was by far the better customer for US goods and was likely to be so for a long time to come. In fact, Japan was America's third best customer overall, as exports to Japan equaled roughly the total of all exports to South America.[70] The much-ballyhooed China market had never materialized. American investments in China in the 1930s averaged only between 200 and 300 million dollars, approximately the same amount invested in Japan, which amounted to only 5 per cent of total foreign investment abroad.[71] Great Britain and Japan, by contrast, each held a much larger economic stake in China.[72]

Insisting on China as the chief cause of the war is all the more perplexing because Japanese imperialism in China had been all but ignored for the better part of a decade following the declaration of the Hoover–Stimson doctrine in 1932. Although the principled opposition to Japanese treaty violations remained, no new initiatives emerged from Washington to do something about them. If anything, the traditional unwillingness to forcefully oppose the diplomacy of imperialism in China was set more firmly in place than ever before. With the brief exception of the Wilsonian moment, the failure of the American foreign-policy establishment to think about East Asian issues outside the boundaries of great power cooperation meant that it was impossible to conceive of China as something for which the US might be willing to go to war.

There were, admittedly, many reasons for Americans to be disturbed by Japanese military expansion in China. The open door, as enshrined in the treaties of the 1920s, was being abused with impunity. A Japanese conquest of China would have frustrated the American cultural effort in that country by replacing it with a Sino-Japanese cultural relationship. A reversal of the Americanization of China would have cast into doubt the global future of East Asia and, by extension, a liberal outlook for the world itself. Not least, a Japanese victory would have buried once and for all the idea of a cooperative phasing out of imperialism in China and in Asia generally. In its place, a more aggressive – and for colonial peoples a more exploitative – kind of imperialist diplomacy would have become the model for other areas of the world.

But these negative consequences, by themselves, were insufficient to trigger a strong American challenge to Japan. The situation in Asia only turned critical toward the end of the 1930s because of its connection, conceptually, with the more serious emergency in Europe. As one historian put it, Japan, "through aligning itself with the Axis, seemed to imperil not merely Asian but world order."[73] It was only in conjunction with Hitler's bid for German hegemony in Europe that Japan's diplomacy of imperialism came to seem intolerable. It would have been impossible for Americans to take so critical a view of the situation in Asia without the crisis in Europe. But it was equally impossible to act boldly in Europe without also taking into account the threatening aspects of the situation in Asia. This critical linkage between the open door in China and the threat in Europe was possible only because the conceptual junction box of Wilsonianism connected the two lines into a single circuit. America's plunge into the maelstrom of global war thus provides a striking illustration of how the Wilsonian analysis of imperialism's role in world politics was put into practice.

Since 1936, when the Anti-Comintern Pact had been signed, FDR sensed that "there was in the making a policy of world domination between Germany, Italy and Japan."[74] As FDR explained about the Japanese: "You never can tell where they are going to stop . . . they might join up the danger from the other side and make it even more difficult to defend ourselves."[75] The signature of the Tripartite Pact in September 1940 by Germany, Japan, and Italy confirmed and further excited this sense of threat. On the eve of war, Secretary of State Cordell Hull voiced the American suspicion to a Japanese emissary that "Hitler proposes to take charge of one-half of the world and Japan proposes to take charge of the other half."[76]

Not only would a Japanese conquest of East Asia and the south-west Pacific deprive Great Britain of imperial resources needed to defeat Germany,[77] but a combined conquest of Europe and Asia by the Axis powers would effectively put an end to a liberal "open world". In a closed world of power politics and imperial expansion dominated by the Axis powers, internationalists believed that the United States would be isolated – politically, economically, and ideologically – more completely than had ever been the case in its history. The nation's political system would be transformed in the direction of militarism and authoritarianism, the economic system would lose its *laissez-faire* character, and the ideological belief in democracy would begin to fade. As one memo put it, the defeat of Great Britain and France would mean "the end of liberalism in trade, in thought and in social organization, and the effects of this would soon penetrate into every American home."[78]

In this crisis, America's identity, the American way of life, was believed to be at risk. Internationalists feared that the US would become a "garrison state," a nation whose survival had been purchased by the surrender of its liberal identity. Unlike the 1890s, when anti-imperialists sought to avert a self-inflicted wound to the nation's sense of self, the danger this time originated abroad. The United States felt threatened by Japanese expansion in East Asia in the 1930s because American images of China fed into a larger, global perspective on international relations; indeed, they always had, though never before in so menacing a way. It was not the loss of the open door in China that led American policy-makers to the point of seriously contemplating a war against Japan. More troublesome was a looming breakdown of civilization that portended a future in which the element of mutualism, the precondition of a positive sense of international identity, might disappear altogether. The loss of China alone would have been painful, but China's connection to the collapse of global civilization was far more distressing.[79] And the course of events in the Far East suggested that such a cataclysmic global meltdown was under way.

It was the assumption that one of the causes of World War I had been imperialism, widely held among Wilsonians, that gave such enormous weight to the crisis in the Far East. FDR, along with fellow internationalists in his administration, increasingly viewed Japanese and German expansion as part of a single global threat to which an Anglo-American division of labor might be applied: the British, and later the Soviets, could take on the Germans, while the Americans could handle the Japanese. This seemed to make sense especially as the Japanese depended on the United States for the bulk of their oil imports and were vulnerable to the threat of an embargo. In such an event, it was widely believed that the Japanese would pull back from their program of expansion. Putting a damper on the diplomacy of imperialism, it was hoped, might also help reduce the pressure of Hitler's expansionism in Europe. As for the possibility of a deal with Japan like those that had often been made in the past – a Pacific variation on the theme of appeasement – that could only make the European situation worse. From this Wilsonian perspective, the breakdown of cooperation in one region was consequentially related to conflict in the other.

The Wilsonian view of the diplomacy of imperialism as a contributory problem in a global crisis helped to tip the scales in favor of American intervention in the conflict. Though one cannot be absolutely certain, it seems likely that FDR would have taken the US into the war with Germany in any case, with or without a war in Asia. Despite Roosevelt's protestations to the contrary, the destroyers-for-bases deal of September 1940, the Lend-Lease Act of March 1941, and FDR's provocative convoying decisions and the revision of the neutrality acts later in the year suggest strongly that he was steering a course for participation in the war on the continent. But the prospect of participating in another European war was enormously controversial at the time. To have entered it solely on the basis of Roosevelt's artful manipulation of his powers as commander-in-chief would have caused problems with national unity and morale.

Would a tough line against Japan alone have been adopted in the absence of the European crisis? Certainly a few Wilsonians, like Stimson in 1931, favored action at a time when Germany was still a law-abiding citizen of the international community. But it is not clear that public support would have been present in an East Asia-only context. Nor is it certain that East Asian specialists in the State Department, contentiously divided between partisans of Japan and China, would have been able to make a united and unambiguous recommendation. One can see why a firm judgment would have been hard to come by, given America's sense of racial and civilizational superiority, its continued participation in the diplomacy of imperialism as a treaty power, the traditional absence of a compelling security stake in the region, and the cross-cutting economic interests in China and Japan. The strategic relevance of the Far Eastern situation, taken on its own regional terms, was far less obvious than the global significance that it derived from being connected via Wilsonian reasoning to the collapse of the European balance of power. Even today, in an era of more thoroughgoing global sensibilities, it is difficult in retrospect to equate Japan and Germany as moral evils or as equivalent geopolitical threats.

The showdown with Japan helped to sort out such difficulties. Complex though its relation to the European war was, it simplified matters enormously by starting the war in a way that instantly brought the support of what had been a seriously divided public opinion. In retrospect, the growth of public support for a tough line against Japan, even at the risk of war, made it easier to enter the global conflict through the Pacific back door. But the vindication of this tactical approach depended ultimately upon a convincing demonstration of the accuracy of the Wilsonian belief that the two explosive crises on different sides of the world were in fact inseparable. Japan's attack on Pearl Harbor and Germany's declaration of war a few days later confirmed the Wilsonian intuition about imperialism's incendiary importance.

The complicated connections between the crises in East Asia and Europe demonstrated in dramatic fashion how the diplomacy of imperialism, which in pre-Wilsonian days was not thought to be worth a war, could serve as a catalyst for a full-blown geopolitical conflagration that was in every way more serious than World War I. By 1941, the East Asian crisis had progressed from being a symbol of discord in the house of the great powers to a cause of their conflict. Inasmuch as the European war and the Sino-Japanese War – which until December 1941 remained two separate conflicts – were joined together by virtue of American participation, it is likely that there would not have been a *World* War II without the

Wilsonian view of imperialism. In the absence of the Wilsonian linkage between the diplomacy of imperialism in Asia and events in Europe, this war, like World War I before it, might have been a transatlantic drama with a Pacific sideshow – though a much larger sideshow, to be sure.[80]

The war marked the end of imperialism as a fashionable ideology and the end of racialism as an official doctrine (though obviously it did not mean the end of racism, which simply went underground). Sensing the ripeness of the historical moment, independence movements marshaled their strength in various colonies during the war, looking forward to decisive contests with their European overlords. This emergence of stiff resistance would sap imperialism of whatever glamour it retained. For their part, in many cases the white colonizers had long since discovered that the image of El Dorado had become, in reality, only an empire of fool's gold. World War II was also a watershed in America's formal relationship to imperialism. "The age of imperialism is ended," declared Undersecretary of State Sumner Welles in 1942.[81] Meanwhile, influential books like Henry Wallace's *The Century of the Common Man* and Wendell Willkie's *One World* openly called for the end of colonialism as a matter of global social justice.

It was no secret that Roosevelt wanted to see colonialism eliminated after the war, but, as with almost every aspect of FDR's policies, one cannot be absolutely certain why he was so set on the idea. No doubt his outlook was influenced by his heightened moral sensitivity to colonialism, fueled in part by growing doubts about the argument from civilization. While FDR possessed his full share of racist views, he was not sure that claims of superiority justified imperial rule. As he told one of his press conferences: "I often wonder what right, inherent right, you and I have to call any other nation backward. Have we a definite right to call any other nation backward? . . . Are they wholly uncivilized people? I wonder."[82]

FDR's moral objections were also aroused by his revulsion against European colonial misrule. "It's just plain exploitation of these people," he remarked after passing through Gambia on the way to Casablanca early in 1943.[83] With an over-the-hill Great Britain as the sole remaining major imperialist power, he felt free to voice ideas about imposing a death sentence upon colonialism that Wilson had been able to entertain only in a guarded way. In 1941 he told reporters that "any nationality, no matter how small, has the right to its own nationhood."[84] Following his chief's lead, Secretary of State Cordell Hull announced in 1942 that other colonial powers should follow the example set by the United States in the Philippines and "earnestly favor freedom for all dependent peoples at the earliest date practicable."[85]

Despite his doubts about its morality, most of FDR's hostility to colonialism was directed against its misapplication rather than against colonialism *per se*. Thus, he felt no embarrassment in advocating United Nations trusteeships – League of Nations mandates, essentially, but with greater international accountability – on the argument that immediate independence was often unrealistic. "For a time at least there are many minor children among the peoples of the world that need trustees," he had said.[86] The method here was also taken from the Wilsonian playbook: great power cooperation, under the mantle of trusteeship, in a "higher imperialism." But as a neo-Wilsonian internationalist it is also likely that he feared that imperialism, like an underground coal fire left unattended, might lead to another global conflagration among the great powers. "To deny the objectives of independence," he said on one occasion, "would sow the seeds of another world war."[87]

Just exactly how this might happen was not explicitly stated, but given FDR's emphasis on great power cooperation as the key to the postwar peace – his "four policemen" concept that found an institutional expression in the Security Council of the United Nations – one can infer his thinking on the dangers posed by imperialism. Because colonialism had come to be associated with exclusivity and selfishness, it was prima facie in tension with great power cooperation. Besides exciting jealously and competition, it set a bad precedent for the Soviet Union and its postwar territorial ambitions. With postwar colonial rebellions well nigh inevitable, the chance existed that the great powers might be sucked involuntarily into a renewed diplomacy of imperialism. Whatever the precise rationale, as the war approached its end, FDR was clearly looking forward to an end of imperialism and all its works.

The Cold War Era

All of FDR's readings of tea leaves failed to anticipate the Cold War with the Soviet Union or its consequences. As a result, policy in the postwar years did not follow the straight-forward anti-imperialist course that Washington had plotted in advance. Quite the contrary, many of the problems of imperialism and anti-imperialism that Americans had hoped would pass away re-emerged, albeit in altered forms, following the war. To a surprising extent, the confrontation between the Soviet Union and the United States, often viewed as a great power conflict whose center was in Europe, also featured an ideologically reshaped revival of the diplomacy of imperialism, thus providing the Cold War with the global dimension that was its most striking feature.

Contrary to expectations, the United States often wound up on the "wrong" side of colonial controversies in the post-war period. As relations with the Soviet Union went rapidly downhill after 1945, the US placed a premium on securing reliable European allies. Just as Wilson in Paris had needed to court the leading colonial powers, Cold War statesmen needed their help to buttress America's position in Europe after World War II. Consequently, if pushing for decolonization was thought likely to damage the political stability of an ally, the United States tended to look the other way. Though this was, in principle, not desirable from the Wilsonian world view – and American policy-makers were acutely conscious that it was not – geopolitical priorities clearly dictated that the US side with its allies. The American attitude, then, was quite conflicted. It was comprised in equal measures of an under-standing of the need for decolonization, a distrust of the political capacity of those same dependent peoples, and a willingness to subordinate anti-imperialist concerns to the exigencies of Cold War globalism.

The story played itself out time and again. In the case of the decolonization of the Netherlands East Indies, the United States was slow to align itself with the independence movement led by Sukarno, for fear that the Dutch government in The Hague, whose support for American policy on the continent was badly needed, might be politically crippled. Similarly with France. Although FDR had been bitterly critical of French rule in Indochina, the dread of undermining shaky pro-western governments in Paris led Washington to acquiesce in the postwar determination of France to forcibly restore its colonial rule in Indochina. South Africa was another case in point. The imposition of the policy of apartheid, a kind of hyper-segregation, by the Afrikaner governments was tolerated by Washington because Pretoria was rabidly anti-communist and because South Africa sat atop huge deposits of valuable strategic minerals.[88]

The episode that ran counter to this screenplay was the Suez crisis of 1956. Outraged by the decision of Egyptian President Gamal Abdal Nasser to nationalize the Suez Canal, the British, French, and Israelis launched an invasion of Suez in an attempt to restore the status quo. Only after President Eisenhower cut off the flow of oil and money to his allies did they agree to withdraw. But even here the United States sided with the Egyptians less out of sympathy for Nasser than from the Cold War fear that much of the "Third World" would gravitate toward the Soviet Union if America simply stood by and allowed its European allies to proceed with their scheme. Relations with the British and French, who were much stronger than they were a decade earlier, could be repaired, but it was not certain that the United States could withstand a global tide of nationalist outrage.

Even as decolonization picked up an irresistible head of steam, thus confirming the American belief that imperialism was a thing of the past, the United States rather unexpectedly became an imperial power of a new sort. In Europe this "empire by invitation" was the result of the continental nations, worried by their inability to fend off a Soviet threat, calling in the new world to redress the balance of the old. The Americans came and, thanks to the length of the Cold War and the willingness of America's allies to see the US shouldering most of the burden, they stayed. American generals commanded multinational NATO armies. American troops occupied Japan and Germany and, once the occupations were formally ended, stayed on to defend those countries from communism.

American troops based in Europe and elsewhere enjoyed imperial-style privileges. The Status of Forces Agreements signed with allies granted to the GIs a modern-day form of extraterritoriality. An educational imperium arose abroad as entrepreneurial colleges and universities sought to profit by providing American-style schooling abroad to GIs eager to get their professional tickets punched. Thus, while the colonial empires of other powers shrank, America's Cold War military imperium grew to huge proportions. By 1960, a million and a half Americans, 1 percent of the population, lived abroad.

This expansion included some new territorial additions. The navy, determined never again to allow another Pearl Harbor, demanded that the US hang on to forward positions it had conquered at great cost in the Pacific. Thus some Pacific islands north of the equator, formerly held by the Japanese were transferred to American control as a "strategic trust" under the supervisory umbrella of the UN Trusteeship Council, "an empire in all but name," according to one scholar.[89] Okinawa remained American-occupied until 1972, when control finally reverted to Japan. But, mostly, the US military gained its overseas footholds by treaty.

Most surprisingly, the Cold War found the United States becoming deeply embroiled as a player in a Cold War variation of the diplomacy of imperialism. As the tense situation in Europe was successfully stabilized in the mid-1950s by the emergence of a workable balance of power, Cold War stresses were displaced to less stable areas of the world, especially Asia and Africa. The confrontation with China over Korea had offered a foretaste of this problem. By 1960, the competition on the periphery had received high-level doctrinal sanction. Stalin's mercurial successor, Nikita Khrushchev, spoke of the ideological necessity of supporting "sacred wars" in the Third World, while John F. Kennedy responded to the challenge by arguing that the Cold War would be won or lost on the periphery. It was well understood in Washington, as one memo put it, that "The heightened appreciation of the fertile field that exists for communist maneuvering in the underdeveloped countries is one of the most radical innovations of the post-Stalin era."[90]

The Cold War challenged the progressive and Wilsonian thesis that conflict over peripheral regions bred even nastier great power confrontations. Actually, it inverted that logic. Great power military conflict, when it occurred at all, took place on the periphery in places like Korea and Indochina in large measure because they were considered unimportant in themselves. A great power war was thought less likely to break out in outlying areas, whereas military incidents in Germany, for example, might easily have triggered an all-out conflagration. Thus, in the absence of European instability, conflict in the Third World could be more readily contained. Nevertheless, it was dangerous enough, especially when the situation in Europe was still unsettled. In its Cold War garb, this geopolitical concern for the allegiance of Third World nations, where the US had few, if any, tangible interests at stake, made the diplomacy of imperialism the most volatile factor in world politics, as it had been for a time at the turn of the century. John Hay's maxim that "the world's peace rests with China" was doubtful when it was made, but it seemed the gospel truth in the 1960s.

The most conspicuous American intervention was in Vietnam. After the French failed to defeat the communist Vietminh and reinstall themselves as colonial masters of the country, they left in 1954 and agreed to a temporary partition between a communist North and an anti-communist South Vietnam.[91] The United States soon began to provide support to the government in the South and, when a rebellion by the communist Viet Cong threatened to swamp the regime, the Kennedy administration began to pour in advisers and equipment. Kennedy's successor, Lyndon Johnson, decided on a large-scale military involvement in 1965 as the only way of heading off a certain defeat. By 1968 more than 500,000 American soldiers were deployed in the country. But Vietnam was only the most conspicuous of a series of interventions, covert and overt, undertaken by the US in the so-called "Third World."

American interventionism generated anti-imperialist reproaches. From Marxist and socialist regimes, this sort of criticism was only to be expected, for their doctrine held that capitalist foreign policy was imperialist by its very nature. But the critique also gained a degree of respectability at home when anti-imperialism as a political and intellectual critique of US foreign policy re-emerged from its long slumber. In the 1950s, the intellectually numbing Cold War consensus had frozen virtually all criticism from the left, but by the 1960s widespread dissatisfaction with the war in Vietnam provided an eager audience for explanations that seemed to make sense of the nation's increasingly unpopular interventionism. A calming of tensions with the USSR, unprecedented domestic prosperity, and the revival of radical domestic idealism left a postwar generation of young people receptive to critiques that challenged the policy consensus.

The opposition to Vietnam was made up of a diverse coalition that included students opposed to the draft, radical young members of the New Left, African-Americans, Cold War establishment types who thought the nation had taken a wrong turn, and conservative realists who saw no national interests at stake in the war. For example, the influential pundit Walter Lippmann, long since having turned conservative, on one occasion wrote scaldingly that America was becoming "a bastard empire that relies upon force to achieve its purposes."[92]

But the chief intellectual critics were members of a neo-progressive "Wisconsin school" whose guru was the historian William Appleman Williams. In his classic work, *The Tragedy of American Diplomacy*, Williams argued that American foreign policy since the nineteenth century had been driven into interventionist predicaments abroad by a powerful ideology of open door expansionism. Setting no store by official protestations to the contrary, Williams and his followers insisted that US foreign policy was imperialistic through and through.[93] "It is time to stop depending so narrowly . . . upon an informal empire for our well-being and welfare," he insisted.[94] This argument was a bit tricky because it rested on the assumption that there was a variety of imperialism, an "imperialism of free trade," that was anti-colonial in form. By this standard, America's relatively hasty retreat from formal imperialism failed to exonerate it of the charges in the indictment. On the contrary, according to this view, this anti-colonial outlook had merely allowed US policy-makers to concentrate on creating a vast "informal empire" by means of economic expansion abroad.[95]

The argument went something as follows. Marching under the allegedly scientific and historically progressive banner of free trade, Americans were confident about the ability of the nation's economic power to control and shape other societies as dependencies in an "open world." This economic conquest of the world was intended to meet the needs of a capitalist system whose domestic crises of overproduction, which were structurally rooted in a maldistribution of income, could be resolved only by opening up new markets overseas. Inevitably, however, Washington's support of American economic interests abroad produced conflict with other nations, generated revolutionary unrest, and in the end led to war. Capitalizing on the widespread dissatisfaction with the Vietnam War, these arguments were successful enough to make them a permanent part of the developing field of US diplomatic history, a scholarly discipline that entered its "take-off" phase in the postwar years.

Despite its growing appeal, the anti-imperialist critique of US policy faced some insuperable problems in its attempt to establish itself as the dominant view of foreign relations. It was, for one thing, extraordinarily dependent upon a single foreign-policy event, the Vietnam War, for its popularity. Although the critique was intended to apply to American foreign policy as a whole, the ferment over Vietnam did not affect core Cold War undertakings like the NATO alliance, the nuclear arms race, or major American commitments in Asia to Taiwan, Japan, and Australia and New Zealand. The success of anti-imperialism as a political movement was attributable almost wholly to the discontent created by Vietnam and not with any deep dissatisfaction with the global assumptions of US foreign policy. Its political support in Congress, moreover, was in many ways ideologically less coherent and less well organized than the progressive coalition of the 1920s. The New Left, represented by the Students for a Democratic Society, was too anarchic in temperament, too radical and ideologically disordered, and too closely tied to young upper-middle-class college students to create a sustainable movement.

Intellectually, too, this brand of anti-imperialism was unable to provide a convincing explanation of foreign-policy behavior. The problem was evident in interpreting the Vietnam War. Time and again, the government denied that the United States was in Vietnam for reasons of naked self-interest. For example, in 1965 President Johnson told the AFL-CIO annual convention: "Everyday someone asks me why we are in Vietnam, and every day I want to answer: Not for economic reasons. We are spending our treasury, not producing it there."[96] Of course, the critical rejoinder was that the US was preserving the economic system rather than defending specific interests, but it was hard to see how a failure to act in Vietnam would have done any serious damage to American capitalism, either directly or indirectly. If anything, involvement, by producing price inflation, was economically far more harmful. The problem with Vietnam was not the transparency of America's economic interests; for most people, the puzzling thing was the absence of *any* perceptible interests, beyond the rather mysterious insistence on preserving "credibility."[97]

The anti-imperialist protests lost their vitality in 1971 after troop withdrawals ordered by President Nixon brought a steep decline in the monthly numbers of US battle deaths. As America's involvement in the war wound down, the anti-imperialist left lost its mass constituency. And as the Cold War evolved into a less confrontational phase in the brief thaw of *détente* that followed, interventions in the Third World declined in number and the kinds of geopolitical complications that bedeviled the country during the early years of the Cold War began to shrink to the vanishing point. By the 1970s, the US felt able to oppose apartheid in South Africa and the break-away white-supremacist settler regime of Ian Smith in Rhode-sia. The "great game" did resume for a time following the collapse of *détente* with Soviet intervention in Afghanistan in 1979 and American opposition to the leftist Sandinista regime in Nicaragua in the 1980s, but under much tighter constraints than in the early years of Cold War – in each case, direct US intervention was out of the question. The end of the Cold War in 1991 essentially ended the Cold War version of the diplomacy of imperialism.

As the twentieth century drew to a close, American foreign policy entered a new era. America's colonial dominion had been reduced to a small number of sparsely inhabited islands and Puerto Rico, which accounted for the bulk of the em-pire's population.[98] The end of the Cold War also shrank America's imperial role abroad by reducing the number of unilateral interventions and by downsizing the nation's over-seas military empire. Though the United States retained lead-ership in NATO, American troop levels in Europe were reduced to less than 20 percent of their historic high, thereby shrink-ing considerably the American imperium in Europe.

Anti-imperialism was also de-fanged as an issue by the con-tinued rapid pace of decolonization. As decolonization ap-proached its limits, anti-imperialism lost its real-world object. With the sum of UN member nations standing at 185, more than 125 sovereign countries had come into being since the end of World War II. To all intents and purposes, colonialism and the geopolitically inspired diplomacy of imperialism had come to an end. For a time in the 1970s, it even appeared to some observers that the global economic balance was shifting in favor of the Third World in the wake of the oil embargo imposed by the Organization of Petroleum Exporting Coun-tries in 1973.

Overall, though, high expectations were disappointed. While a temporary bonanza of oil revenues benefited some developing nations, they did not prove to be a panacea even for the most oil-rich among them. For the oil-poor, the run-up of oil prices imposed yet another massive foreign exchange burden. Many of the new nations fell into civil wars, lapsed into dictatorial rule, or saw their economic output decline in real terms in response to ill-conceived development schemes. Third World debt reached astronomical levels beyond the capacity of many nations to repay, while foreign aid, sometimes in sizable amounts, became a device for avoiding hard and unpopular economic decisions. Population outran resources and overwhelmed the ability of governments, which often demonstrated stunning incompetence, to lead the way to rapid modernization.

For those inclined to point the finger of blame outside their borders, the explanation for this unhappy turn of events appeared to lie in "neo-colonialism," the continuing control by the former mother country by indirect means. Because, according to this view, independence would continue to be a sham until all the economic apron strings had been cut, various forms of economic nationalism and socialism became fashionable. It would take decades of disastrous experimentation with home-grown varieties of socialism before some nations began to conclude that the nationalist cure was worse than the neo-colonial disease.

In the United States, the intellectual critique continued as a minority persuasion among historians of US foreign relations, though it declined in intensity in the aftermath of Vietnam and lost its radical edge. Many members of the open door school became more moderate, while some radical scholars went so far as to reject entirely their fire-breathing analyses of the 1960s. In the early 1980s, talk of a new synthesis suggested that the old debates no longer evoked the same all-or-nothing passions of earlier decades.

In the absence of concrete objects to stimulate interest, anti-imperialist critiques survived by taking on a more abstract form. By the 1990s, new intellectual fashions imported from

France had shifted attention away from hard political and economic critiques to intricate analyses of imperialist "discourses" in which it was hard to identify a villain or to determine if there was any villain at all, for that matter. At the extreme, arcane "post-structuralist" or "deconstructionist" modes of analysis identified language, not brute social facts of power, as the primary site upon which international domination was constructed. From this standpoint, the primary evil-doer was not the United States as a political entity, but impersonal "discourses" in which language governed humans rather than vice versa. This linguistic turn was part of a more general intellectual shift in which the social sciences and the humanities were taking a greater interest in cultural and ideological modes of analysis.

In other ways, though, the critique of American imperialism appeared to be alive and well, at least at first sight. Some of the most emotionally charged conflicts in the post-Cold War era had a decidedly anti-imperialist and anti-American coloration. The tension between Islamic and western values, with the United States usually viewed as the standard-bearer of the west, was only the most spectacular example of culturally defined antagonisms that were, like colonialism and the diplomacy of imperialism, played out in both the First and Third Worlds. Even fully westernized countries like France fretted about the domination of American movies, the infiltration of American words into the French language, the importation of American foods, and the penetration of American pop culture generally into the French way of life. An American ambassador in Paris noted sympathetically the French sense of "a threat to their identity," which made it necessary for them "to counter what they see as a menace to their culture and their society."[99]

Thus, in many quarters globalization was seen as the Americanization of the world. But if this was intended to be a reproach, it fell short of its target, as Americans saw little to be ashamed of in their ambition to recreate the world in the image of their nation. One did not need survey evidence to understand that most Americans continued to feel, deep in their bones, that the American way of life was the nation's chief export. Americans had long since abandoned any love of colonialism as a legitimate foreign-policy activity, but they continued to envision themselves as the champions of a universal empire of the spirit and way of life, the empire of modernity.

But was this imperialism?

6

Beyond Imperialism: The Empire of Modernity

One tends to think of imperialism as a *big* thing, a primal phenomenon. From the panoramic perspective of world history, imperialism is certainly that. But if the American experience with empire is set against the far more imposing European record, it comes off as a rather diminutive affair.[1] Granted, it was hardly insignificant for those peoples who were forcibly colonized by the United States. Yet it is clear that American imperialism was not only a rather frail addition to a family already full of robust and mature European siblings, but that it died during childhood. In retrospect, British journalist John A. Hobson, author of a classic study of imperialism, was far wide of the mark in predicting that "the same forces which are driving European states along the path of territorial expansion seem likely to act upon the United States."[2] By the time he made that forecast, America's imperialist moment had come and gone.

Imperialism was neither an idea with deep intrinsic appeal for Americans, nor a policy driven by powerful special interests. With the exception of the Caribbean, compelling motives of national security were absent. The acquisition of the Philippines was due to some unique circumstances and to the momentary appeal of a larger internationalist vision that had not yet been tested. Its charm faded quickly thereafter as a result of the domestic divisions that it generated and because the unpleasant realities of imperial administration failed to live up to their romantic advance billing. There was no way that the exaggerated claims on behalf of imperialism as a tonic for all that ailed Philippine and American society could be made good. Thus, except for Puerto Rico, which seemed strategically too important to let go, it did not take long before the white man's burden became merely burdensome.

American imperialism would have been short-lived even if it had been confined to a relationship between colonizer and the colonized, but its life span was further shortened by the enforced contact with other powers that came with admission into the imperial family. Imperialism failed to bring the untroubled cooperation and division of labor among the civilized powers that its proponents had anticipated. To nearly everyone's distress, it featured instead a competitive diplomacy of imperialism. In China, the United States as a treaty power found itself arrayed against this diplomacy by asserting, in a principled manner, various versions of the open door policy. In the Caribbean, the nation engaged in pre-emptive imperialism, justified by the communal rhetoric of civilization, as a way of preventing European empires from taking up residence in the western hemisphere. In short, American imperialism was at pains to avoid the diplomacy of imperialism.

Imperialism's luster was further tarnished when American policy-makers began to appreciate its geopolitical hazards. Through the 1920s, the diplomacy of imperialism, distasteful and repugnant as it was, did not constitute a serious threat to American interests or security as then defined. However reprehensible Russian or Japanese expansion into China, it was never considered worth a war. By the late 1930s, however, American internationalists concluded that it was no longer possible to deal with the diplomacy of imperialism by withdrawal or by the launching of principled protests. Because it had come to be viewed as an important element of a global threat to American security, it could not be ignored.

This history of half-hearted involvement and growing aversion might seem to suggest that the annexation of the Philippines was lacking in deep roots of the kind typically found in economic necessity and geopolitical interests. But the ideology that underlay imperialism proved to be quite deep, actually, much deeper and more durable in the end than the economic and geopolitical strategies pursued by the nation over the same span of time. Through all the frustrating encounters with refractory colonial realities and the diplomacy of imperialism, Americans retained their belief in the economic and cultural development of the non-industrial world *and* in the eventual cooperation of like-minded developed societies. Not only did this belief in civilization or modernization, which existed both prior to and after American imperialism, provide the justification for empire, it also furnished the ideological resources to go beyond it.

This is because imperialism, anti-imperialism, and American globalism were all outgrowths of the same underlying world view. America's experiment with imperialism was the product of a belief that it was a progressive policy for both the colonizers and the colonized. The attractiveness of empire lay in the likelihood of fraternal Anglo-American collaboration at the core and the promise of collaboration by the civilized powers at the periphery. In this sense, despite a number of historical accidents on the road to empire, imperialism was not an aberration, but a logical outgrowth of a growing conviction that the nation had a global future in a rapidly modernizing world. But it was not the only possible outcome. When it became clear that imperialism was subverting the vision of great power harmony and cooperation, it was rejected as a bad national policy and as a danger to international society.

Ironically, this abandonment of imperialism and all its works made possible the partial fulfillment of an even more ambitious global destiny. The more Americans distanced themselves from imperialism, the closer they came to reaching the promised land of a world civilization that they originally had hoped to enter by traveling the path of empire. But before a viable internationalism finally came into view, Americans also had to pass through a half-century of military globalism. In the end it was America's behavior as a world power in two world wars and the Cold War that cleared enough political space to allow this supranational idea to stay alive and eventually flourish. Without the American political commitment to internationalism, it is possible that globalization would not have proceeded as rapidly as it did or even that it might have been reversed.

As John Tomlinson has argued, in the modern world "What replaces 'imperialism' is globalisation."[3] As traditional imperialism has been eliminated, the trend toward creating a "global culture" has become a far more potent force for spreading civilization than first-generation imperialists would have imagined possible. Although Americans have turned their backs on colonialism, they have remained unflaggingly eager to modernize other peoples, whatever their level of development. Though critics gag at the enormous hubris of the idea of Americanizing the world, the notion has been enduringly popular, not only with the American public, but to a surprising extent with a world eager to enjoy not only the material benefits of the American way of life, but its cultural trappings as well.

It is globalization that many critics of US foreign relations have in mind today when they accuse the United States of cultural imperialism. But this breathtakingly ambitious empire of modernity is imperialist in only a metaphorical sense, for it is simultaneously more harsh and more tolerant than imperialism, more compelling but with greater scope for accommodation and resistance. Though it is easy to see it as a force making for the continued subaltern status of poorer nations, it is, at the same time, an historical experiment in progress that made possible the creation of an egalitarian world community that earlier imperialists could scarcely have imagined. Even some modern Marxists who see globalism as a new development agree that US "imperial expansion has nothing to do with imperialism."[4]

As a successor to imperialism, globalization is a quite different phenomenon, at the same time more devastating and more benign than its nationalist predecessor. In some ways it is far more encompassing in its reach than traditional methods of colonial control. In fact, modernity is the most destructive consequence that one can imagine of contact between developed and undeveloped societies.[5] That is because modernization is not cultural, but anti-cultural, a "negation of culture,"[6] which makes it much more ambitious and more potent than imperialism.

Globalization is not a temporary occupation of the world that, once lifted, would allow traditional cultural values to reassert themselves. It is, at its most ruthlessly effective, a juggernaut that utterly destroys traditional cultures - witness the declining number of languages spoken in the world today. As globalization gained momentum, traditional cultures were assaulted, transformed, and even annihilated by a steamroller of civilization that flattened everything in its path, including even the culture of the United States. To be sure, the process is far from playing itself out and cultural tenacity remains a basic fact of life, but with the advent of globalization we may be witnessing not only the death of particular cultures but the beginning of the end of culture itself, of the "givenness" of uniqueness and particularity, as the hallmark of the human condition.

And yet, to stress only the negative features of global modernization is clearly to take an unbalanced view, for it is not at all certain that it is a sinister development. For one thing, cultural particularism has had some serious problems of its own, including the tendency to look down upon other peoples and to act accordingly in some very nasty ways. At least the emergence of a world as scrambled as an omelet has helped to spread universal values of freedom, equality, and human dignity whose nobility and widespread appeal are hard to deny. Though quite uneven in its distribution of favors, it has brought once-undreamed-of material benefits to many with the promise of more to come.

Moreover, any critique of globalization that indicts it as the ultimate expression of cultural imperialism ought also to acknowledge, in fairness, that the political values that made globalization triumphant are the same values that put colonialism out of business and defeated the diplomacy of imperialism. In the course of two world wars and the Cold War, these values also vanquished the destructive geopolitics of modernity. In addition to replacing imperialism, then, globalization has also replaced traditional power politics - no small achievement.

Globalization should also not be confused with an Americanization of the world. Yes, the growth of a "global culture" has been stimulated by American economic and military muscle, but no nation has *that* much power. To a significant extent, globalization is the product of the seductiveness of the modern way of life. It differs from previous, and more cruel, conflicts of civilizations in which people were routinely "killed, infected, driven out, or largely replaced."[7] That side of things has not been entirely absent, of course, as native Americans can well attest, but there was another side to the process in which the human desire for personal freedom and material improvement played a part. Despite not infrequent lapses, usually occasioned by security concerns, Americans were guided by the belief that globalization was better promoted by mutual consent than by forcible submission.

While its success in the twentieth century depended on the United States, globalization is American only in a limited sense. Because globalization was always more a global process than an American project, a multi-lane superhighway rather than a one-way street, the American way of life was also transformed by globalization. As one historian has put it, "behind the phenomenon 'Americanization' lies the actual 'Europeanization' of the world."[8] Americanization, westernization, Europeanization, and globalization are just different names for a process that could not be confined to narrow nationalist channels.

The view of globalization as a predatory violator of cultures also fails to give much credit to colonized peoples for the capacity to resist, subvert, and turn to their own uses the policies of the occupiers. For example, according to one unsympathetic definition of imperialism, "while the stronger state's dominance is rarely absolute, it is often the major factor in determining the course and outcome of events within the weaker state."[9] This definition obviously rings true to critics of cultural imperialism, and it is even acceptable to some aggressive modernizers who insist that the United States ought to have been even more aggressive in exporting democracy – that, if anything, it was not imperialist enough.[10]

But culture, even under assault, has remained a potent force in its own right.[11] The power of cultural resistance was something that American proconsuls abroad experienced first hand, as witness the many failed attempts by Americans to produce cultural transformation in the areas under their control.[12] Despite their imperial power, Americans failed to imprint their way of life upon their subalterns. Filipinos remained Filipinos, Cubans became more Cuban than ever, Haitians have remained Haitians, and China created a modern national identity to oppose to the west. Ironically, the United States may have been most successful as a modernizer when not attempting to impose modernization directly upon other societies.

At the end of the twentieth century, it seemed clear that Americans had succeeded in creating a global setting that provided, in theory, a secure platform for market-based development. But, at this point, it was impossible to say with finality whether the experiment had been a success or a failure. And there was no way to foresee whether development would in fact be universalized. One of the few things that can be said with confidence is that we have no searchlights capable of illuminating the future. When it comes to predicting the future, it has been said, the world is divided into those who don't know and those who don't know that they don't know. Speeding down the murky road of history, we are hurtling into a dark tract of time that our weak headlights cannot penetrate.

Of necessity, then, forecasts, no matter how confidently put, are guided more by ideological predilections than by hard knowledge. But it is significant as a measure of the global popularity of modernization that the yardstick by which America is likely to be judged is the high standard that it has set for itself. The real question is whether globalization will produce an equitable global division of labor and a just standard of living for all peoples, along with democratic polities, or whether the system of political economy promoted by the United States will only widen the gap between haves and have-nots, between those who shape history to their own advantage and those who are its victims.

Much depends upon whether international trends will follow and expand upon the pattern of development already experienced by the industrialized nations. Perhaps the world economy, with its disturbing gap between winners and losers, is at a point analogous to that of domestic economies in the early stages of the industrial revolution, when vast disparities in wealth and power were the norm. Should development proceed to the point that most peoples begin to enjoy the benefits of middle-class status, the United States will have contributed to the most far-reaching program of expansion of all, the conquest of the earth by an empire of modernity. If it continues to fall far short of this goal,[13] the argument would swing decisively in favor of those critics who see globalization as a new form of imperial domination and exploitation. Either way, the fate of non-industrialized peoples will continue to be a crucial indicator of the state of modern civilization.

Notes

Notes to the Introduction

1   For a classic indictment of many of the traditional arguments, see James A. Field Jr, "American Imperialism: The Worst Chapter in Almost any Book," *American Historical Review*, 83 (1978), p. 665.

2   In recent years a new approach to the study of imperialism has come into vogue in which the emphasis has been on the study of rhetoric. Some notable examples are Amy Kaplan and Donald Pease (eds), *Cultures of United States Imperialism* (Durham: Duke University Press, 1993); David Spurr, *The Rhetoric of Empire: Colonial Discourse in Journalism, Travel Writing, and Imperial Administration* (Durham: Duke University Press, 1993); and, for Great Britain, Robert H. MacDonald, *The Language of Empire: Myths and Metaphors of Popular Imperialism, 1880–1918* (Manchester: Manchester University Press, 1994). Though they are absorbing and often useful as indicators of the general cultural milieu, cultural studies of this kind have a number of built-in shortcomings for my purposes: they tend to be too far removed from the policy process, which includes official decision-makers, administrators, and various interest groups, to offer convincing explanations of how foreign policy is made; they are too diffuse to explain the specifics of foreign-policy ideologies; they have a weak understanding of social structure and individual psychology; they neglect international politics; and they tend to be indifferent to the unpredictable play of events.

3   Frank Ninkovich, *Modernity and Power: A History of the Domino Theory in the Twentieth Century* (Chicago: University of Chicago Press, 1995), and *The Wilsonian Century: US Foreign Policy since 1900* (Chicago: University of Chicago Press, 1999).

4   See, *inter alia*, Richard Koebner and Helmut Dan Schmidt, *Imperial-*

ism: The Story and Significance of a Political Word, 1840–1960 (Cambridge: Cambridge University Press, 1965); Raymond Williams, *Keywords: A Vocabulary of Culture and Society* (London: Croom Helm, 1976), pp. 132–3; Wolfgang Mommsen, *Theories of Imperialism*, trans. P. S. Falla (New York: Random House, 1980); Jürgen Osterhammel, *Colonialism: A Theoretical Overview*, trans. Shelley L. Frisch (Princeton, NJ: M. Wiener, 1996).

5 Richard J. Barnet, *Roots of War* (Baltimore, MD: Penguin, 1971), p. 237.

6 For more complexities and imponderables, see the argument by David S. Landes, *The Wealth and Poverty of Nations* (New York: W. W. Norton, 1998), p. 37, which suggests that the collapse of the Roman empire may have been a calamity in the short run, but over the long haul "Europe's great good fortune lay in the fall of Rome and the weakness and division that ensued."

7 William H. McNeill, *The Shape of European History* (New York: Oxford University Press, 1974), pp. 173–4.

Notes to Chapter 1

1 D. K. Fieldhouse, *The Colonial Empires: A Comparative Survey from the Eighteenth Century* (New York: Delacorte Press, 1965), p. 178; Samuel Huntington, *The Clash of Civilizations and the Remaking of World Order* (New York: Simon and Schuster, 1991), p. 51.

2 William H. McNeill, *The Pursuit of Power: Technology, Armed Force, and Society since AD 1000* (Chicago: University of Chicago Press, 1982), pp. 260–1.

3 Walter Bagehot, *Physics and Politics* (New York: Knopf, 1946), p. 215.

4 Theodore Roosevelt, "Biological Analogies in History," in *The Works of Theodore Roosevelt* (National Edition, New York: C. Scribner's Sons, 1926), vol. 12, p. 49.

5 Alfred Thayer Mahan, who a decade later would be closely identified with the navalist rationale for imperialism, was at this time arguing, in his most famous work, that the role of a modern navy was to thwart blockades and keep open the approaches to the nation's seaports. But he concluded that "The motive, if any there be, which will give the United States a navy, is probably now quickening in the isthmus." See Mahan, *The Influence of Sea Power upon History, 1660–1805* (Englewood Cliffs, NJ: Prentice-Hall, 1980), p. 61.

6 Richard Olney to Philander Knox, January 29, 1912, Knox Papers, Library of Congress Manuscript Division, no. 16.

7 Quoted in H. W. Brands, *The Reckless Decade* (New York: St Martin's Press, 1995), p. 301.

8   Charles W. Eliot, *American Contributions to Civilization and Other Essays* (New York: Century, 1898), p. 377.

9   George F. Kennan, *American Diplomacy 1900–1950* (Chicago: University of Chicago Press, 1950), p. 8.

10   Or, as one formulation puts the classical alternatives, "predatory drive and preclusive defense." See George Liska, *Career of Empire: America and Imperial Expansion Over Land and Sea* (Baltimore, MD: The Johns Hopkins University Press, 1978), p. 108.

11   David S. Landes, "The Nature of Economic Imperialism," in Kenneth E. Boulding and Tapan Muskerjee (eds), *Economic Imperialism: A Book of Readings* (Ann Arbor: University of Michigan Press, 1972), pp. 134–8, rightly points out that special interests are always to be found, but that it is foolish to conclude from this that imperial policy was made exclusively on their account. To do so would be to confuse the part with the whole.

12   Indeed, that was the chief reason why a critic like John Hobson, in his classic work, *Imperialism: A Study* (London: J. Nisbet, 1902), believed that imperialism could easily be eliminated – the solution was simply to target and expose the few well-placed parasitic groups that were feeding off the body politic.

13   Kenneth R. Hoover, with James Marcia and Kristen Parris, *The Power of Identity: Politics in a New Key* (Chatham, NJ: Chatham House, 1997), p. 3. Among other works that stress the importance of identity are Peter J. Katzenstein (ed.), *The Culture of National Security: Norms and Identity in World Politics* (New York: Columbia University Press, 1996); Yosef Lapid and Friedrich Kratochwil (eds), *The Return of Culture and Identity in IR Theory* (Boulder, CO: Lynne Rienner, 1996); William Bloom, *Personal Identity, National Identity, and International Relations* (New York: Cambridge University Press, 1990); Lucian Pye, "Identity and the Political Culture," in Leonard Binder et al. (eds), *Crises and Sequences in Political Development* (Princeton, NJ: Princeton University Press, 1971), pp. 101–35. I would go even farther in asserting the importance of identity issues. In the modern era, thanks to the growing influence of ideology in international relations, identity issues have become more and more prominent. Identity is synonymous with modernity in many ways because it becomes problematic for the first time in modern times at the individual and social levels once society was desacralized and social status became a matter of achievement. Once national identity was rooted in the people, the changing definition of the people makes national identity problematic. If one were forced to list some of the factors that have produced this shift toward identity politics in international relations in the modern era, here are some suggestions, for starters: the rise of nationalism; the growing importance of universalist ideologies like liberalism and imperialism; the impact of decolonization; a decline in the incidence of territorial

expansion; the growing importance of public opinion; and the emergence of international organization. In combination, these developments have eased survival concerns while shifting the emphasis to problems of national self-definition. Indeed, the most grave foreign-policy crises through which the United States passed in the twentieth century were framed not in terms of survival, but instead focused on the survival of "the American way of life" – a cultural/ideological definition of security. According to Samuel Huntington, "efforts to define national interest presuppose agreement on the nature of the country whose interests are to be defined. National interest derives from national identity." See his "The Erosion of American National Interests," *Foreign Affairs*, 76 (September/October 1997), p. 28. That being said, identity is not the opposite of security, for the two quite clearly overlap in most cases. Thus, if a lobster fisherman were to discover that a disease organism was wiping out his supply of crustaceans, he would be losing both his means of subsistence and his way of life.

14   William James, "The Moral Equivalent of War," in *Memories and Studies* (New York: Longmans, Green, and Co., 1934), p. 281.

15   For a discussion of state weakness and growth in the late nineteenth century, see Fareed Zakaria, *From Wealth to Power: The Unusual Origins of America's World Role* (Princeton, NJ: Princeton University Press, 1998), pp. 90–127.

16   Kristin Hoganson, *Fighting for American Manhood: How Gender Politics Provoked the Spanish-American and Philippine-American Wars* (New Haven, CT: Yale University Press, 1998), pp. 132, 36.

17   For the argument that aggressiveness in foreign policy is to a significant extent rooted in the biological imperatives of the male sex, see Francis Fukuyama, "Women and the Evolution of World Politics," *Foreign Affairs*, 77 (September/October 1998), pp. 24–40. On the other hand, many feminists would argue that international violence is the result of male cultural conditioning rather than inborn drives.

18   Theodore Roosevelt, "Biological Analogies in History," in *Works of Theodore Roosevelt*, vol. 12, p. 55.

19   Theodore Roosevelt, "Washington's Forgotten Maxim," in *American Ideals and Other Essays, Social and Political*, rev. edn (New York: Knickerbocker Press, 1903), p. 258. For a work that puts some social-psychological meat on the bones of TR's masculine rhetoric, see Sarah Watts, "Rough Rider in the White House: Theodore Roosevelt and the Politics of Desire," unpublished MS, now in press.

20   Benedict Anderson, *Imagined Communities: Reflections on the Origins and Spread of Nationalism* (London and New York: Verso, 1991).

21   Quoted in Walter LaFeber, *The New Empire: An Interpretation of American Expansion 1860–1898* (Ithaca, NY: Cornell University Press, 1963), p. 250. Although the importance of public opinion and chance as causes of war are downplayed in a critique offered by Luis A. Pérez

Jr, *The War of 1898: The United States and Cuba in History and Historiography* (Chapel Hill, NC: University of North Carolina Press, 1998), pp. 57–80, it is still worth asking: would a war with Spain over Cuba have been possible, or desirable, without a strong shove from public opinion? Or, in the absence of a public outcry, would the prospect of a rebel victory on the island have been sufficient reason to intervene? I think not.

22 Julius Pratt, *Expansionists of 1898* (New York: Quadrangle Books, 1936), pp. 230–59.

23 From Morton Keller's summary of the Spanish-American War on the History Channel web site (at http://thehistorychannel.com/).

24 Quoted in William E. Leuchtenberg, "Progressivism and Imperialism: The Progressive Movement and American Foreign Policy, 1898–1916," *The Mississippi Valley Historical Review*, 39 (June 1952), p. 497.

25 Margaret Leech, *In the Days of McKinley* (New York: Harper, 1959), p. 179.

26 Quoted in Frank Freidel, *The Splendid Little War* (Boston: Little, Brown, 1958), p. 6.

27 Elihu Root to Cornelius N. Bliss, April 2, 1898, Root Papers, Library of Congress, as quoted in David Healy, *Drive to Hegemony: The United States in the Caribbean 1898–1917* (Madison: University of Wisconsin Press, 1988), p. 40.

28 However, the debate continues. The 1976 findings of a review initiated by Admiral Hyman Rickover in H. G. Rickover, *How the Battleship Maine was Destroyed* (Washington, DC: Government Printing Office, 1976) have recently been challenged by those who insist that the evidence is not inconsistent with an underwater mine as the cause of the explosion. See Thomas B. Allen (ed.), "A Special Report: What Really Sank the Maine," US Naval Institute, *Naval History Magazine* (at http://www.usni.org/Naval_History/NHallen.html). See also Steve Vogel, "The Maine Attraction: Historians, Engineers again Debating Cause of Explosion that Sank Battleship," *The Washington Post*, April 23, 1998.

29 Joseph E. Wisan, "The Cuban Crisis as Reflected in the New York Press," in Theodore P. Greene (ed.), *American Imperialism in 1898* (Boston: D. C. Heath, 1955), p. 42.

30 Spain declared war first on April 24. Madrid's willingness to accommodate American demands did not extend to the point of agreeing to US mediation, which would have been to relinquish Spanish sovereignty.

31 The Senate vote was 42–35; in the House, it was 311–6. The problem in the Senate was the war resolution's ambiguity about Cuba's status. Populists, silver Republicans, and many Democrats wanted recognition of the revolutionary Cuban government.

32 For the best account of the military side of the war, see David Trask,

The War with Spain in 1898 (New York: Macmillan, 1981).

33 Quoted in Sebastian Balfour, *The End of the Spanish Empire, 1898–1923* (Oxford: Clarendon Press, 1997), p. 44n.

34 Quoted in Ivan Musicant, *Empire by Default* (New York: Henry Holt, 1998), p. 518.

35 Of the total of 4,100 American military casualties, fewer than 400 soldiers died in battle and about 1,600 were wounded. The cost of the war was approximately 250 million dollars.

36 Quoted in Robert H. Ferrell, *American Diplomacy: The Twentieth Century* (New York: W. W. Norton, 1988), p. 43.

37 Geoffrey Perrett, as quoted in John Tebbel, *America's Great Patriotic War with Spain* (Manchester, VT: Marshall Jones Co., 1996), p. i.

38 In a classic essay on "Cuba, the Philippines, and Manifest Destiny," in *The Paranoid Style in American Politics and Other Essays* (New York: Vintage Books, 1997), pp. 145–87, Richard Hofstadter located the source of American imperialism in what he called the "psychic crisis" of the 1890s. Given the enduring power of Hofstadter's subtle and wide-ranging analysis, it is only fair to ask: does identity really improve conceptually upon his formulation? I believe that it does mark an advance, in a number of respects. First, identity faces simultaneously in two directions, inward and outward, whereas the analytical searchlight of the "psychic crisis" approach is aimed primarily at internal factors to the neglect of the international dimension. Second, identity-based foreign-policy behavior like the decision for imperialism does not necessarily require a sense of crisis. As I will argue later, the "normal" yearning for positive identification can be a powerful identity motive. Third, notwithstanding Hofstadter's fondness for sociological concepts, identity points to the need for a broad analysis of social and ideological factors such as race, history, territoriality, religion, ideology, gender, race, and class, whereas "psychic crisis" is more psychological in bent. Fourth, as an analytical tool, identity is more usefully contrasted as an alternative to traditional foreign-policy concerns with survival or security. Fifth, in the modern era, given the growing importance of ideology in international relations, it could be argued that there has been a shift to identity politics as traditional security issues have faded into the background. If this is indeed so, imperialism takes on a rather different, and far more complicated, meaning when viewed from a broader historical context than when viewed as the product of a "psychic crisis" unique to the 1890s.

39 For an argument that stresses positive identification with outsiders as a central aspect of identity formation, see, for example, Alexander Wendt, "Identity and Structural Change in World Politics," in Lapid and Kratochwil (eds), *The Return of Culture and Identity in IR Theory*. On p. 52, Wendt argues as follows: "I define self- and collective interest as effects of the extent to and manner in which social identities

involve an *identification* with the fate of the other ... In any given situation (it is the nature of identification [positive or negative] that determines how the boundaries of the self are drawn." See also George Herbert Mead, *Mind, Self, and Society* (Chicago: University of Chicago Press, 1934), on the importance of a "generalized other" to identity formation. What Erik Erikson had to say about individuals needing to build identity through identification with others applies equally to nations. See Erik H. Erikson, *Young Man Luther: A Study in Psychoanalysis and History* (New York: W. W. Norton, 1962), pp. 115, 117. For a more traditional, and limited, view of the identification dynamic as a process that works "towards internal group integration and cooperativeness, as well as towards external group aggressiveness," see Bloom, *Personal Identity, National Identity*, p. 113. Positive external identification, he believes (pp. 151–3), is at this stage only a desirable possibility.

40   Quoted in Leech, *In the Days of McKinley*, p. 323.

41   Straus to McKinley, May 12, 1898, in Ernest May, *Imperial Democracy: The Emergence of the United States as Great Power* (New York: Harper Torchbooks, 1973), p. 246.

42   In Pratt, *Expansionists of 1898*, p. 326.

43   Baron von Holstein to Bülow, in Holger Herwig, *Politics of Frustration: The United States in German Naval Planning, 1898–1941* (Boston: Little, Brown, 1976), pp. 32–3.

44   Quoted in Trask, *The War with Spain in 1898*, p. 454.

45   Lodge to TR, May 24, 1898, in Lodge, *Selections from the Correspondence of Theodore Roosevelt and Henry Cabot Lodge, 1884–1918* (New York: Scribner, 1925), vol. 1, p. 313.

46   Cited in Robert Kelley, *The Transatlantic Persuasion: The Liberal-Democratic Mind in the Age of Gladstone* (New York: Knopf, 1969), p. 345.

47   John Braeman, *Albert Beveridge: American Nationalist* (Chicago: University of Chicago Press, 1971), pp. 27–8.

48   Bayard Taylor, *A Visit to India, China, and Japan, in the Year 1853* (New York: G. P. Putnam, 1855), p. 268. See also Akira Iriye, *From Nationalism to Internationalism: Foreign Policy to 1914* (London: Routledge and Kegan Paul, 1977), p. 65.

49   Thomas Noer, *Briton, Boer, and Yankee: The United States and South Africa, 1870–1914* (Kent, Ohio: Kent State University Press, 1978), p. 40.

50   "How Colonies are Made: Great Britain's Wonderful Success in that Direction," *The New York Times*, August 9, 1895.

51   For republican expansionism, see Bradford Perkins, *The Creation of a Republican Empire, 1776–1865*, volume 1: *The Cambridge History of American Foreign Relations*, ed. Warren I. Cohen (New York: Cambridge University Press, 1993).

52 The continuities and discontinuities between earlier American expansion and the colonialism of the 1890s is another topic that cries out for deeper evaluation by historians.

53 Daniel T. Rodgers, *Atlantic Crossings: Social Politics in a Progressive Age* (Cambridge, MA: Harvard University Press, 1998), p. 52.

54 Herbert Croly, *The Promise of American Life* (Indianapolis: Bobbs-Merrill, 1965), p. 297.

55 William Justin Mann, *America in its Relation to the Great Epochs of History* (Boston: Little, Brown, 1902), p. 224.

56 Ernest May, *American Imperialism: A Speculative Essay* (New York: Atheneum, 1968), pp. 228–9. See also Christopher Endy, "Travel and World Power: Americans in Europe, 1890–1917, *Diplomatic History*, 22 (Fall 1988), p. 565; Others, like Milton Plesur, *America's Outward Thrust* (DeKalb, IL: Northern Illinois University Press, 1971), p. 236, see the expansionism of the 1890s as based on an "aversion to a world-wide imperialism from which we were excluded economically." Though I would bet my money on May's thesis, a definitive judgment on American perceptions of European imperialism awaits deeper research into late nineteenth-century sources. Amazingly, given the often desperate hunt by graduate students and scholars for workable research topics, the hypothesis ventured by May in *American Imperialism* remains untested.

57 Richard Olney, "Growth of our Foreign Policy," *The Atlantic Monthly* (March 1900) (at http://www.theatlantic.com/atlantic/election/connection/ foreign/olney.html). On Olney's complex, changing views, particularly on the Philippines and China policy, see Gerald G. Eggert, *Richard Olney: Evolution of a Statesman* (University Park, PA: Pennsylvania State University Press, 1974), pp. 179–81, 284–92.

58 Quoted in James C. Bradford (ed.), *Admirals of the New Steel Navy: Makers of the American Naval Tradition, 1880–1930* (Annapolis, MD: Naval Institute Press, c.1990), p. 42, also in Walter A. McDougall, *Promised Land, Crusader State: The American Encounter with the World since 1776* (Boston: Houghton Mifflin, 1997), p. 104.

59 Quoted in Julius Pratt, *America's Colonial Experiment: How the United States Gained, Governed, and in Part Gave Away its Colonial Empire* (New York: Prentice-Hall, 1950), p. 61.

60 Richard H. Miller (ed.), *American Imperialism in 1898: The Quest for National Fulfillment* (New York: John Wiley, 1970), p. 128.

61 On the logistics of the China trade, see James A. Field Jr, "American Imperialism: The Worst Chapter in Almost any Book," *American Historical Review*, 83 (1978), p. 667n.

62 Herbert Squiers to Andrew D. White, August 9, 1898, in Glenn C. Altschuler, *Andrew D. White: Educator, Historian, Diplomat* (Ithaca, NY: Cornell University Press, 1979), p. 246.

63 Rhoda E. A. Hackler, "The United States Presence in the Northern

Philippines prior to 1898 (II): The Political and Career Consuls," *Bulletin of the American Historical Collection*, 18 (1) (January–March 1990), pp. 49–72. My thanks to Ed Miller of Harvard University for pointing out this source.

64 Lewis L. Gould, *The Presidency of William McKinley* (Lawrence: University of Kansas Press, 1980), pp. 136–43.

65 Robert C. Bannister, *Social Darwinism: Science and Myth in Anglo-American Social Thought* (Philadelphia: Temple University Press, 1979), pp. 226–42. For the confusion between Darwinism and Spencerianism, see Peter J. Bowler, *The Non-Darwinian Revolution: Reinterpreting a Historical Myth* (Baltimore, MD: The Johns Hopkins University Press, 1988), pp. 156–65. Darwinism, it now seems clear, was part of a wider current of evolutionist thought in the late nineteenth century, much of which was progressive in character and which could easily take an anti-imperialist turn. In support of this view, see Paul Crook, *Darwinism, War and History: The Debate over the Biology of War from the 'Origin of Species' to the First World War* (Cambridge: Cambridge University Press, 1994), pp. 93–7. For other discussions of evolutionism, see George W. Stocking Jr, *Race, Culture, and Evolution: Essays in the History of Anthropology* (New York: Free Press, 1968) and *Victorian Anthropology* (New York: Free Press, 1987); and J. W. Burrow, *Evolution and Society: A Study in Victorian Social Theory* (Cambridge: Cambridge University Press, 1966).

66 A. E. Campbell, "The Paradox of Imperialism: The American Case," in Jürgen Osterhammel and Wolfgang J. Mommsen (eds), *Imperialism and After: Continuities and Discontinuities* (London: Allen and Unwin, 1986), pp. 35–6. See chapter 5 for a more detailed discussion of imperialist internationalism.

67 The margin was not quite as close as the numbers would at first seem to indicate. A few senators would have been willing to vote for the treaty if absolutely necessary to prevent its defeat. Then, too, eight anti-imperialist senators would not be returning to the next Congress.

68 Quoted in Daniel Schirmer, *Republic or Empire: American Resistance to the Philippine War* (Morristown, NJ: Schenkman, 1972), p. 108.

69 The racial critique leveled some 30 years earlier by the eloquent "48-er," Carl Schurz, in discussing the implications of annexing the Dominican Republic, still had appeal in the 1890s: "Have you thought of it, what this means? . . . fancy ten or twelve tropical States added to the southern States we already possess; fancy the Senators and Representatives of ten or twelve millions of tropical people, people of Latin race mixed with Indian and African blood . . . fancy them sitting in the halls of Congress, throwing the weight of their intelligence, their morality, their political notions and habits, their prejudices and passions, into the scale of the destinies of this Republic; and, what is more, fancy the Government of this Republic making itself responsible for order and

security and republican institutions in such States, inhabited by such people; fancy this, and then tell me, does not your imagination recoil from the picture?" Quoted in Robert L. Beisner, *Twelve against Empire: The Anti-imperialists, 1898–1900* (New York: McGraw-Hill, 1971), pp. 23–4.

70 Edwin Burritt Smith, "Shall the United States Have Colonies?," address to the Second National Social and Political Conference, Detroit, Michigan, June 29, 1901 (at http://www.boondocksnet.com/ailtexts/ ebs0601.html) in Jim Zwick (ed.), *Anti-imperialism in the United States, 1898–1935* (at http://www.boondocksnet.com).

71 William B. Gatewood Jr, *Black Americans and the White Man's Burden 1898–1903* (Urbana: University of Illinois Press, 1975), p. 180.

72 Frederick Merk, *Manifest Destiny and Mission in American History: A Reinterpretation* (New York: Vintage Books, 1963), p. 247.

73 The imperialist position on race was moderate in the overall scheme of things. Analytically, the possibilities were: (1) a hard racism that ruled out any possibility of closing the gap in civilization among races; (2) Lamarckism, a hybrid concept that combined race and culture so that learned characteristics were thought to be hereditarily transmissible; and (3) a cultural view that saw non-white societies as historically retrograde but capable of learning. Most imperialists seemed to favor Lamarckism, which was the reigning scientific outlook in the 1890s. On the emergence of Lamarckism, see Stocking Jr, *Race, Culture, and Evolution*, and Peter J. Bowler, *The Eclipse of Darwinism: Anti-Darwinian Evolution Theories in the Decade around 1900* (Baltimore, MD: The Johns Hopkins University Press, 1983).

74 Quoted in David Healy, *US Expansionism: The Imperialist Urge in the 1890s* (Madison: University of Wisconsin Press, 1970), p. 33.

75 Bradford Perkins, *The Great Rapprochement: England and the United States 1895–1914* (New York: Atheneum, 1968), p. 83, argues convincingly that "race" as used then actually translated into what today we would call cultural solidarity. For the early development of the sense of global Anglo-Saxon mission, see Reginald Horsman, *Race and Manifest Destiny: The Origins of American Racial Anglo-Saxonism* (Cambridge, MA: Harvard University Press, 1981), pp. 272–97. See also the chapter on Anglo-American amity in Charles S. Campbell, *The Transformation of American Foreign Relations 1865–1900* (New York: Harper and Row, 1976), pp. 319–37.

76 Louis Fischer, *Gandhi: His Life and Message for the World* (New York: Mentor Books, 1960), p. 61.

77 Beisner, *Twelve against Empire*, p. 15.

78 Quoted in Schirmer, *Republic or Empire*, p. 116.

79 Letter to Boston *Evening Transcript*, March 1, 1899, in Daniel B. Schirmer and Stephen Rosskamm Shalom (eds), *The Philippines Reader: A History of Colonialism, Neocolonialism, Dictatorship, and Resist-*

ance (Boston: South End Press, 1987), p. 29.

80   Roosevelt to Mahan, December 13, 1897, in Elting E. Morison (ed.), *The Letters of Theodore Roosevelt* (Cambridge, MA: Harvard University Press, 1951), vol. 1, p. 741.

81   William C. Widenor, *Henry Cabot Lodge and the Search for an American Foreign Policy* (Berkeley, CA: University of California Press, 1980), p. 112n.

82   Quoted in May, *Imperial Democracy*, p. 259.

83   Quoted in Anders Stephanson, *Manifest Destiny: American Expansion and the Empire of Right* (New York: Hill and Wang, 1995), p. 88.

84   Quoted in Michael Schaller, *The United States and China in the Twentieth Century* (New York: Oxford University Press, 1980), p. 16.

Notes to Chapter 2

1   Leon Wolff, *Little Brown Brother: How the United States Purchased and Pacified the Philippines* (New York: Oxford University Press, 1991), p. 16.

2   Henry Norman, *The Peoples and Politics of the Far East* (New York: C. Scribner's Sons, 1895), p. 175.

3   Alden March, *The History and Conquest of the Philippines and our Other Island Possessions* (New York: Arno Press, repr. edn, 1970), p. 244.

4   Quoted in Henry F. Graff (ed.), *American Imperialism and the Philippine Insurrection* (Boston: Little, Brown, 1969), p. 33.

5   Glenn Anthony May, "The Unfathomable Other: Historical Studies of US-Philippine Relations," in Warren I. Cohen (ed.), *Pacific Passages: The Study of American-East Asian Relations on the Eve of the Twenty-first Century* (New York: Columbia University Press, 1996), p. 286; Ken De Bevoise, *Agents of Apocalypse: Epidemic Disease in the Philippines* (Princeton, NJ: Princeton University Press, 1995).

6   Fred Poole and Max Vanzi, *Revolution in the Philippines: The United States in a Hall of Cracked Mirrors* (New York: McGraw-Hill, 1984), p. 171.

7   Daniel Headrick, *The Tools of Empire: Technology and European Imperialism in the Nineteenth Century* (New York: Oxford University Press, 1981), pp. 58–73.

8   Quoted in Kristin Hoganson, *Fighting for American Manhood: How Gender Politics Provoked the Spanish-American and Philippine-American Wars* (New Haven, CT: Yale University Press, 1998), p. 184.

9   Ibid., p. 188.

10   Richard E. Welch Jr, *Response to Imperialism: The United States and*

the Philippine War, 1899–1902 (Chapel Hill, NC: University of North Carolina Press, 1965), pp. 98–9.

11 Hoganson, *Fighting for American Manhood*, p. 199.

12 See Glenn Anthony May, *Social Engineering in the Philippines: The Aims, Execution, and Impact of American Colonial Policy, 1900–1913* (Westport, CT: Greenwood Press, 1980), p. xvii.

13 Cited in Theodore Friend, *Between Two Empires: The Ordeal of the Philippines, 1929–46* (New Haven, CT: Yale University Press, 1965), p. 35.

14 Julius Pratt, *America's Colonial Experiment: How the United States Gained, Governed, and in Part Gave Away its Colonial Empire* (New York: Prentice-Hall, 1950), p. 163.

15 Quoted in Peter Stanley, *A Nation in the Making: The Philippines and the United States, 1899–1921* (Cambridge, MA: Harvard University Press, 1974), pp. 60–1.

16 Newspaper report of a lecture in Harrisburg, Pennsylvania [February 24, 1900], in Arthur Link et al. (eds), *The Papers of Woodrow Wilson* (Princeton, NJ: Princeton University Press, 1966–94), vol. 11, p. 440.

17 Quoted in Emily Rosenberg, *Financial Missionaries to the World: The Politics and Culture of Dollar Diplomacy 1900–1930* (Cambridge, MA: Harvard University Press, 1999), p. 39.

18 In Graff, *American Imperialism and the Philippine Insurrection*, p. 124.

19 Quoted in Stanley, *A Nation in the Making*, p. 56.

20 Quoted in Bonifacio S. Salamanca, *The Filipino Reaction to American Rule, 1901–1913* (Hamden, CT: The Shoe String Press, 1968), p. 64.

21 Sung Yong Kim, *United States-Philippine Relations, 1946–1956* (Washington, DC: Public Affairs Press, 1968), p. 15.

22 H. W. Brands, *Bound to Empire: The United States and the Philippines* (New York: Oxford University Press, 1992), p. 67.

23 Pratt, *America's Colonial Experiment*, p. 201.

24 Brands, *Bound to Empire*, p. 75.

25 Wolff, *Little Brown Brother*, p. 17.

26 See Kenton J. Clymer, "Protestant Missionaries and American Colonialism in the Philippines, 1899–1916: Attitudes, Perceptions, Involvement," in Peter W. Stanley (ed.), *Reappraising an Empire: New Perspectives on Philippine-American History* (Cambridge, MA: Harvard University Press, 1984), pp. 144–70.

27 Brands, *Bound to Empire*, p. 70.

28 Quoted in Stuart Creighton Miller, *"Benevolent Assimilation": The American Conquest of the Philippines, 1899-1903* (New Haven, CT: Yale University Press, 1982), p. 139.

29 Quoted in Stanley, *A Nation in the Making*, p. 14.

30 V. G. Kiernan, *America: The New Imperialism* (London: Zed Press, 1978), p. 1.

31 Brands, *Bound to Empire*, p. 78.

32 Ibid., p. 96.

33 Tony Smith, *The Pattern of Imperialism: The United States, Great Britain, and the Late-Industrializing World since 1815* (New York: Cambridge University Press, 1981), pp. 150–1.

34 Robert Pringle, *Indonesia and the Philippines: American Interests in Island Southeast Asia* (New York: Columbia University Press, 1980), p. 121.

35 Tony Smith, *America's Mission: The United States and the Worldwide Struggle for Democracy in the Twentieth Century* (Princeton, NJ: Princeton University Press, 1994), pp. 54–5.

36 Pratt, *America's Colonial Experiment*, p. 294.

37 From the Boston *Evening Transcript*, June 3, 1898, in Daniel B. Schirmer and Stephen Rosskamm Shalom (eds), *The Philippines Reader: A History of Colonialism, Neocolonialism, Dictatorship, and Resistance* (Boston: South End Press, 1987), p. 21.

38 Brands, *Bound to Empire*, p. 163.

39 Reed J. Irvine, "American Trade with the Philippines," in Robert J. Barr (ed.), *American Trade with Asia and the Far East* (Milwaukee, WI: Marquette University Press, 1959), p. 175.

40 Brands, *Bound to Empire*, p. 68.

41 Quoted in Roxanne Lynn Doty, *Imperial Encounters: The Politics of Representation in North-South Relations* (Minneapolis: University of Minnesota Press, 1996), p. 36.

42 Stanley, *A Nation in the Making*, p. 32.

43 According to a census document: "[with] the establishment of more rapid and frequent means of communication, whereby they could be brought into more frequent contact with each other, and with the general spread of education, the tribal distinctions which now exist will gradually disappear and the Filipino will become a numerous and homogeneous English-speaking race, exceeding in intelligence and capacity all other peoples of the Tropics." From Vicente L. Rafael, "White Love: Surveillance and Nationalist Resistance in the US Colonization of the Philippines," in Amy Kaplan and Donald Pease (eds), *Cultures of United States Imperialism* (Durham: Duke University Press, 1993), p. 196.

44 Salamanca, *The Filipino Reaction to American Rule*, p. 79.

45 Quoted in May, *Social Engineering*, pp. 91–2.

46 Ibid., p. 101.

47 Quoted in Doty, *Imperial Encounters*, p. 39.

48 Jürgen Osterhammel, *Colonialism: A Theoretical Overview*, trans. Shelley L. Frisch (Princeton, NJ: M. Wiener, 1996), p. 102.

49 Quoted in Ralph Eldin Minger, *William Howard Taft and United States Foreign Policy: The Apprenticeship Years, 1900–1908* (Urbana: University of Illinois Press, 1975), p. 52.

50 Quoted in Schirmer and Shalom (eds), *The Philippines Reader*, p. 26.

51 TR to Taft, August 21, 1907, in Elting E. Morison (ed.), *The Letters of Theodore Roosevelt* (Cambridge, MA: Harvard University Press, 1951), vol. 5, pp. 761–2.

52 From a strategic standpoint, probably the most sensible proposal for the future of the islands, although one that stood no chance of success, was briefly entertained by Henry Cabot Lodge: turn over the Philippines to the British in exchange for some of Britain's holdings in the Caribbean. See William C. Widenor, *Henry Cabot Lodge and the Search for an American Foreign Policy* (Berkeley, CA: University of California Press, 1980) p. 115.

53 William J. Pomeroy, *American Neo-colonialism: Its Emergence in the Philippines and Asia* (New York: International Publishers, 1970), pp. 222–3.

54 Annual message of December 3, 1901, quoted in David H. Burton, *Theodore Roosevelt: Confident Imperialist* (Philadelphia: University of Pennsylvania Press, 1968), p. 84.

55 TR to Silas McBee, August 27, 1907, in Morison (ed.), *Letters*, vol. 5, p. 776.

56 Theodore Roosevelt, *Autobiography* (New York, 1913), reprinted in *The Works of Theodore Roosevelt* (National edition, New York: C. Scribner's Sons, 1926), vol. 20, p. 492.

57 Stanley Karnow, *In our Image: America's Empire in the Philippines* (New York: Random House, 1989), pp. 251–2.

58 Pratt, *America's Colonial Experiment*, p. 302.

59 Theodore Roosevelt Jr, *Colonial Policies of the United States* (New York: Doubleday, Doran, 1937), p. 179.

60 Inasmuch as it was the global dimension of the American position in China that was responsible for the war with Japan, the Philippines proved to be irrelevant to the core issues of East Asian politics – hence another anti-imperialist prediction was completely off base. For China's role in US diplomacy in the 1930s, see chapter 5.

61 Karnow, *In our Image*, pp. 330–2.

62 *Foreign Relations of the United States, 1950*, volume 6: *Eastern Europe; The Soviet Union* (Washington, DC: USGPO, 1969), pp. 1514–20.

63 Nick Cullather, *Illusions of Influence: The Political Economy of United States–Philippines Relations, 1942–1960* (Stanford, CA: Stanford University Press, 1994), p. 140.

64 Brands, *Bound to Empire*, p. 337.

65 *TIME ASIA*, April 27, 1998, vol. 151, no. 16 (at http://cgi.pathfinder.com/time/asia/magazine/1998/980427/philippines4.html).

66 Quoted in *The New York Times*, July 27, 1999, A: 17.

67 *Asiaweek*, May 8, 1998 (at http://members.tripod.com/~chapelnet_2/asiaweek1.html).

68 For definitions and examples of the varieties of indirect rule, see

Osterhammel, *Colonialism*, pp. 51–2.

69 On this point, see Pierre Bourdieu, *Distinction: A Social Critique of the Judgment of Taste*, trans. Richard Nice (Cambridge, MA: Harvard University Press, 1984), p. 23.

70 Akira Iriye, "Robinson and Gallagher in the Far East: Japanese Imperialism," in Wm Roger Louis (ed.), *Imperialism: The Robinson and Gallagher Controversy* (New York: New Viewpoints, 1976), p. 224.

71 Cullather, *Illusions of Influence*, p. 153.

72 Shirley Jenkins, *American Economic Policy toward the Philippines* (Stanford, CA: Stanford University Press, 1954), p. 166.

Notes to Chapter 3

1 It is still difficult to quarrel with Julius Pratt's judgment that "the dominant motive was clearly political and strategic rather than economic": Julius Pratt, *America's Colonial Experiment: How the United States Gained, Governed, and in Part Gave Away its Colonial Empire* (New York: Prentice-Hall, 1950), p. 116. Unfortunately, this approach makes it seem as if American vital interests in the region during these years were self-evident and constant when, in fact, the nation's regional stake was periodically being redefined in global terms that differed substantially from the rationale for regionalism offered, say, in 1823. Because American internationalism as a whole had an unsettled definition of the national interest throughout at least the first half of the twentieth century, that indeterminacy also carried over to the way in which it defined US interests in Latin America. In a modern context, determining what was "political" and what was "strategic" could be very puzzling. For a more detailed argument, see Frank Ninkovich, *Modernity and Power: A History of the Domino Theory in the Twentieth Century* (Chicago: University of Chicago Press, 1995).

2 See Ninkovich, *Modernity and Power*, and Frank Ninkovich, *The Wilsonian Century: US Foreign Policy since 1900* (Chicago: University of Chicago Press, 1999).

3 See chapter 5 for a discussion of such complexities.

4 Quoted in Peter H. Smith, *Talons of the Eagle: Dynamics of US–Latin American Relations* (New York: Oxford University Press, 1996), p. 63.

5 Cole Blasier, *The Hovering Giant: US Responses to Revolutionary Change in Latin America, 1910–1985*, rev. edn (Pittsburgh, PA: University of Pittsburgh Press, 1985), pp. 5, 100.

6 John H. Coatsworth, *Central America and the United States: The Clients and the Colossus* (New York: Twayne, 1994), p. 10.

7 Memo by Alvey Adee, in Richard D. Challener, *Admirals, Generals, and American Foreign Policy, 1898–1914* (Princeton, NJ: Princeton University Press, 1973), p. 265.

8   Quoted in David Spurr, *The Rhetoric of Empire: Colonial Discourse in Journalism, Travel Writing, and Imperial Administration* (Durham: Duke University Press, 1993), p. 31.

9   Knox speech, June 15, 1910, Knox Papers, Library of Congress Manuscript Division, box 45.

10 It is impossible to quarrel with the unpleasant evidence produced by critical histories such as Mark T. Berger's, *Under Northern Eyes: Latin American Studies and US Hegemony in the Americas 1898–1990* (Bloomington, IN: Indiana University Press, 1995). In this case, however, I would take issue with one of his central contentions: that the "ideas central to any discourse usually remain unexamined" (p. 9). Not only were they often articulated early in the twentieth century, most people would hew to these ideas today, even with the benefits of discursive analysis to point out their biases. Indeed, in the case of attitudes toward Africa, they have made an amazingly open comeback.

11 TR to Charles W. Eliot, April 4, 1904, in Elting E. Morison (ed.), *The Letters of Theodore Roosevelt* (Cambridge, MA: Harvard University Press, 1951), vol. 4, p. 769.

12 John H. Johnson, *Latin America in Caricature* (Austin: University of Texas Press, 1980), offers abundant evidence from the cartoon literature of the many ways in which Latin Americans were stereotyped.

13 Senator Teller of Colorado was himself motivated in part by the desire to protect beet sugar interests in his state that might have suffered in the event of Cuba's annexation.

14 Quoted in Richard Olney, "Growth of our Foreign Policy," *Atlantic Monthly*, 85 (March 1900), p. 291.

15 Quoted in Smith, *Talons of the Eagle*, p. 51.

16 Quoted in Louis A. Pérez Jr, *Cuba under the Platt Amendment, 1902–1934* (Pittsburgh, PA: University of Pittsburgh Press, 1986), p. 51.

17 Major J. E. Runcie, "American Misgovernment of Cuba," *North American Review*, 170 (February 1903), as quoted in Akira Iriye, *From Nationalism to Internationalism: US Foreign Policy to 1914* (London: Routledge and Kegan Paul, 1977), p. 316.

18 Root to Leonard Wood, February 9, 1901, in David A. Healy, *The United States in Cuba, 1898–1902* (Madison: University of Wisconsin Press, 1963), pp. 156–7.

19 *Literary Digest*, 22 (February 21, 1901), p. 152, in Healy, *The United States in Cuba*, p. 158.

20 Quoted in Walter LaFeber, *The Cambridge History of American Foreign Relations*, volume 2: *The American Search for Opportunity, 1865–1913* (New York: Cambridge University Press, 1993), p. 130.

21 Shafter to Adjutant General of the Army, August 16, 1898, quoted in José M. Hernández, *Cuba and the United States: Intervention and Militarism, 1868–1933* (Austin: University of Texas Press, 1993), p. 60.

22 Hernández, *Cuba and the United States*, p. 58.

23 Lars Schoultz, *Beneath the United States: A History of United States Policy toward Latin America* (Cambridge, MA: Harvard University Press, 1998), p. 128.

24 Quoted in LaFeber, *The American Search for Opportunity*, p. 149.

25 Quoted in Luis A. Pérez Jr, *The War of 1898: the United States and Cuba in History and Historiography* (Chapel Hill, NC: University of North Carolina Press, 1998), p. 49.

26 Wood to TR, July 12, 1899, as quoted in Jack C. Lane, *Armed Progressive: General Leonard Wood* (San Rafael, CA: Presidio Press, 1978), p. 91.

27 Hermann Hagedorn, *Leonard Wood: A Biography* (New York: Kraus Reprint Co., 1969), vol. 1, p. 333.

28 Lester D. Langley, *The Banana Wars: An Inner History of American Empire, 1900–1934* (Lexington, KY: University Press of Kentucky, 1983), p. 46.

29 David Lockmiller, *Magoon in Cuba: A History of the Second Intervention, 1906–1909* (Chapel Hill, NC: University of North Carolina Press), 1938), p. 185.

30 For an account sympathetic to the technocratic reformism of the US army, see Allan Reed Millett, *The Politics of Intervention: The Military Occupation of Cuba 1906–1909* (Columbus: Ohio State University Press, 1968).

31 Quoted in Pérez, *Cuba under the Platt Amendment*, p. 32.

32 *The New York Times*, November 20, 1898.

33 Pérez, *Cuba under the Platt Amendment*, pp. 188–9.

34 Luis A. Pérez Jr, *Cuba and the United States: Ties of Singular Intimacy* (Athens: University of Georgia Press, 1990), p. 146.

35 David McCullough, *The Path between the Seas: The Creation of the Panama Canal 1870–1914* (New York: Simon and Schuster, 1977), p. 613.

36 Quoted in Schoultz, *Beneath the United States*, p. 153.

37 San Francisco speech of May 7, 1912, Knox Papers, box 46.

38 Albert Bushnell Hart, *The Foundations of American Foreign Policy* (New York: Macmillan, 1901), p. 238.

39 Alfred Thayer Mahan, "Hawaii and our Future Sea Power," in *The Interest of America in Sea Power, Present and Future* (Boston: Little, Brown, 1898), p. 52.

40 John Major, *Prize Possession: The United States and the Panama Canal 1903–1979* (New York: Cambridge University Press, 1993), p. 44.

41 Quoted in J. Michael Hogan, *The Panama Canal in American Politics: Domestic Advocacy and the Evolution of Policy* (Carbondale, IL: Southern Illinois University Press, 1986), p. 65.

42 Major, *Prize Possession*, p. 57.

43 Letter of December 15, 1903, quoted in Lawrence O. Ealy, *Yanquí*

Politics and the Isthmian Canal (University Park, PA: Pennsylvania State University Press, 1971), p. 63.

44 As usual, historians are a contentious lot, and not all are quick to condemn TR's actions in this affair. Frederick W. Marks Jr, *Velvet on Iron: The Diplomacy of Theodore Roosevelt* (Lincoln: University of Nebraska Press, 1979), pp. 96–105, makes a spirited defense of TR's seizure of Panama, while Richard H. Collin, *Theodore Roosevelt, Culture, Diplomacy, and Expansion: A New View of American Imperialism* (Baton Rouge: Louisiana State University Press, c.1985), emphasizes the sincerity of the argument from civilization.

45 Major, *Prize Possession*, p. 72.

46 Quoted in Walter LaFeber, *The Panama Canal: The Crisis in Historical Perspective* (New York: Oxford University Press, 1989), p. 63.

47 Quoted in Walter LaFeber, *Inevitable Revolutions: The United States in Central America* (New York: W. W. Norton, 1984), p. 37.

48 Emily Rosenberg, *Financial Missionaries to the World: The Politics and Culture of Dollar Diplomacy 1900–1930* (Cambridge, MA: Harvard University Press, 1999), p. 50.

49 Nancy Mitchell, *The Danger of Dreams: German and American Imperialism in Latin America* (Chapel Hill, NC: University of North Carolina Press, 1999).

50 See chapter 5 for an explanation of how the Roosevelt Corollary was part of a larger global response to the diplomacy of imperialism.

51 Quoted in Langley, *The Banana Wars*, p. 66.

52 Knox to Taft, September 28, 1909, Knox Papers, box 28.

53 David Trask, *The War with Spain in 1898* (New York: Macmillan, 1981), p. 366.

54 Alfred T. Mahan, *Lessons of the War with Spain* (Boston: Little, Brown, 1899), p. 30.

55 Puerto Ricans cannot vote in US presidential elections while residing in Puerto Rico, but they are eligible to do so upon moving to the US and establishing residency as variously defined by the states.

56 Rexford Guy Tugwell, *Changing the Colonial Climate* (New York: Arno Press, 1970), p. 9.

57 Henry Wells, *The Modernization of Puerto Rico: A Political Study of Changing Values and Institutions* (Cambridge, MA: Harvard University Press, 1969), p. 93.

58 Robert David Johnson, *Ernest Gruening and the American Dissenting Tradition* (Cambridge, MA: Harvard University Press, 1988), p. 143.

59 Quoted in Wells, *The Modernization of Puerto Rico*, p. 226.

60 The number of Puerto Rican New Yorkers declined by 96,000 in the 1990s, however. The decrease was attributable to suburbanization, movement to other areas of the US, and a growing reverse migration of Puerto Ricans born in the US.

61 Quoted in Ronald Fernandez, *The Disenchanted Island: Puerto Rico*

and the United States in the Twentieth Century (Westport, CT: Praeger, 1992), p. 249.

62 As of 1995, Puerto Rico's per capita GDP ranked slightly lower than that of the Bahamas, but was much higher than that of countries like Mexico, Argentina, and Brazil.

63 Eileen J. Findlay, "Love in the Tropics: Marriage, Divorce, and the Construction of Benevolent Colonialism in Puerto Rico, 1898–1910," in Gilbert M. Joseph, Catherine C. Legrand, and Ricardo D. Salvatore (eds), *Close Encounters of Empire: Writing the Cultural History of US–Latin American Relations* (Durham: Duke University Press, 1998), pp. 139–72.

64 Fernandez, *The Disenchanted Island*, p. 244.

65 Frederick S. Calhoun, *Power and Principle: Armed Intervention in Wilsonian Foreign Policy* (Kent, Ohio: Kent State University Press, 1986), p. 88.

66 TR to Kermit Roosevelt, November 14, 1906, in Morison (ed.), *Letters of Theodore Roosevelt*, vol. 5, p. 495.

67 Calhoun, *Power and Principle*, p. 101.

68 Paul Drake, "From Good Men to Good Neighbors," in Abraham Lowenthal (ed.), *Exporting Democracy: The United States and Latin America* (Baltimore, MD: The Johns Hopkins University Press, 1991) p. 25.

69 The standard account is Hans Schmidt, *The United States Occupation of Haiti, 1915–1934* (New Brunswick, NJ: Rutgers University Press, 1971).

70 Walter Weyl, *America's World Policies* (New York: Macmillan, 1917), p. 211.

71 Quoted in Schmidt, *The United States Occupation of Haiti*, p. 205.

72 Quoted in Whitney T. Perkins, *Constraint of Empire: The United States and Caribbean Interventions* (Westport, CT: Greenwood Press, 1981), p. 160.

73 Quoted in Drake, "From Good Men to Good Neighbors," p. 32.

74 Quoted in Calhoun, *Power and Principle*, p. 103.

75 One should note, however, that Haitian immigrants to the United States have compiled a commendable record of socioeconomic improvement as a consequence of their work ethic.

76 Quoted in Smith, *Talons of the Eagle*, p. 62.

77 Bruce J. Calder, *The Impact of Intervention: The Dominican Republic during the US Occupation of 1916–1924* (Austin: University of Texas Press, 1984), p. 239.

78 Ibid., p. 38.

79 Ernest H. Gruening, "Haiti and Santo Domingo Today – I," *The Nation*, 114 (February 8, 1922), in Jim Zwick (ed.), *Anti-imperialism in the United States, 1898–1935* (at http://www.boondocksnet.com/ailtexts/gruening220208.html).

80 Collin, *Theodore Roosevelt*, p. 188.

81 Ernest May essay (at http://gi.grolier.com/ presidents/ea/side/ mondoc.html).

82 Frederic Austin Ogg, *National Progress, 1905–1917* (New York: Harper, 1918), p. 246.

83 James William Park, *Latin American Underdevelopment: A History of Perspectives in the United States, 1870–1965* (Baton Rouge: Louisiana State University Press, 1995), pp. 100–31.

84 Robert David Johnson, "The Transformation of Pan-Americanism," in Robert David Johnson (ed.), *On Cultural Ground: Essays in International History* (Chicago: Imprint Publications, 1994), p. 173.

85 See the 1940 survey by the Office of Public Opinion Research in John J. Johnson, *A Hemisphere Apart: The Foundations of United States Foreign Policy toward Latin America* (Baltimore, MD: The Johns Hopkins University Press, 1990), p. 194.

86 Johnson, *Ernest Gruening*, p. 112.

87 Pérez, *Cuba under the Platt Amendment*, p. xvii.

88 For some surprising twists and turns in the US government's relationship with United Fruit, see Paul J. Dosal, *Doing Business with the Dictators: A Political History of United Fruit in Guatemala, 1899–1944* (Wilmington, DE: Scholarly Resources, 1993).

89 Memorandum of National Security Council meeting, December 5, 1963, as quoted in Michael E. Latham, "Panama Crisis: Johnson and the 'Chiari Problem' of 1964" unpublished MS.

90 W. W. Rostow, *The Stages of Economic Growth: A Non-Communist Manifesto* (Cambridge: Cambridge University Press, 1971), p. 166. For a closer look at academically inspired modernization strategies, see Michael E. Latham, *Modernization as Ideology: American Social Science and 'Nation Building' in the Kennedy Era* (Chapel Hill, NC: University of North Carolina Press, 2000).

91 Tony Smith, "The Alliance for Progress," in Lowenthal (ed.), *Exporting Democracy*, p. 73.

92 Quoted in Mark T. Gilderhus, *The Second Century: US–Latin American Relations since 1889* (Wilmington, DE: Scholarly Resources, 2000), p. 174.

93 Stephen G. Rabe, *The Most Dangerous Area in the World: John F. Kennedy Confronts Communist Revolution in Latin America* (Chapel Hill, NC: University of North Carolina Press, 1999), pp. 168–70.

94 Quoted in Michael E. Latham, "Ideology, Social Science, and Destiny: Modernization and the Kennedy-era Alliance for Progress," *Diplomatic History*, 22 (Spring 1998), p. 225.

95 Quoted in David F. Schmitz, *Thank God They're on our Side: The United States and Right-wing Dictatorships, 1921–1965* (Chapel Hill, NC: University of North Carolina Press, 1999), p. 165.

96 *The Rockefeller Report on the Americas* (Chicago: Quadrangle Books, 1969), p. 17.

97 Jorge I. Domínguez, Robert A. Pastor, and R. DeLisle Worrell (eds), *Democracy in the Caribbean: Political, Economic, and Social Perspectives* (Baltimore, MD: The Johns Hopkins University Press, 1993), esp. pp. 1–25.

98 Pérez, *Cuba under the Platt Amendment*, p. 337.

99 For a fine overview, see Thomas F. O'Brien, *The Revolutionary Mission: American Enterprise in Latin America, 1900–1945* (New York: Cambridge University Press, 1996).

100 Ernest May, "The Alliance for Progress in Historical Perspective," in Akira Iriye (ed.), *Rethinking International Relations: Ernest R. May and the Study of Foreign Affairs* (Chicago: Imprint Publications, 1998), p. 23.

101 For an approving view of this approach, see Millett, *The Politics of Intervention*, p. 267.

Notes to Chapter 4

1 See Trumbull White, *Glimpses of the Orient* (Philadelphia: P. W. Ziegler, 1897), p. 3 for a typical nineteenth-century inventory of cultural contrasts.

2 John King Fairbank, *The United States and China*, 4th edn (Cambridge, MA: Harvard University Press, 1983), p. 160.

3 Michael Hunt, *The Making of a Special Relationship: The United States and China to 1914* (New York: Columbia University Press, 1983), pp. 7–8.

4 There was one significant exception: the British received Hong Kong as an entrepôt and governed it as a crown colony until it was retroceded to China in 1997.

5 Eileen P. Scully, "Taking the Low Road in Sino-American Relations: 'Open Door' Expansionists and the Two China Markets," *Journal of American History*, 82 (June 1995), pp. 62–83.

6 Hunt, *The Making of a Special Relationship*, pp. 148–9.

7 See the somewhat more optimistic figures in Charles S. Campbell Jr, *Special Business Interests and the Open Door Policy* (New Haven, CT: Yale University Press, 1951), p. 11.

8 Jonathan G. Utley, "American Views of China, 1900–1915: The Unwelcome but Inevitable Awakening," in Jonathan Goldstein, Jerry Israel, and Hilary Conroy (eds), *America Views China: American Images of China Then and Now* (Bethlehem, PA: Lehigh University Press, 1991), p. 122.

9 For a discussion of some of the tensions and contradictions that plagued the simultaneous pursuit of treaty port imperialism and developmental idealism, see David L. Anderson, *Imperialism and Idealism:*

American Diplomats in China, 1861–1898 (Bloomington, IN: Indiana University Press, 1985).

10   Murray A. Rubinstein, "American Board Missionaries and the Formation of American Opinion toward China, 1830–1860," in Goldstein et al. (eds), *America Views China*, p. 77.

11   Richmond Croom Beatty, *Bayard Taylor, Laureate of the Gilded Age* (Norman: University of Oklahoma Press, 1936), p. 139.

12   Morrell Heald and Lawrence S. Kaplan, *Culture and Diplomacy: The American Experience* (Westport, CT: Greenwood Press, 1977), p. 103.

13   John King Fairbank, *The Great Chinese Revolution 1800–1985* (New York: Harper and Row, 1987), p. 125.

14   According to one count, by 1949 there were approximately 1 million Protestant and 3 million Roman Catholic converts in China. See Francis P. Jones, "American Religious Influence on China," in Chi-Pao Cheng (ed.), *Chinese-American Cultural Relations* (New York: China Institute in America, 1965), p. 134.

15   Quoted in Paul Varg, *Missionaries, Chinese, and Diplomats: The American Protestant Missionary Movement, 1890–1952* (Princeton, NJ: Princeton University Press, 1958), p. 89.

16   James C. Thomson Jr, Peter. W. Stanley, and John Curtis Perry, *Sentimental Imperialists: The American Experience in East Asia* (New York: Harper and Row, 1982), pp. 51, 58.

17   Quoted in Jerry Israel, *Progressivism and the Open Door: America and China, 1905–1921* (Pittsburgh, PA: University of Pittsburgh Press, 1971), p. 21.

18   Anderson, *Imperialism and Idealism*, pp. 5–6.

19   Thomas McCormick, *The China Market: America's Quest for Informal Empire, 1893–1901* (Chicago: Quadrangle Books, 1967), pp. 65–6.

20   *Journal of the American Association of China* (1908), quoted in Akira Iriye (ed.), *Mutual Images: Essays in American–Japanese Relations* (Cambridge, MA: Harvard University Press, 1975), p. 88.

21   Ernest D. Burton, quoted in Varg, *Missionaries, Chinese, and Diplomats*, p. 91.

22   Quoted in Mary Brown Bullock, *An American Transplant: The Rockefeller Foundation and Peking Union Medical College* (Berkeley, CA: University of California Press, 1980), p. 35.

23   Francis Anthony Boyle, *Foundations of World Order: The Legalist Approach to International Relations, 1898–1922* (Durham: Duke University Press, 1999), p. 96.

24   Quoted in Delber L. McKee, *Chinese Exclusion Versus the Open Door Policy 1900–1906* (Detroit: Wayne State University Press, 1977), p. 194.

25   Michael H. Hunt, *Frontier Defense and the Open Door: Manchuria in Chinese–American Relations, 1885–1911* (New Haven, CT: Yale University Press, 1973), p. 78.

26 Charles Morris, *Man and his Ancestors* (New York, 1900), p. 194, as quoted in John S. Haller Jr, *Outcasts from Evolution: Scientific Attitudes of Racial Inferiority* (Urbana, IL: University of Illinois Press, 1971), p. 152.

27 W. I. Thomas, in Haller, *Outcasts from Evolution*, p. 149.

28 In Akira Iriye, *Across the Pacific: An Inner History of American-East Asian Relations* (New York: Harcourt, Brace, 1967), p. 119.

29 One should note, however, that other nations exercised considerable cultural influence as well. By 1905, Japan was playing host to some 20,000 Chinese students.

30 Taft, address to Lowell, MA Board of Trade, February 19, 1908, series 95, reel 565, Taft Papers.

31 Taft, Shanghai speech, October 7, 1907, Taft Papers.

32 *London Daily News*, January 10, 1910, clipping in Knox Papers, box 28.

33 Taft, address to Lowell, MA Board of Trade, February 19, 1908, series 95, reel 565, Taft Papers.

34 Quoted in Frank Ninkovich, "The Rockefeller Foundation, China, and Cultural Change," *Journal of American History*, 70 (March 1984), p. 801.

35 House Con. Res. 22, January 3, 1912.

36 Jonathan G. Utley, "American Views of China, 1900–1915: The Unwelcome but Inevitable Awakening," in Goldstein et al. (eds), *America Views China*, p. 125. See the discussion of the public reaction in James Reed, *The Missionary Mind and American East Asia Policy 1911–1915* (Cambridge, MA: Harvard University Press, 1983), pp. 120–35.

37 *Outlook*, 97 (February 4, 1911), pp. 249–50.

38 D. W. Y. Kwok, *Scientism in Chinese Thought 1900–1950* (New York: Biblo and Tannen, 1971), p. 11.

39 Ray Stannard Baker, *Woodrow Wilson and World Settlement* (Gloucester, MA: Peter Smith, 1960), vol. 2, p. 252.

40 Wilson to Joseph Tumulty, April 30, 1919, in Ray Stannard Baker and William E. Dodd (eds), *The Public Papers of Woodrow Wilson*, volume 5: *War and Peace* (New York: Kraus Reprint Co., 1970), p. 475.

41 Akira Iriye, *After Imperialism: The Search for a New Order in the Far East, 1921–1931* (Chicago: Imprint Publications, 1990), p. 20.

42 Quoted in Harold Isaacs, *Scratches on our Minds: American Views of China and India* (Armonk, NY: M. E. Sharpe, 1980), p. 151.

43 John King Fairbank, *Chinese–American Interactions: A Historical Summary* (Rahway, NJ: Rutgers University Press, 1975), p. 55.

44 On this point, see chapter 5.

45 Warren Cohen, *East Asian Art and American Culture* (New York: Columbia University Press, 1992).

46 The civil engineer Oliver Todd, as quoted in Jonathan Spence, *To*

Change China: Western Advisers in China 1620–1960 (Boston: Little, Brown, 1969), p. 211.

47　For an overview, see James C. Thomson Jr, *While China Faced West: American Reformers in Nationalist China, 1928–1937* (Cambridge, MA: Harvard University Press, 1969).

48　Ibid., p. 18.

49　Barbara W. Tuchman, *Stilwell and the American Experience in China* (New York: Macmillan, 1971), p. 131.

50　John King Fairbank memo of November 19, 1943, quoted in Frank Ninkovich, "Cultural Relations and American China Policy, 1942–1945," *Pacific Historical Review*, 49 (August 1980), p. 480.

51　John King Fairbank, *Chinabound: A Fifty Year Memoir* (New York: Harper and Row, 1982), p. 244.

52　Quoted in Michael Schaller, *The US Crusade in China, 1938–1945* (New York: Columbia University Press, 1979), p. 111.

53　Memo by John Stewart Service, September 3, 1944, *Foreign Relations of the United States* (1994), vol. 6, p. 616.

54　Quoted in Schaller, *The US Crusade in China*, p. 192.

55　Warren I. Cohen, "The United States and China Since 1945," in Warren Cohen (ed.), *New Frontiers in American–East Asian Relations* (New York: Columbia University Press, 1983), p. 134.

56　*The China White Paper, August 1949* (Stanford, CA: Stanford University Press, 1967), p. 383.

57　Quoted in Michael H. Hunt, "The American Remission of the Boxer Indemnity: A Reappraisal," *The Journal of Asian Studies*, 31 (May 1972), p. 541.

58　Akira Iriye, "Americanization of East Asia: Writings on Cultural Affairs since 1900," in Cohen (ed.), *New Frontiers in American–East Asian Relations*, p. 63.

59　Henry P. Van Dusen, as quoted in T. Christopher Jesperson, *American Images of China 1931–1949* (Stanford, CA: Stanford University Press, 1996), p. 151.

60　Quoted in Tang Tsou, *America's Failure in China, 1941–1950* (Chicago: University of Chicago Press, 1963), p. 509.

61　Acheson speech at the National Press Club, January 12, 1950, *Department of State Bulletin*, January 23, 1950, p. 114.

62　*China White Paper*, p. xvi.

63　Even Stalin thought it was obvious. "If socialism is victorious in China and our countries follow a single path then the victory of socialism in the world will be virtually guaranteed," he predicted. Quoted in John Lewis Gaddis, *We Now Know: Rethinking Cold War History* (Oxford: Clarendon Press, 1997), p. 66.

64　Harold Isaacs, as quoted in Jesperson, *American Images of China*, p. 174.

65　Dean Rusk, address to China Institute dinner, May 17, 1951, as quoted in David Allan Mayers, *Cracking the Monolith: US Policy against the Sino-Soviet Alliance, 1949–1955* (Baton Rouge: Louisiana State University Press, 1986), p. 104.

66 On one occasion, Eisenhower tried to turn a racialist public opinion against the interventionists in his administration by remarking that "Letters to him constantly say what do we care what happens to those yellow people out there?" NSC meeting of September 12, 1954, Papers of Dwight D. Eisenhower, Ann Whitman File, NSC series, box 6.

67 Gordon H. Chang, *Friends and Enemies: The United States, China, and the Soviet Union, 1948–1972* (Stanford, CA: Stanford University Press, 1990), p. 173.

68 *Executive Sessions of the Senate Foreign Relations Committee* (Historical Series), vol. VI, February 24, 1954, p. 158.

69 In Nancy Bernkopf Tucker, "Cold War Contacts: America and China, 1952–1956," in Harry Harding and Yuan Ming (eds), *Sino-American Relations, 1945–1955: A Joint Reassessment of a Critical Decade* (Wilmington, DE: Scholarly Resources, 1989), p. 257.

70 DDE to Churchill, December 14, 1954, Papers of Dwight D. Eisenhower, Ann Whitman File, DDE diary series, box 7.

71 Interview with Anna Louise Strong, August 1946, in Leonard Roy Frank, *Random House Webster's Quotationary* (New York: Random House, 1999), p. 561.

72 Gordon H. Chang, "JFK, China, and the Bomb," *Journal of American History*, 74 (March 1988), pp. 1287–1310.

73 Richard Nixon, *RN: The Memoirs of Richard Nixon* (New York: Grossett and Dunlap, 1978), p. 882.

74 Papers of LBJ, Congressional Briefings on Vietnam, Dean Rusk briefing for new Congressmen, January 13, 1965.

75 Warren I. Cohen, *Dean Rusk* (New York: Cooper Square, 1980), p. 288.

76 Quoted in Robert D. Schulzinger, *Henry Kissinger: Doctor of Diplomacy* (New York: Columbia University Press, 1989), p. 76.

77 Statement by George Ball, Papers of LBJ, Congressional Briefings on Vietnam, February 9, 1965.

78 Richard Nixon, "Asia after Vietnam," *Foreign Affairs*, 45 (October 1967), p. 122.

79 Jonathan D. Pollack, *The Lessons of Coalition Politics: Sino-American Security Relations* (Santa Monica, CA: The Rand Corporation, 1984).

80 For the best analysis, see Lowell Dittmer, *Sino-Soviet Normalization and its International Implications, 1945–1990* (Seattle: University of Washington Press, 1992).

81 Nixon, *Memoirs*, p. 553.

82 Gerald Strober and Deborah H. Strober, *Nixon: An Oral History of his Presidency* (New York: Harper Collins, 1964), p. 133.

83 John King Fairbank, "China: Time for a Policy," *The Atlantic Monthly* (April 1957) (at http://www.theatlantic.com/unbound/flashbks/china/fairbank.html).

84 It should be noted that Taiwan also benefited from (1) the developmentalist legacy of Japanese colonial rule between 1895 and 1945, especially infrastructure, public health, and literacy; and (2) the flow of talented *émigrés* fleeing the communists on the mainland.

85 Warren Cohen, "While China Faced East: Chinese-American Cultural Relations, 1949–71," in Joyce K. Kallgren and Denis Fred Simon (eds), *Educational Exchanges: Essays on the Sino-American Experience* (Berkeley, CA: Institute of East Asian Studies, 1987), p. 49.

86 Ibid., p. 53.

87 Editor's note, in Patrick M. Boarman (ed.), *Trade with China: Assessments by Leading Businessmen and Scholars* (New York: Praeger, 1974), p. ix.

88 *The New York Times*, November 16, 1999, A: 16.

89 Minxin Pei, "Is China Democratizing?" *Foreign Affairs*, 77 (January/February 1998), p. 78.

90 James A. Baker III, *The Politics of Diplomacy: Revolution, War and Peace, 1989–1992* (New York: G. P. Putnam, 1995), p. 106.

91 Clinton radio address, June 27, 1998, White House web site.

92 Madeleine Albright, "The Testing of American Foreign Policy," *Foreign Affairs*, 77 (November/December 1998), p. 57.

93 Hunt, *The Making of a Special Relationship*, p. 302.

Notes to Chapter 5

1 For some recent textbook examples, see Thomas A. Bailey, *A Diplomatic History of the American People*, 10th edn (Englewood Cliffs, NJ: Prentice-Hall, 1980), p. 483; Robert D. Schulzinger, *American Diplomacy in the Twentieth Century* (New York: Oxford University Press, 1984), p. 16; H. William Brands, *The United States in the World*, vol. I (Boston: Houghton Mifflin, 1994), p. 222.

2 Archibald Cary Coolidge, *The United States as a World Power* (New York: Macmillan, 1908), p. 132.

3 William L. Langer, *The Diplomacy of Imperialism*, 2nd edn (New York: Knopf, 1972), p. 96.

4 Quoted in David S. Patterson, *Toward a Warless World: The Travail of the American Peace Movement 1887–1914* (Bloomington, IN: Indiana University Press, 1976), p. 73.

5 Quoted in Stanley Karnow, *In our Image: America's Empire in the Philippines* (New York: Random House, 1989), p. 171.

6 Robert Wiebe, *The Search for Order, 1877–1920* (New York: Hill and Wang, 1967). See also n. 63 in chapter 1, above.

7   Quoted in Peter H. Smith, *Talons of the Eagle: Dynamics of US–Latin American Relations* (New York: Oxford University Press, 1996), p. 50.

8   TR to Cecil Spring Rice, January 18, 1904, in Elting E. Morison (ed.), *The Letters of Theodore Roosevelt* (Cambridge, MA: Harvard University Press, 1951), vol. 3, p. 699.

9   Quoted in Anders Stephanson, *Manifest Destiny: American Expansion and the Empire of Right* (New York: Hill and Wang, 1995), p. 88.

10 The Reverend Josiah Strong, as quoted in Robert C. Bannister, *Social Darwinism: Science and Myth in Anglo-American Social Thought* (Philadelphia: Temple University Press, 1979), pp. 226–42.

11 Jon Tetsuro Sumida, *Inventing Grand Strategy and Teaching Command: The Classic Works of Alfred Thayer Mahan Reconsidered* (Baltimore, MD: The Johns Hopkins University Press, 1997).

12 Ibid., p. 87.

13 TR to Henry White, August 12, 1906, in Morison (ed.), *Letters of Theodore Roosevelt*, vol. 5, p. 359.

14 Walter Weyl, *American World Policies* (New York: Macmillan, 1917), p. 215.

15 Cited in Norman E. Saul, *Concord and Conflict: The United States and Russia, 1867–1914* (Lawrence, KS: University Press of Kansas, 1996), p. 472.

16 Ibid., p. 188.

17 Quoted in Edward A. Zabriskie, *American–Russian Rivalry in the Far East 1895-1914: A Study in Power Politics and Diplomacy* (Westport, CT: Greenwood Press, 1976), p. 94.

18 TR to George von Lengerke Meyer, December 26, 1904, quoted in Zabriskie, *American–Russian Rivalry*, pp. 179–80.

19 John King Fairbank, *Chinese–American Interactions: A Historical Summary* (Rahway, NJ: Rutgers University Press, 1975), p. 57.

20 Quoted in Walter LaFeber, *The Cambridge History of American Foreign Relations*, volume II: *The American Search for Opportunity, 1865–1913* (New York: Cambridge University Press, 1993), p. 175.

21 *The Education of Henry Adams* (New York: Time Inc., 1946), vol. 2, p. 145.

22 Frank Ninkovich, "Theodore Roosevelt: Civilization as Ideology," *Diplomatic History*, 10 (Summer 1986), pp. 221–45.

23 TR to Hermann Speck von Sternberg, October 11, 1901, in Morison (ed.), *Letters of Theodore Roosevelt*, vol. 3, p. 172.

24 TR to Andrew D. White, November 2, 1914, in ibid., vol. 5, p. 25.

25 Raymond A. Esthus, *Theodore Roosevelt and Japan* (Seattle: University of Washington Press, 1966), p. 308. Esthus emphasizes, however, that Elihu Root, then serving as secretary of state, was very careful not to compromise the open door as a matter of principle.

26 Charles Neu, "1900–1913," in Ernest May and James C. Thomson Jr (eds), *American-East Asian Relations: A Survey* (Cambridge, MA: Harvard University Press, 1957), p. 157.

27 TR to Sir Edward Grey, December 18, 1906, in Morison (ed.), *Letters of Theodore Roosevelt*, vol. 5, p. 528.

28 On this point, see Kathleen Dalton, "Between the Diplomacy of Imperialism and the Achievement of World Order by Supranational Mediation: Ethnocentrism and Theodore Roosevelt's Changing Views of World Order," paper delivered at a conference on Ethnocentrism et Diplomatie: L'Amerique et Le Monde au Xxème Siècle, University of Paris, January 14–15, 2000.

29 I know, I know. "But TR was a *realist*" many will continue to insist. However, given TR's actions, that is true only if one defines a hemispheric approach – in other words, isolationism – as realism. What then becomes of Roosevelt's much talked-about *Weltpolitik*? And what, then, are we to make of all his talk of civilization?

30 TR to Cecil Spring Rice, December 27, 1904, in Morison (ed.), *Letters of Theodore Roosevelt*, vol. 4, p. 1087.

31 Knox speech, December 11, 1909, Knox Papers, box 45.

32 William Howard Taft, address to Tippecanoe Club, Cleveland, Ohio, January 29, 1908, Taft Papers, series 9A, reel 564.

33 Knox to H. M. Hoyt, October 8, 1909, Knox Papers.

34 Knox's suggested reply to Roosevelt's letter of December 22, 1910, Taft Papers, reel 454, case file no. 26.

35 Knox to Taft, August 26, 1909, Knox Papers, box 27.

36 J. K. Ohl to Knox, April 10, 1911, Knox Papers, no. 14.

37 Knox speech, April 25, 1911, Asiatic Association, NYC, Knox Papers, box 45.

38 Jerry Israel, *Progressivism and the Open Door: America and China, 1905–1921* (Pittsburgh, PA: University of Pennsylvania Press, 1971), p. 84.

39 *The China Press*, September 29, 1912, copy in the Knox Papers, no. 18.

40 Letter draft, Knox to Taft [1911?], Knox Papers.

41 Knox speech, June 15, 1910, Knox Papers, box 45.

42 Knox speech draft, May 1910, Knox Papers, box 28.

43 Robert David Johnson, *The Peace Progressives and American Foreign Relations* (Cambridge, MA: Harvard University Press, 1995), p. 26.

44 A Commemorative Address, "The Ideals of America" [December 26, 1901], in Arthur Link et al. (eds), *The Papers of Woodrow Wilson* (Princeton, NJ: Princeton University Press, 1966–1994), vol. 12, p. 223.

45 William E. Leuchtenberg, "Progressivism and Imperialism: The Progressive Movement and American Foreign Policy, 1898–1916," *The Mississippi Valley Historical Review*, 39 (June 1952), pp. 483–504.

46 Willard Range, *Franklin D. Roosevelt's World Order* (Athens: University of Georgia Press, 1959), p. 103.

47 Christopher Lasch, *The American Liberals and the Russian Revolution* (New York: McGraw-Hill, 1972), pp. x–xi. N. Gordon Levin Jr also captured this ideological bifurcation when he argued that "Wilsonian ideology sought essentially to end traditional imperialism and the balance of power." See N. Gordon Levin Jr, *Woodrow Wilson and World Politics: America's Response to War and Revolution* (New York: Oxford University Press, 1968), p. 8.

48 Walter Lippmann, *The Stakes of Diplomacy* (New York: Macmillan, 1932 [1917]), pp. xix, 108, 124.

49 Weyl, *American World Policies*, pp. 18, 165, 188.

50 An address, Baltimore, April 6, 1918, in Link et al. (eds), *Papers of Woodrow Wilson*, vol. 47, p. 270.

51 Ray Stannard Baker, *Woodrow Wilson and World Settlement* (Gloucester, MA: Peter Smith, 1960), vol. 2, p. 11. Obviously, the views of Wilson and the progressive anti-imperialists differed in the way that Joseph Schumpeter differed from John Hobson.

52 For this distinction, see Frank Ninkovich, *The Wilsonian Century: US Foreign Policy since 1900* (Chicago: University of Chicago Press, 1999), p. 12.

53 The Fourteen Points speech, January 8, 1918, in Ray Stannard Baker and William E. Dodd (eds), *The Public Papers of Woodrow Wilson*, volume 5: *War and Peace* (New York: Kraus Reprint Co., 1970), pp. 159-61.

54 Ibid., p. 252.

55 Ibid., p. 262.

56 Ibid., p. 266.

57 Charles H. Sherrill, *Modernizing the Monroe Doctrine* (Boston: Houghton Mifflin, 1916), p. 154.

58 From Charles Seymour, *The Intimate Papers of Colonel House* (Boston and New York: Houghton Mifflin, 1928), vol. 4, p. 195.

59 By far the best treatment of progressive anti-imperialism during these years is Johnson, *The Peace Progressives*. But see also Emily Rosenberg, *Financial Missionaries to the World: The Politics and Culture of Dollar Diplomacy 1900–1930* (Cambridge, MA: Harvard University Press, 1999), pp. 122-50.

60 Charles Beard and Mary Beard, *The Rise of American Civilization*, volume 2: *The Industrial Era* (New York: Macmillan, 1928), p. 526.

61 John Dewey, "Imperialism is Easy," *The New Republic*, 50 (March 23, 1927) (at http://home.ican.net/~fjzwick/ailtexts/dewey.html) in Jim Zwick (ed.), *Anti-imperialism in the United States, 1898–1935* (at http://home.ican.net/~fjzwick/ail98-35.html) (January 10, 1999).

62 Scott Nearing and Joseph Freeman, *Dollar Diplomacy: A Study in American Imperialism* (New York: Modern Reader, 1969), p. xiii.

63 Senator Hiram Bingham, as quoted in Robert David Johnson, "The Politicization of Cultural Diplomacy," in Liping Bu and Frank

Ninkovich (eds), *The Cultural Turn: Essays in the History of US Foreign Relations* (Chicago: Imprint Publications, 2000).

64   Quoted in Richard N. Current, *Secretary Stimson: A Study in Statecraft* (New York: Archon Books, 1970), p. 102.

65   Waldo Heinrichs, *American Ambassador: Joseph C. Grew and the Development of the United States Diplomatic Tradition* (New York: Oxford University Press, 1986), p. 220.

66   Jürgen Osterhammel, "Semi-colonialism and Informal Empire in Twentieth Century China: Towards a Framework of Analysis," in Jürgen Osterhammel and Wolfgang J. Mommsen (eds), *Imperialism and After: Continuities and Discontinuities* (London: Allen and Unwin, 1986), p. 300.

67   Dorothy Borg, *The United States and the Far Eastern Crisis of 1933–1938* (Cambridge, MA: Harvard University Press, 1964).

68   In Irwin F. Gellman, *Good Neighbor Diplomacy: United States Policies in Latin America, 1933–1945* (Baltimore, MD: The Johns Hopkins University Press, 1979), p. 65.

69   Beatrice Bishop Berle and Travis Beal Jacobs (eds), *Navigating the Rapids 1918–1971: From the Papers of Adolf A. Berle* (New York: Harcourt Brace Jovanovich, 1973), pp. 231–2.

70   Heinrichs, *American Ambassador*, p. 267.

71   The investments differed, however. In China, it was direct investment; in Japan, it took the form of purchasing Japanese bonds.

72   For figures, see John King Fairbank, *The United States and China*, 4th edn (Cambridge, MA: Harvard University Press, 1983), pp. 324–7.

73   Frank Freidel, *Franklin D. Roosevelt: A Rendezvous with Destiny* (Boston: Little, Brown, 1990), p. 379.

74   Doc. 1565, FDR conference with Senate Military Affairs Committee, January 31, 1939, in Donald B. Schewe (ed.), *Franklin D. Roosevelt and Foreign Affairs*, vol. 4, *January 1937–August 1939* (New York: Garland Books, 1979).

75   Doc. 1744, FDR press conference, April 20, 1939, in ibid.

76   Memo of conversation, November 18, 1941, in Akira Iriye, *Pearl Harbor and the Coming of the Pacific War: A Brief History with Documents and Essays* (Boston: Bedford/St Martin's, 1999), p. 46.

77   Ironically, opposing the diplomacy of imperialism required, for the moment, supporting the British empire. These kinds of dilemmas would become even more apparent during the Cold War. See my discussion below.

78   Doc. 1616a, memo from Joseph P. Kennedy to FDR [March 3, 1939] in Schewe, *Franklin D. Roosevelt and Foreign Affairs*, volume 9, *December 1938–February 1939*.

79   Melvyn P. Leffler, *A Preponderance of Power: National Security, the Truman Administration, and the Cold War* (Stanford, CA: Stanford University Press, 1992), p. 22. For the larger argument, see Frank

Ninkovich, *Modernity and Power: A History of the Domino Theory in the Twentieth Century* (Chicago: University of Chicago Press, 1995), pp. 112–21.

80 In signing the Tripartite Pact in September 1940, Germany and Japan each hoped to deter the United States from entering *its* particular war by offering this suggestion of a strategic linkage between Asia and Europe. It is clear that the assumption backfired by increasing American involvement, but it is worth pointing out why this should have happened. While other powers were using global calculations for the furtherance of essentially regional interests, the United States was viewing separate regional events through a global lens. The Tripartite Pact thus aroused the kinds of internationalist fears that fed the interventionist impulse.

81 Quoted in Robert J. McMahon, *The Limits of Empire: The United States and Southeast Asia since World War II* (New York: Columbia University Press, 1999), p. 10.

82 Doc. 1744, FDR press conference, April 20, 1939, in Schewe, *Franklin D. Roosevelt and Foreign Affairs*, volume 4: *January 1937–August 1939*.

83 Range, *Franklin D. Roosevelt's World Order*, p. 105.

84 Quoted in Christopher Thorne, *Allies of a Kind: The United States, Britain, and the War against Japan, 1941–1945* (New York: Oxford University Press, 1978), p. 103.

85 Cited in Robert J. McMahon, *Colonialism and Cold War: The United States and the Struggle for Indonesian Independence, 1945–1949* (Ithaca, NY: Cornell University Press, 1981), p. 55.

86 Allan M. Winkler, "American Opposition to Imperialism During World War II," in Rhodri Jeffreys-Jones (ed.), *Eagle Against Empire: American Opposition to European Imperialism* (Aix-en-Provence: Université de Provence, 1983), p. 84.

87 Quoted in Wm Roger Louis, *Imperialism at Bay: The United States and the Decolonization of the British Empire, 1941–1945* (New York: Oxford University Press, 1978), p. 538. See also Warren Kimball's judgment that "In Roosevelt's mind, the monster of colonialism threatened to bite if not devour the world by plunging it into another huge war." Warren F. Kimball, *The Juggler: Franklin D. Roosevelt as Wartime Statesman* (Princeton, NJ: Princeton University Press, 1991), p. 128

88 Scott Bills, *Empire and Cold War: The Roots of US–Third World Antagonism, 1945–1947* (New York: St Martin's Press, 1990); H. W. Brands, *The Specter of Neutralism: The United States and the Emergence of the Third World, 1947–1960* (New York: Columbia University Press, 1989); McMahon, *Colonialism and Cold War*; Thomas Borstelmann, *Apartheid's Reluctant Uncle: The United States and South Africa in the Early Cold War* (New York: Oxford University Press,

1993), p. 109; Peter L. Hahn, *The United States, Great Britain, and Egypt, 1945–1946: Strategy and Diplomacy in the Early Cold War* (Chapel Hill, NC: University of North Carolina Press, 1991).

89 David A. Lake, *Entangling Relations: American Foreign Policy in its Century* (Princeton, NJ: Princeton University Press, 1999), p. 14.

90 Untitled paper on Soviet foreign policy n.d. [but analyzing a Khrushchev speech of January 1961], Papers of John F. Kennedy, National Security File, box 176, Kennedy Library.

91 The 1954 crisis in Indochina was particularly dicey because of the unstable situation in Europe, in which the future of the western alliance appeared to be up for grabs.

92 Walter Lippmann, "The American Promise," *Newsweek* (October 9, 1967).

93 Paul M. Buhle and Edward Rice-Maximin, *William Appleman Williams and the Tragedy of Empire* (New York: Routledge, 1995). A good introduction to his work is Henry W. Berger, *A William Appleman Williams Reader: Selections from his Major Historical Writings* (Chicago: Ivan R. Dee, 1992).

94 William Appleman Williams, *The Tragedy of American Diplomacy* (New York: Delta Books, 1962), p. 305.

95 The argument is also tricky in its treatment of motives. US policy-makers are accused of imperialism despite their protestations to the contrary. This implies that the critics have a better grasp of objective reality than the policy-makers, who are presumed to be misrepresenting the facts or suffering from delusion.

96 A thoroughgoing critique could easily consume another book. But I think it only fair to list my principal objections to the thesis that the desire for commercial expansion translates into imperialism, however defined. (1) The open door perspective is primarily a domestic critique, but its validity depends ultimately on an assessment of the international consequences of US trade policy. Any judgment of the effectiveness, duration, benefits, and drawbacks of economic imperialism must be based on what happens abroad, not on an analysis of domestic factors. (2) An imperialism of free trade does not necessarily develop between countries that specialize in the production of primary products and those that export finished goods. Sometimes it does and sometimes it doesn't, depending on all kinds of circumstances. Even in cases where such an unequal relationship does develop initially, it is bound to change over time. (3) For those nations that have not been able to flourish under an open global trading regime, it is impossible to demonstrate that they would have fared better under some other system, although one could always maintain that they might have prospered. As far as I know, there is no objective way of settling this argument. (4) The argument that US economic expansion was needed to shore up the domestic economy seems doubtful. While it is certainly true that

the United States has been the principal champion of an open world without which the modern world economy could not have been created, it is difficult to see this as a case where the US acted on behalf of its economic interests, narrowly conceived. Given the long heritage of protectionism and its appeal to politically powerful interest groups, it was hardly the course of least resistance. The argument seems even more out of place in the late twentieth century when, as the US began to run massive trade deficits, its commitment to an open world economy increased. (5) Despite its preoccupation with economic matters, the open door argument is not about economic necessities, as its Marxist critics well knew, but about a state of mind. Because the need for expansion is cast in subjective terms as the product of an ideology, its connection to hard material interests is far from clear. The (allegedly) irresistible appeal of the objectively insignificant China market provides the best-known illustration of this problem. Indeed, as soon as one starts to think about it, the intellectual snarls become quite formidable. For example: according to this argument, Americans mistakenly believed that they were anti-imperialist. But if this allegation of imperialism is based only on the analysis of an ideology, how does one prove that it is not imperialist without going into the two-way details of particular relationships? (6) The open door economic outlook, though certainly present, is not a complete ideological world unto itself. It is in fact part of a much larger world view, which also happens to be the same outlook that generated a hostility to the diplomacy of imperialism and opposition to Nazi Germany's expansionism. It needs to be evaluated, then, from a broader perspective. (7) The open door interpretation has a blind spot when it comes to geopolitics. It assumes a fundamentally benign world in which the US faced no fundamental threats to its security; not surprisingly, then, its interpretations of the intentions of overseas actors and the consequences of events abroad tend to downplay danger. Thus the tendency to see Stalin as a moderate, the USSR as a state driven by non-ideological and local security interests, and Third World revolutions as strategically inconsequential. This propensity to ignore or downplay the dangers from Japan, Germany, or the USSR comes close to being an ideological taboo against considering the possibility that the dangers deserved to be taken seriously. But whatever the merits of the particular cases might be, the assumption that a culturally and politically plural world is a secure place is not necessarily true. On the contrary, it would seem more natural to suppose that national and cultural differences tend to make for conflict rather than cooperation among peoples. (9) It neglects the phenomenon of globalization, which, because it was to some degree independent of American foreign policy, allows for the possibility, at least in principle, that an open world would have developed in any case; and (10) with reference to the chief theme of this book: because there is nothing inherent in commercial expansion that, of itself, translates into a desire for territorial possession and control, it does not explain American colonialism. To be sure, economic expansion can take a colonial form, but the liberal version found in the United States has been predominantly non-territorial. While the open door critique is of limited help in explaining American imperialism or foreign relations in general, it is only fair to note that it may, in the end, prove to be correct on a global scale as a description of the relationship between developed and underdeveloped sections of the world. On this possibility, see my concluding paragraphs.

97   The narrowly economic argument was more appropriate to the era of classical imperialism, when special interests could often be found pulling strings behind the scenes, than to the era of globalism, in which policy seemed to be based on empyrean abstractions.

98   A list of its possessions includes the following: American Samoa; Baker Island; Guam; Howland Island; Jarvis Island; Johnston Atoll; Kingman reef; Midway Islands; Navassa island; the Commonwealth of the Northern Mariana Islands, which include the islands of Rota, Saipan, Tinian, Pagan, Guguan, Agrihan, and Aguijan; Palmyra Atoll; The Virgin Islands; Wake Island; and Puerto Rico.

99   Statement by Felix Rohatyn in *The New York Times*, December 2, 1999, A: 2.

Notes to Chapter 6

1   See the chronology in D. K. Fieldhouse, *The Colonial Empires: A Comparative Survey from the Eighteenth Century* (New York: Delacorte Press, 1965), pp. 138–47, or the scant mention of the United States in Michael Doyle, *Empires* (Ithaca, NY: Cornell University Press, 1986). A. E. Campbell, *America Comes of Age* (New York: American Heritage Press, 1971), p. 96, who calls American imperialism both "hesitant and relatively insignificant," is typical of the dismissive attitude of many historians.

2   John Hobson, *Imperialism:A Study* (London: J. Nisbet, 1902), p. 23.

3   John Tomlinson, *Cultural Imperialism: A Critical Introduction* (Baltimore, MD: The Johns Hopkins University Press, 1991), p. 175.

4   Michael Hardt and Antonio Negri, *Empire* (Cambridge, MA: Harvard University Press, 2000), p. 145.

5   "Cultural genocide" some might call it, but that strikes me as a loaded way of putting the matter.

6   Jonathan Friedman, *Cultural Identity and Global Process* (London: Sage, 1994), p. 81.

7   Jared Diamond, *Guns, Germs, and Steel: The Fates of Human Societies* (New York: Norton, 1999), p. 102.

8 Reinhold Wagnleitner, *Coca-Colonization and the Cold War: The Cultural Mission of the United States in Austria after the Second World War* (Chapel Hill, NC: University of North Carolina Press, 1994), p. 6.

9 Jules Benjamin, *The United States and Cuba: Hegemony and Dependent Development, 1880–1934* (Pittsburgh: University of Pittsburgh Press, 1977), p. xi.

10 See, e.g., Joshua Muravchik, *Exporting Democracy: Fulfilling America's Destiny* (Washington, DC: AEI Press, 1991); Tony Smith, *America's Mission: The United States and the Worldwide Struggle for Democracy in the Twentieth Century* (Princeton, NJ: Princeton University Press, 1994).

11 For some stimulating thoughts on how culture as a primordial expression of "situated difference" is being tranformed into culturalism, a form of identity politics, see Arjun Appadurai, *Modernity at Large: Cultural Dimensions of Globalization* (Minneapolis: University of Minnesota Press, 1996).

12 See, e.g., the essays in Gilbert M. Joseph, Catherine C. Legrand, and Ricardo D. Salvatore (eds), *Close Encounters of Empire: Writing the Cultural History of US–Latin American Relations* (Durham and London: Duke University Press, 1998).

13 Despite some impressive advances in health, education, and nutrition, the income gap between the developed and underdeveloped nations continued to grow through the 1990s. Details can be found in the *Human Development Report 1999* (New York: Oxford University Press, 1999). For some unsettling descriptions of globalization's problems, see Saskia Sassen, *Globalization and its Discontents* (New York: New Press, 1998), and William Greider, *One World, Ready or Not: The Manic Logic of Global Capitalism* (New York: Simon and Schuster, 1999).

Index

acculturation, 89
Acheson, Dean, 182, 185
Adams, Henry, 209
Adams, John Quincy, 94, 156
Aguinaldo, Emilio, 42, 50, 51, 54, 58, 73
Albizu Campos, Pedro, 127
Aldrich, Nelson W., 22
Alger, Russell A., 21
Alliance for Progress, 147–9
American Asiatic Association, 159
American Council of Learned Societies, 176
Americanization and globalization, 245–54
Anglo-Japanese alliance, 166, 222
Anglo-Saxonism, see race
Anti-Comintern Pact (1936), 230
anti-imperialism: and anti-colonialism, 200–1; in Caribbean region, 14; as cause of World War II, 227–34; in China, 174–8, 210–14, 219–22, 224–6; and civilization, 144; in Cold War, 237–43; conservative (Mugwump) anti-imperialism, 43–7, 200, 204, 205, 215; cooperative (open door) anti-imperialism, 201–2, 203–14, 221–2, 225–6; and cultural relations, 224; and geopolitics, 236–7; and identity issues, 41–7; as opposition to diplomacy of imperialism, 201; and Philippine annexation, 43; post-Cold War, 243–6; progressive anti-imperialism, 202, 214–17, 222–4, 226, 286n; race, 43–4; and racialism, 35–6, 220; and Treaty of Versailles, 219–20; and US foreign policy, 3; and Vietnam War, 240–3; Wilsonian anti-imperialism, 217–21, 227–36
anti-imperialist league, 43
Aquino, Corazon, 85, 87
Atkinson, Fred W., 69, 70

Bagehot, Walter, 10
Baker, James, 196
Baker, Ray Stannard, 220
Ball, George, 188
Barrows, David R., 70
Batista, Fulgencio, 104
Beals, Carlton, 145
Beard, Charles, 223
Beard, Mary, 223
Beisner, Robert, 45

Bell Trade Act (1946), 80
Berle, Adolf, 228
Betancourt, Romulo, 148
Beveridge, Albert, 33, 34, 72, 95
Bidlack's treaty (1846), 105, 109
Bonifacio, Andres, 58
Boxer indemnity, 169
Boxer Rebellion (1900), 73, 164–5
Brooke, General John R., 99
Bryan, William Jennings, 17; and
  China, 168; and Philippines,
  41–3, 46
Bryan–Chamorro treaty (1916),
  122
Buckley, William F., Jr, 117
Bunau-Varilla, Philippe, 108, 109–
  10
Bundy, McGeorge, 147
Bureau of Insular Affairs, 55
Burgess, John W., 47
Burke, Edmund, 50
Burlingame treaty (1868), 166
Bush, George H., 117, 195
Butler, Smedley, 92

Caperton, William B., 135
Caribbean region: in Cold War,
  145–9; fear of European
  imperialism in, 120–1; and
  Monroe Doctrine, 13; in 1920s,
  142; and Platt amendment, 98;
  and Roosevelt Corollary,
  119–20, 208–9
Carnegie, Andrew, 203
Carter, Jimmy, 116, 191
Cass, Lewis, 106
Castro, Fidel, 146, 148
Central Intelligence Agency, 82,
  117; and Cuba, 147; and
  Guatemala, 146
Chennault, Claire, 179
China: American images of, 38,
  167, 168–9, 171, 175, 187,
  192–4; and banking
  consortiums, 171, 172; Boxer

Rebellion, 73, 164–5; and
  boycott movement, 167; and
  Canton system, 155; civil war,
  177; compared with Latin
  America and Philippines, 91,
  153; cultural relations with,
  192–4; and diplomacy of
  imperialism, 38–9, 174–8,
  210–14, 219–22, 224–34;
  economic interests in, 38; and
  education, 161, 167;
  extraterritoriality in, 157, 158;
  global significance of, 182, 184;
  and human rights, 196; and
  Korean War, 185–6; and League
  of Nations, 173–4; loss of,
  183–4; and modernization,
  161–3, 176, 177, 180–1, 190–9;
  and oriental exclusion, 18; post-
  World War I, 219–21; revolution
  of 1911, 169, 171; scholarly
  study of, 175–6, 192–3; treaty
  port system, 157–8; treaty tariff,
  158; and "tribute system,"
  154–5; and World War II,
  178–81, 228–9
China, People's Republic of, 80–1;
  American trade with, 194–5; and
  anti-imperialism, 183; creation
  of, 182; and cultural
  imperialism, 183; as global
  power, 197; global significance
  of, 189–90; modernization of,
  188–99; non-recognition of,
  182–3, 186–7; and Sino-Soviet
  pact, 186; and Soviet
  imperialism, 185, 186; and
  USSR, 188–9; and Vietnam War,
  187–8
China Aid Act (1948), 182
China market, 153, 156, 159,
  194–5, 228–9
China White Paper, 184
Chinese Communist Party, 174
Churchill, Winston, 188

civilization: and Anglo-Saxonism, 44–5; and China, 154; and globalization, 249–54; and imperialism, 41, 209–10; and Panama Canal, 106, 110–11; and Philippines, 39–40, 46–7, 52–4; and Theodore Roosevelt, 120–1, 209–10

civilizing mission: in Cuba, 98–100; in Latin America, 91–3, 143–4; in Philippines, 33, 87–90

Clark Memorandum, 142

Clayton–Bulwer treaty (1850), 105

Cleveland, Grover, 12, 13, 18; and Cuba, 22–4, 97; and Philippines, 35, 51, 97

Clinton, Bill, 195, 197, 198

Cold War: and anti-imperialism, 236–7; and China, 181–8; in Latin America, 145–9; and Philippines, 79–82, 90

Colombia, 105, 108–10

Committee on Cultural Relations with the PRC, 192

Congress, US, and economic exploitation, 66, 67

Coolidge, Archibald Cary, 201

Croley, Herbert, 36

Crowder, Enoch, 103

Cuba: annexation of discussed, 94–5; anti-Americanism in, 103; before 1898, 94; Castro's revolution, 146–7; civilizing mission in, 98–100; and Cleveland administration, 22–4; domestic political importance of, 24; educational reforms in, 99–100; in 1890s, 21–8; and Grant administration, 21–2; occupation of (1898–1902), 96–100; occupation of (1906–8), 100–2; statehood discussed, 95; and Teller amendment, 31; US cultural impact, 103; US economic interests in, 102–3; US

stake in, 22

cultural imperialism: and China, 183, 198; and globalization, 253; in Latin America, 152

cultural relations, 89, 143–4; and anti-imperialism, 224

cultural revolution, 188

culture and globalization, 252–4

Cushing, Caleb, 158

customs receiverships, 118–22

Dartiguenave, Philippe, 134

Darwinism, reform, 203, 204

Darwinism, social, 40–1

Davies, John Paton, 181

De Lôme letter, 25

decolonization, 79, 243; and geopolitics, 236–7

deconstructionism, 244

Denby, Charles, 162

Deng Xiao Ping, 190

deracination, 88

détente, 189, 190, 243

Dewey, George, 27, 31, 51; on Filipinos, 50

Dewey, John, 223

Díaz, Adolfo, 121, 122

diplomacy of imperialism: in Cold War, 185, 186; in Manchuria, 205–8; and open door policy, 164–5; *see also* anti-imperialism

dollar diplomacy: in China, 168–72; in Latin America 121–2; in Manchuria, 211–14

Dominican Republic: customs receivership in, 119–20; economic reforms, 140; and Grant administration, 35; invasion (1965), 147; modernization efforts in, 138–40; occupation of, 137–41; resistance in, 140–1

Downes v. *Bidwell* (1901), 55–6

DuBois, W. E. B., 70

Dulles, John Foster, 146, 187

Dunne, Finley Peter, 69
Dupuy de Lôme, Enrique, 25

education: and acculturation, 89;
in China, 161–3, 169; in Cuba,
99–100; in Dominican Republic,
139–40; in Haiti, 135; in
Philippines, 68–72, 89; in Puerto
Rico, 131–2
Eisenhower, Dwight D., 186, 187
Estrada, Joseph, 87
Estrada Palma, Tomás, 100
Europe, public opinion toward, 36
extraterritoriality, 157, 158, 238

Fairbank, John King, 175, 176,
180, 192, 207
Firestone, Harvey, 66
Foraker Act (1900), 124
Forbes, W. Cameron, 65, 76, 136
Ford, Gerald R., 190
Foster, John W., 95
Four Modernizations, 190–1
Frye, Alexis, 99

gender concerns, 19–20
Germany, 230; and Caribbean,
119–20; and Philippines, 33
global culture, 252
globalization, 245–54; post-
imperialist variety, 250–4; as
source of imperialism and anti-
imperialism, 249–50
Goethals, George W., 112
Gómez, José Miguel, 100
Gómez, Máximo, 22, 97
good neighbor policy, 122, 144,
226–7
Gorgas, William L., 112
Grant administration, 35
Grau San Martín, Ramón, 104
Great Britain: and Anglo-Japanese
alliance, 166; cedes US primacy
in Caribbean, 107; and China,
156–7; as civilizing power, 35;

and Clayton–Bulwer treaty, 105;
and Philippines, 33; and US
public opinion, 14; and
Venezuela crisis, 13
Great Proletarian Cultural
Revolution, 188
Grenada, 147
Gruening, Ernest, 127, 141
Guantánamo Bay, 98
Guatemala, 149

Haiti: economic interests in,
133–4; modernization efforts in,
135; occupation of, 132–7;
racial tensions, 135–6; strategic
fears, 133; UN intervention,
150; withdrawal from, 137
Hanna, Marcus, 22
Harding, Warren G., 76
Harrison, Francis Burton, 60
Hart, Albert Bushnell, 106
Hart, Sir Robert, 158
Hawaii, and US annexation,
11–12, 28–9
Hay, John, 45, 239; and China,
204–5, 207–8; and open door
notes, 165; and Panama,
109–10; and Spanish-American
War, 29
Hay–Bunau-Varilla treaty (1903),
110, 116
Hay–Herrán treaty (1903), 108
Hay–Pauncefote treaty (1901), 107
Hayes, Rutherford B., 105
Hearst, William Randolph, 26
Hitler, Adolf, 230
Hoar, George F., 45–6; and Cuba,
98
Hobson, John A., 247
Hofstadter, Richard, 260n
Homestead Strike (1892), 17–18
Hoover, Herbert, 175, 224–5; and
Haiti, 136
Hoover–Stimson doctrine, 225,
229

Hu Shih, 173, 175
Hughes, Charles Evans, 174
Hukbalahop, 78, 79, 82–3
Hull, Cordell, 230, 235
Hull–Alfara treaty (1936), 115
Hurley, Patrick, 181

identity: and China, 153–4;
  defined, 15–16; and gender
  concerns, 19–20; and
  internationalism, 30–1, 36–7;
  and World War II, 230–1
ilustrados, 49
immigration, 18; from China,
  166–7; in Hawaii, 29; from
  Philippines, 76, 78, 87
imperialism: American and
  European compared, 10, 247;
  and anti-imperialism, 248–9; as
  cause of war, 204–6, 235–6;
  causes of, 2; and colonialism, 6;
  and commercial expansion,
  240–1, 286n; and cultural
  relations, 143–4; defined, 5–6;
  diplomacy of imperialism, 6;
  European, 9–10; and
  globalization, 245–54; and
  identity issues, 30–41; and
  interests, 16; and international
  identity, 36–7, 40, 46;
  internationalism in 1920s, 143;
  in late-nineteenth century, 9; and
  Latin American policy, 91–4,
  150–2; morality of, 6–7; no
  longer fashionable, 143, 247–8;
  pre-emptive, 91–2; profitability
  of, 66, 67; and public opinion,
  14–15; and race, 35–6, 44–5;
  reasons for decline, 248–9; and
  republican expansion, 35; US
  empire in Europe, 237–8; and
  US foreign policy, 3–5; *see also*
  anti-imperialism
imperialism, diplomacy of, 6; and
  China, 38–9; and east Asia,
  126–34; opposition to in
  Caribbean, 91; and Philippines,
  32–3
indirect rule, in Philippines, 88
Indochina, 237; *see also* Vietnam
Institute of Pacific Relations, 176
interests, 16; in China, 198; in
  Latin America, 91–2; and
  Philippine annexation, 37–8
internationalism, and anti-
  imperialism, 201–2, 203–14,
  217–22, 225–36, 237–43; and
  imperialism, 36–7, 40, 46

James, William, 46
Japan, 166, 238; and China, 164,
  171–2, 173, 177–8; and Hawaii,
  29; and Korea, 67; and
  Manchuria, 72, 205–7, 210–14,
  224–5; and Philippines, 33, 73,
  74, 76, 78–9, 86; and Russo-
  Japanese War, 166; and
  Shantung, 219–21; war planning
  against, 73; and World War II,
  227–34
Jefferson, Thomas, 208
Jiang Ching-kuo, 192
Jiang Kai-shek, 174, 175, 178,
  179, 181, 182
Jiang Kai-shek, Mme, 175
Jiang Tso-lin, 161
jingoism, 19, 25–6
Johnson, Lyndon B.: and Alliance
  for Progress, 149; and
  Dominican Republic, 147; and
  Panama, 116; and Vietnam 240,
  242
Jones Act (1916), 75
Jones Act (1917), 124–5
Jones–Costigan Act (1934), 126

Katipunan, 49–50
Kennedy, John F., 239
Khrushchev, Nikita, 239
Kipling, Rudyard, 46

Kissinger, Henry, 116, 189
Knox, Philander, 93, 106, 121, 170; and Dominican Republic, 138; and Manchuria, 212, 213, 214
Knox–Castrillo convention (1911), 121
Korean War (1950–3), 80, 185–6
Kuomintang, 80, 174, 175–7

Lamarck, Jean-Baptiste, 70
Lamarckism, 70, 264n
Langer, William, 203
Lansing–Ishii accord (1917), 172
Lasch, Christopher, 216
Latin America: compared with China, 153; compared with Philippines, 91; cultural imperialism, 152; and economic imperialism, 145
Laurel–Langley agreement, 83
Leo XIII, Pope, 63
Lesseps, Ferdinand de, 105
liberalism, Cobden–Bright variety, 12, 40
Liliuokalani (queen of Hawaii), 11
Lin Piao, 188
Lippmann, Walter, 216
Lodge, Henry Cabot, 13, 21, 29; and Cuba, 23, 24, 95; and Panama Canal, 106; and Philippines, 31–2, 34–5, 67, 71; and Puerto Rico, 28
Lodge, Henry Cabot, Jr, 146
Long, John D., 31
Luce, Henry, 178

MacArthur, Arthur, 54, 72, 203
MacArthur, Douglas, 77, 78, 79
Machado, Gerardo, 103–4
McKinley, William, 19–20, 25, 30, 31, 39, 40, 52, 74, 98, 102; and Boxer Rebellion, 73; and Cuba as protectorate, 95–6; and decision to annex Philippines,

30–5; and Hawaii, 29; manhood questioned, 24; and Teller amendment, 94–5
McKinley tariff (1890), 11
Magoon, Charles, 101–2
Magsaysay, Ramon, 82–3
Mahan, Alfred Thayer: on imperialism, 37; and isthmian canal, 106; and Manchuria, 170–1, 181, 185, 205–7, 210–14, 224–6; and Puerto Rico, 123
Manglapus, Raul, 85
Mann, Thomas, 149
Mao Zedong, 81, 182, 183, 188, 189, 190; on nuclear war, 187
Marcos, Ferdinand, 84
Marcos, Imelda, 84–5
Marroquín, José Manuel, 108
Marshall, George C., 181
Martí, Jose, 96
May, Ernest, 36, 262n
May 4th movement, 173, 174, 221
Micronesia, 80, 238
Miles, Nelson A., 123, 124
missionaries: in China, 160–3; in Philippines, 32, 39–40
modernization: and China, 161–3, 176–7; rebirth of, 188ff; theory, 147–9
Monroe Doctrine, 13; in 1920s, 142; and Platt amendment, 98; and Roosevelt Corollary, 119–20, 208–9
Mott, John R., 161
Mugwumps, 43–7, 204, 205, 215
Muñoz Marin, Luis, 126, 127–8, 129

Napoleon, 68
Nasser, Gamal Abdal, 237
national character, *see* identity
National Education Association, 176
National Library Association, 176

NATO, 197, 237, 243
Nearing, Scott, 223
Nehru, Jawaharlal, 187
neo-colonialism, 244
Netherlands East Indies, 237
Neu, Charles, 210
New Left, 240–1
New Panama Canal Company,
  107–8, 109
Nicaragua: as canal route, 108;
  customs receivership in, 121–2;
  Sandinista revolution, 147
nine-power treaty (1922), 174, 222
Nixon, Richard M., 243; and
  Alliance for Progress, 149; and
  China, 189, 190; and Latin
  America, 146
Noriega, Manuel, 117, 149

Office of Strategic Services, 181
Okinawa, 238
Olney Corollary, 12–13, 37, 45;
  and Cuba, 95
OPEC, 243
open door anti-imperialism, 201–2,
  203–14, 221–2, 225–6
open door imperialism, 286–8
open door policy, 72; and
  diplomacy of imperialism,
  165–6; as essence of US
  imperialism, 206, 286n;
  internationalization of, 174; and
  Manchuria, 171–2; and
  modernization, 164–73; and
  modernization of China, 170–2;
  in 1920s and 1930s, 173–8; and
  World War II, 227–34
Operation Bootstrap, 128
Opium War (1839–42), 156–7
Organic Act (1902), 59
Organization of American States,
  146
Osmeña, Sergio, 59–60, 79
Otis, Elwell S., 51

Panama: as American protectorate,
  115–16; economic dependence
  on US, 114
Panama Canal, 104–18, 150;
  acquisition, 107–12;
  administration, 113–14;
  construction, 112–13;
  divestiture, 117–18; early
  interest in, 104–5; strategic
  importance of, 106–7, 118;
  tensions with Panama, 114–16;
  as work of civilization, 106
party politics: and Philippine
  annexation, 41–3, 76–7; and
  Spanish-American War, 24
Payne–Aldrich tariff (1909), 65
Pearl Harbor, 73
Philippine-American War (1899–
  1902), 42, 50–4
Philippines: annexation of, 30–5;
  base negotiations, 80, 81, 84,
  85–6; and Boxer Rebellion, 73;
  and China trade, 64; and Cold
  War, 79–82; compared with
  Latin America and China, 91,
  153; constitutional status of,
  55–6; and democracy, 59–60;
  development policy in Cold War,
  82; and diplomacy of
  imperialism, 32–3; economic
  problems, 77; educational
  policy, 68–72; failure to
  modernize, 86–90; and
  Germany, 33; and Great Britain,
  33; independence of, 60–1, 64,
  67, 75–9; and Japan, 33; land
  reform, 63–4; and missionary
  impulse, 32; and policy of
  "attraction," 57–9, 66; post-
  independence relationship,
  79–90; profitability of, 74; racial
  composition of, 48–9; racial
  views of, 56–7; religious issues,
  62–4, 69; under Spanish rule,
  49–50; standard of living, 68;

statehood discussed, 55; strategic
status of, 72–4, 78, 81–2; trade
and economic policy, 64–8,
76–7; and underdevelopment,
86–7; US interests in, 39; US
investments in, 66–7; in World
War II, 78–9
Platt, Orville H., 22, 95, 96
Platt amendment (1901), 97–8,
100; and Monroe Doctrine, 98;
revoked, 144
Populism, 17, 18, 24
poststructuralism, 244
protectorate status: of Cuba, 95–6,
97–8; of Panama, 115–16; of
Philippines, 80
public opinion, 14, 25–6; and
imperialism, 35; and Philippines,
34–5, 37, 72–3
Puerto Rican Reconstruction
Administration (PRRA), 126
Puerto Rico, 123–33, 243;
annexation of, 123–4;
commonwealth status, 129;
constitutional status of, 56;
culture and education, 131–3;
economic development, 125–6,
128, 130–1; immigration to US,
128; invaded, 28; political
options, 126–7, 129–30;
political system, 124; social
problems, 130–1; strategic
importance of, 123, 129
Pullman boycott (1894), 18

Quezon, Manuel, 61, 65, 66, 75–6,
77

race: American views of Cubans,
95, 97; American views of
Filipinos, 56–7; and Anglo-
Saxonism, 44–5; and anti-
imperialism, 35–6, 43–4, 220;
and Dominican Republic, 138;
and educational policy in

Philippines, 69–70; and Haiti,
133, 135–6; and imperialism,
44–5; and Latin America in
1920s, 143; nineteenth-century
views, 264n; and Panama,
113–14; and Philippines, 52, 55,
56–7, 78; and Puerto Rico, 123
Range, Willard, 215
Reagan, Ronald, 117, 147
Reciprocal Trade Agreements Act
(1934), 145
Reed, Thomas, 39
Remington, Frederick, 26
Rhodes, Cecil, 40
Rizal, José, 49
Rockefeller Commission on the
Americas, 149
Rockefeller Foundation, 163, 176
Roosevelt, Franklin D., 77; and
anti-imperialism, 234–6; and
diplomacy of imperialism in
Asia, 225, 227–34; and Haiti,
134, 137; Latin American policy,
144; and Nicaragua, 122; and
Philippine independence, 67,
77–8
Roosevelt, Theodore, 10, 25, 26,
27, 34, 93, 215, 225; on China,
167; and civilization, 209–10;
concerns for national character,
20–1; and Cuba, 23, 100–1; on
Haiti, 133; on imperialism as
civilization, 203–4; and Japan,
72–3; and Manchuria, 205–7,
210; and Panama Canal, 106,
107–12, 118; and Philippines,
31–2, 51–2, 72–3, 75; and
Puerto Rico, 28; racial views,
108–9; and William Howard
Taft, 210–14
Roosevelt, Theodore, Jr, 77
Roosevelt Corollary, 119–20;
abandonment of, 142; and
Monroe Doctrine, 208–9
Root, Elihu: on constitutionality of

colonialism, 56; and Cuba, 24, 96, 98; and Panama Canal, 111; and Philippine statehood, 55
Rostow, Walt W., 147
Rusk, Dean, 185, 186, 188
Russia, and Manchuria, 205–7
Russo-Japanese War, 166

Salisbury, Robert Gascoyne-Cecil, marquis, 13
Sandino, Augusto César, 122
Schurman, Jacob Gould, 57
Schurz, Carl, 43, 263–4
sectionalism, 18–19
Seward, William H., 36
Shafter, William R., 96
Shanghai communiqué (1972), 189
Shantung issue, 219–21
Shinshu Maru incident (1897), 29
Sino-Japanese War (1894–5), 164, 178
six-power consortium, 213
social Darwinism, 40–1, 51, 203
Somosa, Anastasio, 122
South Africa, 35
Soviet Union, *see* USSR
Spain, policy in Cuba, 23, 26
Spanish-American War (1898): causes of, 15–26; economic motives, 22–3; military highlights, 26–7; and need for isthmian canal, 106; and yellow journalism, 25–6
Spear, Robert E., 203–4
Spencer, Herbert, 40
Status of Forces Agreements, 238
Stevens, John L., 11
Stilwell, Joseph, 179–80
Stimson, Henry, 224–5; and China, 175; and Nicaragua, 122; and Philippine independence, 76
Straus, Oscar S., 31
Strong, Josiah, 204
Suez Canal, 105, 237

Suez crisis, 237
Sukarno, Achmed, 237
Sumner, William Graham, 51

Taft, William Howard, 20, 205, 225; and China, 168–72; and Cuba 100; and Dominican Republic, 138; and Nicaragua, 121–2; and Panama Canal, 112, 113; and Philippines 52, 55, 57–8, 61, 64–5, 66, 68; and Theodore Roosevelt, 210–14
Taiwan, 182, 186, 191–2, 197
Taiwan Relations Act, 191
tariff policy: and Cuba, 21; and Hawaii, 11; and Panama, 113; and Philippines, 64–5
Taylor, Bayard, 35
Teller, Henry, 95
Teller amendment, 31, 94, 95, 98
Third World, 243
Thomasites, 69
Tiananmen Square "massacre," 196
Tomlinson, John, 250
Torrijos, Omar, 116
Treaty of Nanjing (1842), 157
Treaty of Paris (1898), 33
Treaty of Versailles (1919), 220–1
Treaty of Wanghia (1844), 158
treaty port system, 157–8
Tripartite Pact (1940), 230
Triple Intervention, 164
Trujillo, Rafael, 139, 141
Truman, Harry S., 79, 129, 181, 182
trusteeship, 221
Twenty-one Demands, 171–2
Tydings, Millard, 127
Tydings–McDuffie Act (1934), 67, 77, 127
Tyler, John, 158

United Fruit Company, 102, 114, 146

United Nations Trusteeship Council, 238
US–Cuban Reciprocity Treaty of 1903, 102
US navy, 10–11, 106–7
US Senate: and Dominican Republic, 35–6; and Treaty of Paris, 41–2
US Supreme Court, and colonialism, 55–6
USS Maine, 23, 25, 259n
USSR, 196; and China, 185, 186, 187, 188–9

Venezuela crisis (1895), 12–13
Viet Cong, 239
Vietnam War, 187–8, 239–43

Washington, Booker T., 69, 70
Washington conference (1921–2), 74, 222
Washington treaties (1922), 174
Welles, Sumner, 234
Weyl, Walter, 134, 206, 217
Weyler, Valeriano, 23
Wherry, Kenneth, 183
White, William Allen, 136
"white man's burden," 46–7, 90

Williams, Frederick Wells, 208
Williams, William Appleman, 240–1
Willkie, Wendell, 234
Wilson, Woodrow, 60; and anti-imperialism, 217–21; and China, 172, 174; and Fourteen Points, 219; and Haiti, 132, 134; and Panama Canal, 115; and Philippines, 56, 75, 215; *see also* anti-imperialism
Wilson–Gorman tariff (1894), 21
Wilsonianism, and World War II, 227–34
Wisconsin school, 240–1
Wood, Leonard, 95, 98–100, 102
World War II, anti-imperialism in, 234–6

yellow journalism, 25–6
YMCA, 161, 162
Yüan Shi-kai, 171
Yung Wing mission, 161

Zelaya, José Santos, 121
Zhou Enlai, 189
Zhu Rongji, 195